TABLE OF CONTENTS

BRITISH ISLES   1
    English   2
    Irish   6
    Scottish   7

SCANDINAVIAN   11

WESTERN EUROPEAN   17
    French   17
    Belgian   24
    Dutch   26
    Germanic   30
    Swiss   35

EASTERN EUROPEAN   41
    Croatian   41
    Czech   44
    Hungarian   45
    Polish   47
    Ukrainian/Russian   51

MEDITERRANEAN   55
    Portuguese   55
    Spanish   59
    Italian   62
    Greek   72

AFRICAN   77

MIDDLE-EASTERN   85
    Arabic   85
    Lebanese   87
    Iranian   88
    Afghani   93
    Jewish   94

INDO-ASIAN   103
    East Indian   103
    Fijian   118
    Sri Lankan   119

SOUTHEAST ASIAN   121
    Vietnamese & Cambodian   121
    Thai, Singaporean, Malaysian & Indonesian   129
    Thai   130
    Singaporean   132
    Malaysian   134
    Indonesian   136
    Filipino   137

CHINESE   145

FAR EASTERN   174
    Japanese   174
    Korean   189

LATIN AMERICAN   193
    Mexican   194
    Central & South American   199

CARIBBEAN   205

NORTH AMERICAN FIRST NATIONS   213

Calendar of Ethnic Celebrations and Festivals   222

Index   234

Feedback   254

Order Form   255

EXPLORING
ETHNIC VANCOUVER

"A British Columbian," wrote local author Barry Mather, "smokes Virginia cigarettes, drinks South American coffee, eats Ontario cheese, California oranges, Norwegian sardines and Alberta butter."

Furthermore, Mather mused, "At noon, a British Columbian will either eat in a cafe owned by a Greek specializing in confusing the public by using French words to describe American foods — or, he will go to the luncheon of some service club founded in the U.S.A. and listen to a European tell how he escaped the Russians in Bulgaria."

Mather wrote that in 1958 in *British Columbia: A Centennial Anthology* — with his tongue firmly in his cheek. But exaggeration-for-effect aside, he was certainly on to something. British Columbians, and particularly those in the Greater Vancouver area, are keenly aware that they are live in an international community whose values, habits and opportunities are inexorably shaped by a multitude of cultures. Life here, more than 25 years after Mather's whimsical observation, is truly a *smorgasbord*. A *pot pourri*. Now, as we stroll our city's streets, odds are that that sari-clad woman on Fraser Street or that Cantonese-speaking cafe customer near Lonsdale Quay is no camera-toting tourist but someone who has lived here for years.

This book is a celebration of Vancouver's spectacular multicultural diversity, and a guide for residents and visitors alike to the ethnic groups that make us a truly world-class city, a special place far greater than the sum of its myriad parts. *Exploring Ethnic Vancouver* came about because, when we were researching our other urban-access books, we were constantly being asked — and asking ourselves — questions about ethnic life here: What's the best Greek restaurant in town? Where can I buy an authentic gift for a homesick Polish friend? Does the Italian community here have any special celebrations? And on and on.

As we delved into finding the answers, we soon realized that an exhaustively comprehensive tome would readily resemble the Vancouver phone book itself. (Indeed, some of the city's largest ethnic groups — Italian, Polish, Greek, etc. — actually publish their own telephone directories.) So, we present *Exploring Ethnic Vancouver* as a passport to, shall we say, the *crème de la crème* of each nationality — a way by which you can thoroughly but conveniently immerse yourself for as little as an hour or as long as a week in a society you may be curious about for any number of reasons. For the larger groups, where there's a specific geographical hub and the sheer variety can seem both exciting yet imposing — East Indian, say, or Italian — we'll direct you to the best slice of life there. On the other hand, perhaps you're planning a trip to Prague and want to acquaint yourself with its cuisine? This book can guide you the one truly authentic Czech restaurant in all of Greater Vancouver. You've recently returned from the Philippines and want to relive the experience by, say, listening to the music you heard there? We tell you the best half-dozen places to buy Philippine tapes and CDs. But this isn't "just" a shopping directory. For those keen on thoroughly experiencing particular lifestyles, *Exploring Ethnic Vancouver* also directs you to cultural centres, annual festivals, foreign-language and bilingual newspapers, radio and television programming, and places of worship — all of which will enhance your understanding of the international fabric of Vancouver.

For further reading about our ethnic diversity, the public library is an invaluable source, as are the libraries of the larger cultural centres. For those interested in the historical and political background of these communities — both in their native lands and since their arrival in British Columbia — we highly recommend Kevin Griffin's *Vancouver's Many Faces* (Whitecap Books). In a sense, this book picks up where his concludes.

One note about the comparative size of the write-ups in this book. Although some of Vancouver's ethnic groups (Chinese, say, or East Indian) are obviously large and require extensive coverage, other smaller groups (for example, Caribbean) may make up in community spirit and visibility what they lack in sheer numbers. Still other large groups — like the Dutch — may live more unobtrusively, not operating all sorts of restaurants and stores, nor holding annual festivals. We elected to concentrate our efforts on those groups whose cultural life and enterprises are readily there for you to access and enjoy — regardless of mere population figures.

That said, if you think we have overlooked a gem, some aspect of the Lower Mainland's multicultural scene that genuinely bespeaks authenticity and a unique contribution to the quality of life in our area, please write to us, and we will consider your suggestion for inclusion in a subsequent edition of *Exploring Ethnic Vancouver.* You'll find a convenient form on the last page of this volume. Photocopy it, share it with your friends, and then mail or fax it to us.

In the meantime, enjoy exploring ethnic Vancouver.

Anne Garber, John T.D. Keyes, Lorraine Gannon
Vancouver, 1995

* * *

As with all of our books, this one would not have been possible without the tips and inside information of our own multicultural friends and colleagues.

Our special thanks for their gracious assistance goes to Marilyn Abundo, Arthur Achiam, Judy Ahola, Denise Anderson, James Barber, Herb Barbolet, Shirley & Peter Barnett, Renee Blackstone, Bernie Bomers, Adelia Carreira, Peter Clough, Ronit Cohen,

Linda Conway, John Crawford, Lydia Soltys Dahl, Patricia de Haas, Judith Der, Stuart Derdyn, Enrico Diano, Molly Diaz, Erwin & Josette Doebeli, Barbara Downs, Liz Engel, Joan Fader, Deb Faurot, Ashley Ford, Verena Foxx, Simon Garber, Bob and MaryEllen Gillan, Donald Gislason, Irv & Noreen Glassner, Kevin Griffin, Paul Haym, Sophie & Chris Dikeakos, Damian Inwood, Dan Isserow, Becky Johnson, Ted Johnson, Amarjit (Amy) Kaur, Alix Kerr, Celia Lam, Teresita Landingin, Judith Lane, Linda Lee, Geneviève Lemarchand, Murray McMillan, Lynne McNamara, Rafe Mair, Lorne Mallin, Ramona Mar, Vic Marks, Susan Mendelson, Kerry Moore, Donald Morin, Kamal Mroke, Angela Murrills, Travis Neel, Salman Nensi, Peter C. Newman, Linda Olivier, Jancis O'Mara, Gunargie O'Sullivan, Jeanne Polich, Marilyn Rapanos, Bachan Singh Rapsha, Jeani Read, Kim Richards, Volkmar Richter, Richard Rochard, Mike Roberts, Michiko Sakata, Joanna Saparas, David Spence, Sonia & Rick Takhar, Tommy Tao, Albert van der Heide, Pat & Dave Valjacic, Rino Vultaggio, Tony Wanless, Ray Wargo, Casey White, Sandra Wilking, Kevin Williams, Kasey Wilson and Stephen Wong.

BRITISH ISLES

As one of the founding ethnic groups in British Columbia — ever since George Vancouver landed here in 1792 — the British (there are almost 400,000 claiming such heritage in the Lower Mainland) can maintain their social and cultural links through an archipelago of clubs and organizations.

The **WISE Club**, which stands for Welsh, Irish, Scottish and English, is located at 1882 Adanac St (254-5858); Celtic music groups and the Morris Dancers practise here. It also incorporates the Rogue Folk Club. Call 254-5858 for information on performances and other activities.

The **British Ex-Serviceman's Association**, at 1143 Kingsway (874-6510), is open to all former members of Commonwealth armed forces, although you do not have to be member to partake of refreshments; just sign in. The cook writes up a menu of the home-cooked British dishes every day.

Naturally, each country in the British Isles has — you'll forgive the phrase, given the weather there — its own umbrella organization. Even within a country, there are groups representing a specific skill or even a frame of mind.

The Celtic Connection is a free newspaper published 10 times a year with a target audience of all those claiming Celtic descent. There are articles from Ireland and Scotland, as well as coverage of local events. Sometimes there are offerings of videos (by mail), such as the recent release of a documentary film, *"An Gorta Mor"* (the Great Famine). If you don't find a copy of the Celtic Connection at one of the shops or pubs listed below, write 741, 916 West Broadway, Vancouver V5Z 1K7 (731-4261; fax 731-5043). Editor is Allcia Martin.

ENGLISH

The **Society of Saint George** is an information clearinghouse for anyone of English extraction or inclination. Write P.O. Box 91334, West Vancouver V7V 3N9 or call 987-8900.

STORES

R B Gourmet Butchers
Robson Market, 1610 Robson St (685-6328)

Featuring English favourites like lamb chops and prime rib of beef, this place also sells individual meat pies (like steak and kidney) and Melton Mowbray pie, on special order or they "make 'em special for the festive season."

The British Home Store
3986 Moncton St, Richmond (274-2261)

In addition to a tiny restaurant section (where you can enjoy a "cream tea — scones with jam and Devon cream and a pot of tea), this operation imports foodstuffs from England, including mixes for making your own trifle (a cake and custard dessert) and shepherd's pie, hard and soft candy (sold by the quarter-pound, just like in any village tobacconist shop "Back 'ome"), English chocolate bars to eat while you browse your English papers, freshly baked meat pies and pasties (meat, potato and vegetables in pastry), blood sausage and even haggis.

Crabtree & Evelyn
Oakridge Centre, 203, 650 West 41st Ave (263-4323)

When you enter the shop, two sensations are immediately apparent: One is visual, thanks to the myriad colour in rich package design reminiscent of the Victorian era, when intricate patterns of flowers and butterflies mingled in lush illustration; the other is the heady scent of potpourri in giant jars, everything from the romantic perfume of rose petals to the coy fragrance of jasmine and cinnamon. If you are generally befuddled by gift-giving, here is inspiration for every taste and interest — all of it presented so beautifully that it seems a pity to add gift wrap and ribbons. There are spices and unusual kitchen condiments, luxurious soaps and grooming aids, and choose-them-yourself sachets — plus helpful staff who seem always ready to serve, yet never in your way.

Kerrisdale Meat Market
2070 West 41st Ave (261-8755)

They bill themselves here as "the British banger butcher shop," and they are definitely the place to go if you want some bangers (sausages) to go with your mash (mashed potatoes). They offer Cambridge (pure pork, recipe from southern England "where they like things mild"), Dorking (from just south of London, in the county of Surrey, mildly spiced pork with lots of herbs), Epping (pork with double-smoked bacon), Oxford (pure pork with a hint of lemon), Ilkey (Yorkshire) sausage (very spicy pork, "good for those cold, wet mornings"), Cumberland ("made the same way as in the old days in the north of England;" pork, beef and lamb; traditionally sold by length), Manchester (northern England; heartier spiced), and Morley (pork with a good hint of English beer; "a favourite pub lunch in the northwest of England").

Marks and Spencer
2333 Guildford Town Centre, Surrey (584-1042)
Lansdowne Park Shopping Centre, 5300 No 3 Road, Richmond (278-7796)
Oakridge Centre, 650 West 41st Ave (255-3015)
Park Royal Shopping Centre, 950 Park Royal South, West Van (925-1104)

At this venerable British family department store, much of the clothing is imported from England. The food department is the most interesting; at Oakridge, it's in a separate but adjacent store. You'll find excellent frozen entrees, like bangers and mash and shepherd's pie; such frozen fish as plaice and kippers; and even desserts like the raisin-filled spotted dick pudding. The store always has a wide selection of tinned biscuits (and extra strong tea bags for the killer brew to dip the biscuits in!), packets of crisps (potato chips) in unusual flavours (roast chicken, spring onion, roast beef with mustard), condiments and candy.

RESTAURANTS

Fish & Chips

Perhaps no food style is more immediately identifiable as British than that slice of Blighty, fish and chips. Folks will drive from one end of town to the other in search of the perfect crispy batter, the tangiest tartar sauce, the most outlandish "over 'ome" atmosphere or the place that gets the mushy peas just right.

Best bets for the "real thing" are **Cockney Kings Fish and Chips** at 6574 East Hastings St, Burnaby (291-1323); **King's Fare**, 1320 West 73rd Ave (266-3474); **Olympia Oyster & Fish Co**, 1094 Robson St (685-0716); **Pajo's** — open only Easter to Thanksgiving on the Steveston Docks (no phone) and Rocky Point, Port Moody (469-2289); **Penny Farthing**, at 5212 Kingsway (434-3616); **Petticoat Lane** number one in a recent newspaper poll at 1863 Marine Drive, West Van (926-4158); and **Windjammer Inn**, 3219 Oak St (733-5312).

Small Restaurants and Tea Shops

Cheshire Cheese Inn
4585 Dunbar St (224-2521)
5645 West Boulevard (261-2834)

Lonsdale Quay Market 123 Carrie Cates Court, North Van (987-3322)

This chain of comfortable restaurants offers a selection of traditional British dishes — steak and kidney pie, fisherman's pie (seafood), toad-in-the-hole (sausage in Yorkshire pudding), Cornish pasty, Welsh rarebit (a fancy version of cheese on toast) — all to be washed down with Shaftesbury Cream Ale and Harp Lager.

Cottage Tea Room
100, 12220 2nd Ave, Steveston (241-1853)

This tiny shop, decorated with commemorative tea towels from Back 'ome, serves the classic English high tea: chocolate, scones, cookies, finger sandwiches, Devon cream and jam. There are also homemade soups and pies, and an assortment of slightly out-of-date English magazines and newspapers to read while you're waiting for the tea to steep.

The Diner
4556 West 10th Ave (224-1912)

You'll know you're here when you see the string of Union Jacks across the front of the building; inside, examine the walls covered in horse brasses, signs and other mementoes from England. Even the placemats are from the London Underground. The Diner serves traditional British fare for breakfast, lunch and dinner here (get Stella to pour you a proper "cuppa") — like oatmeal porridge and bacon and eggs, Salisbury steak, liver and onions, beefsteak pie, and roast beef and Yorkshire pudding every Sunday. You can order a side dish of mushy peas to go with your halibut and chips.

Pollyanna's English Tea Shoppe & Restaurant
15228 Russell Ave, White Rock (536-4322)

Serving high tea all day, seven days a week (except Monday, when they close at 3), this place accepts bookings for groups from 10 am to 7pm. Classic English tea is served with finger sandwiches, scones and Devon cream in a lace-curtained, classic tea shoppe environment.

English-style Pubs

The qualifier "style" is the operative one in many of Vancouver's "English-style" pubs. Many of them appear authentic, but don't serve much in the way of English food—their customers seemingly demanding more trendy fare. Here are a few spots that combine good Brit beer, traditional pub grub and a dart board or two. Check out **The Dover Arms** (961 Denman St, 683-1929); **The Jolly Coachman Pub** (19167 Ford Rd, Pitt Meadows, 465-9911); **The Jolly Taxpayer** (828 West Hastings, 681-3574); **Mountain Shadow Inn** (7174 Barnet Rd, Burnaby, 291-9322); **The Rusty Gull Neighbourhood Pub** (175 East 1st St, North Van, 988-5585); **Queen's Cross Neighbourhood Pub** (2989 Lonsdale Ave, North Van, 980-7715); **Robin Hood Pub** (13468 72nd Ave, Surrey, 594-5474).

IRISH

Irish organizations are represented by the apolitical **Federation of Irish Associations and Societies**. Its mailing address is 1433 Hamilton St, New Westminster V3M 2N5; for information, call 521-8556. The **Stage Eireann Dramatic Society** is devoted to promoting Irish culture through the performing arts; for performance details, call 228-9527.

RESTAURANTS & PUBS

The Blarney Stone
216 Carrall St (687-4322)

There's Galway Bay fish and chips and Irish Stew on the menu, live Irish-style music Tuesday through Saturday, and Guinness and Harp ales on tap seven days a week.

O'Hare's Pub
5131 Steveston Hwy, Richmond (277-2305)

The specialty is homemade meat pies— steak and kidney, steak and mushroom, shepherds. There are also daily specials; Tuesday's, for example, is Georgie Porgie Pies with mushy peas, and chips or bangers and mash. Or try the Dublin stout pies or giant spuds.

STORES

Irish Fancy Store
110, 3866 Bayview St, Steveston (272-1101; fax 263-8328)
You'll find a magnificent array of imported Irish goods here, most of it handmade, certainly in the clothing department. There are tweed ties and Irish walking hats from Donegal, Blarney Castle knitwear, wool coats and sweaters and Celtic jewellery. In the culture category, there are music tapes and books on Irish life and history. On the quaint side, there are shamrock seeds and all manner of St. Patrick's Day items all year round. Check out the Duiske glassware.

ACTIVITIES

Interested in Gaelic football? Join the fun and the "craic" with the **Irish Sporting & Social Club** (everyone welcome). Call Tom O'Sullivan at 875-0507 for info. Irish Dancing? Call **Violet Moore**, 7943 17th Ave, Burnaby (522-0445) for details on instruction.

SCOTTISH

The **United Scottish Cultural Society** represents all smaller (sometimes niche) Scottish groups in B.C. and runs the Scottish Cultural Centre at 8886 Hudson St. For details about upcoming events, call 263-9911 or 263-6955. **The Sons of Scotland Benevolent Assn** (James Sim at 985-5250 or call 1-800-661-0293) also organizes social events. A highlight of the Scottish Canadian year is the **B.C. Highland Games**, usually held in June at the Coquitlam Town Stadium; the immensely popular festival features athletic events like the caber toss and hammer throw;

staged entertainment — fiddling and sword dancing and the like; and the ever-awesome massed pipe bands. For details, call 263-9911 or 263-6955.

STORES

Edinburgh Tartan Gift Shop
375 Water St (681-8889)

Naturally, you'll find plenty of tartan here, in the form of scarves, ties and kilts; the latter are tagged with the name of the clan represented. Books (check out the Scotch whiskey cookbook!), tapes and CDs from the Auld Sod, jewellery (especially kilt pins), and all sorts of golfing accessories, since St. Andrew's is (of course) where the game got started.

House of McLaren
125, 131 Water St (681-5442)

There's exquisite imported Scottish china at this shop, plus books, tapes and CDs, tartan tams and ties, shortbread moulds and tea cozies, and candy galore: imported bulk sweets, individual chocolate bars and other packaged goodies.

The Scotch Shop
674 Seymour St (682-3929)

This is where you can get yourself outfitted in a kilt and all the accessories; the store both sells and rents their clothing. (Check out the large wall chart explaining the clan names and the tartan is associated with them.) Also in stock: Scottish music on tape and CD, and stationery with clan crests.

BAKERIES

Brig-a-Doon Bakery
12847 96th Ave, Surrey (584-9313)

Here's the place to get your Scottish bread, which is denser than regular bread; a customer assures us it makes absolutely the best toast. There are also scones, almond tarts, Empire biscuits (glazed shortbread with a jam filling), thick Scotch meat pies, steak and kidney pie, *bridies* (half circles of flaky pastry filled with ground beef and onion), black or white puddings (sausages) and Ayrshire bacon and ham.

Laidlaw's Scottish Bakery
8269 Oak St (263-0563)

Longtime customers come here for Aberdeen or cheese *rowies* (rich buns that have lots of butter cut into them), scones (soda, Scotch or sultana), and Scottish bread and rolls. There's a full counter of cookies (baked by Jock) that include oatmeal cookies and shortbread imprinted with the Scottish thistle; another counter is filled with Scottish meat pies, bridies, and pasties. Laidlaw's also sells a number of newspapers from the U.K., including the *Daily Record* from Scotland.

Plum puddings and Eccles cakes are a British treat—and many say are never made better than by the Scots. Dependable sources include **Qualitie-Made Bakeries** (2068 West 41st, 261-7010, and 4474 Dunbar St (733-3737); **Moore's Bakery & Delicatessen** (2128 West 41st, 261-2922); and **MacKinnon Bakery** (2715 Granville, 738-2442).

BUTCHER

Peter Black & Sons
21M, Park Royal South, West Van (926-3462)

This thoroughly Scottish butcher carries haggis, Scottish sausages, Ayreshire bacon, Scotch meat pies and some baked goods like Scottish loaves and oatcakes. Their big seasons for specialty items are, naturally enough, Robbie Burns Day and Christmas. Find them in the Park Royal market area.

MISCELLANEOUS ENTERTAINMENT

If you play the bagpipes but don't know where to play them, Capt. Dick Huggett of the **78th Fraser Highlanders** would like to recruit you. You'll get to wear the same uniform and kilt as the soldiers who fought at the Battle of the Plains of Abraham — and play to your heart's content. Call 597-1558.

The **Scottish Cultural Society** sponsors Scottish country dancing in Ceperley Park (Stanley Park), Monday nights, June through mid-August.

OTHERS

The **Welsh Society of Vancouver** works out of the Cambrian Hall (acoustically perfect for the group's various choirs) at 215 East 17th Ave; for details, call 876-2815.

A fine example of a niche group would be the **Vancouver Manx Society**, for people who hail from (or are interested in finding out if they hail from) the Isle of Man. You can contact them by writing 3142 West 32nd Ave, Vancouver, V6I 2C1 or by phoning 522-7651 or 263-1485.

SCANDINAVIAN

There are approximately 23,000 Scandinavian Canadians throughout the Lower Mainland—with the Swedes, Norwegians and Danes each numbering 6000 and up, the Finns 4000 or so, and the Icelandic fewer than 2000.

Each group supports some sort of community association that assists recent immigrants, coordinates business initiatives and organizes festivals.

The **Scandinavian Canadian Chamber of Commerce** is a good source of information at 822, 602 West Hastings St (669-4428; fax 669-4420). The **Sweden House Society** (vice-president Anders Neumueller can be reached at 731-6361) is working to establish a full-fledged Swedish community centre, in concert with the **Swedish Cultural Society (Svenska Kulturforeningen)**; contact Maria Schindel at 984-9873 for details. The latter group organizes the annual Lucia Festival, a traditional Christmastime celebration held thus far at a Vancouver hotel. The **Swedish Canadian Rest Home and Manor** at 1800 Duthie St in Burnaby (420-3222) currently serves as something of a cultural centre. It maintains a

Swedish-language library and is where the **Runeberg Choir** meets Wednesdays at 7:30 pm; for information about choir performances or membership, call Greta Nelson at 433-4070.

The **Sons of Norway Sleipner Lodge** and **Roald Amundsen Centre** at 6540 Thomas St in Burnaby is the centre of organized Norwegian social life. The Norwegian equivalent of Canada Day is celebrated on the closest Sunday to May 17 every year at the Amundsen Centre. For details, call the Sons of Norway at 294-2880.

The **Danish Community Centre of Vancouver** is located at 17672, 57th Ave in Surrey. Call 576-1962 for upcoming activities, especially regarding Danish Constitution Day (June 5), generally celebrated on the first Sunday in June. Many Danish Vancouverites worship at one of two Lutheran churches — at 6010 Kincaid St in Burnaby (298-6112) or 9243, 152nd St in Surrey (581-0628); at both churches, Danish-language services are heard every other Sunday.

At press time, the **Vancouver Finlandia Club** had relocated to an apartment building at 833 East Broadway, and the outgoing message at 874-3626 was only in Finnish. We recommend pursuing Finnish activities through one of the community's three churches: **Finnish Bethel** at 1920 Argyle Drive (325-5414), **Finnish Lutheran** at 6344 Sperling Ave in Burnaby (521-0533) or **Finnish Mission Assembly** at 112371, 96th Ave in Surrey (585-9786); all three hold Finnish-language services on Sunday.

About 500 Icelandic Canadians are members of the **Icelandic Canadian Club of British Columbia**, at 939, 6th St in New Westminster, which offers language classes on weekends and celebrates Independence Day (freedom from Danish rule) on June 17. Its festival to celebrate the end of winter is called *thorrablot* and is held in a local hall annually on a date falling anytime between the end of February and the end of March. For details, call the association at 522-2290.

In print, the **Swedish Press/Nya Svenska Pressen**, established in 1929, is bilingual monthly magazine useful for its classified advertisements and news of community events; to locate copies, write 1294 West 7th Ave Vancouver V6H 1B6; call 731-6381; fax 731-2292; or e-mail swepress@unix.infoserve.net.

The **Rogers Multicultural Channel** airs *Scandinavian Journey* on Friday, Saturday, Sunday and Tuesday; producer Peter Praegel can be reached at 520-7078, fax 540-0135. On radio, AM 1470 (103.3 FM), there is a one-hour Scandinavian block, beginning at 7 pm: Finnish on Monday, Danish and Icelandic on Tuesday, and Swedish and Norwegian on Wednesday.

SHOPPING

Scandinavian Arts
648 Hornby St (688-4744)

This downtown retail outlet is as glorious as an art gallery, thanks to its presentation of Georg Jensen silver jewellery and ornaments, Orrefors clocks from Sweden, Mats Jonasson's exquisitely etched crystal, and a vast array of rich blue Royal Copenhagen porcelain.

Touch of Sweden
2163 West 4th Ave (731-1314)

Kitsilano is home to this emporium of Scandinavian—mostly Swedish—arts and crafts selected by owner Louise Persson: Traditional carved wooden candelabra, a complete range of Swedish clogs (very different from Dutch clogs, says Persson), linens from the prestigious Linnevaveriet firm (est. 1660) and crystal by Kosta Boda (est. 1742). The classic sweaters are from Norway.

The **Swedish Press** magazine ($1.95) can be bought here.

FOOD STORES

Delicatessens

Two Vancouver-area delis offer just about everything a Scandinavian visitor might be missing from back home. In fact, one owner says that Norwegian charter tours have actually included his shop on their itineraries.

La Charcuterie
3665 Kingsway (439-DELI; fax 439-7715)

Although Lebanon-born Salam Kahil long ago bought out his Scandinavian partner, he still maintains probably the finest close-to-downtown source of Scandinavian food stuffs. From Denmark: ginger snacks, chocolate, cheese, mayonnaise, marinated herring and hard candy. From Norway: chocolate, mackerel, jam, cheese. From Sweden: coffee, water, mustard, soft drinks. From Finland: spices, herring and cheese. Deli-counter takeout, like Danish pork roll or *sauna lenkii* (Finnish sausage traditionally cooked by tossing it on sauna coals), can also be enjoyed at tables outside.

Jolly Foods
North Van: 111 Charles St (929-7937)

The North Shore's only complete Scandinavian deli is hard to find, hidden away in a commercial cul-de-sac off Riverside, south of Dollarton Hwy. There you'll find everything: Swedish ginger snaps, coffee and bulk soft candies; Danish bitters, beer sausage and head cheese; innumerable brands of tinned skinless cod roe and codfish balls; Icelandic herring; Danish and Finnish caviar; frozen meatballs and dumplings, and a lovely selection of Danish linen.

Bakeries

Danish pastries are, of course, delicious and deservedly world-famous. Three local bakeries specialize in them and other baked treats: **Danish Bakery**, 4021 Macdonald St (738-4228); the **Danish Pastry Shop**, 3105 Edgemont Blvd, North Van (987-1323); and **Steveston Danish Bakery**, 3420B Moncton St, Steveston (277-2253).

RESTAURANTS

Ikea
3200 Sweden Way (273-2051)

The world-famous home decor store recently closed its snack bar next to the checkout, so you now have to wander through the upstairs maze of furniture and household accessories to get to the restaurant, but it's worth the trip if you want Swedish dry goods and fresh meals prepared daily. On the shelves are Ramlosa water and the traditional apres-ski drink Glogg; various brands of oat brand crisps, lingonberry sauce, tuna and crab creams in tubes, herring of every description; and chocolates, candy and mints. The self-serve sit-down restaurant offers starters like *gravad lax* (smoked salmon), a smorgasbord (you pay by weight), Swedish meatballs with lingonberries, and Swedish waffles.

The Tivoli Restaurant & Catering
750 West Pender St (683-6219)

This business-district establishment offers an extensive menu of Scandinavian delicacies. The cold open-faced sandwiches (*Smorrebrod*) include *gravlax* (cured salmon with dill-and-mustard sauce), *rullepølse* (spiced veal roll with onions and aspic) and smoked eel with egg custard. Among the hot sandwiches are *stjerneskud* (a fillet of sole with shrimp, mushrooms, sliced egg and caviar) and *frikadelle* (Danish fried meatball and red cabbage on rye). Entrees include Swedish meatballs with red cabbage, potatoes and lingonberry sauce; a Copenhagen platter of smoked salmon with caviar and Black Forest ham with Italian salad; and various meat platters.

WESTERN EUROPEAN

FRENCH

Vancouver's French community exists in an interesting conundrum: On one hand, many are tied to family and friends in Quebec; on another, some instead feel direct kinship to France and Europe. They agree on one thing, however: wonderful breads and fine wines and food. Some things cannot and should not be compromised.

Though Vancouver's French originally concentrated their settlement in the Maillardville area, population there has declined dramatically in recent years. The Vancouver French enclave used to be clustered in the stretch of 16th Avenue between Oak and Cambie (so much so that it was known as "the 16th arrondissement").

Our French community is served by a number of private libraries, such as **Maison de la Francophonie**, with some 5000 volumes at 1551 West 7th Ave (736-9806; fax 736-4661) and **Société**

d'Histoire des Franco Columbiens, 2555, 1555 West 7th Ave (a library of 1000 volumes, 732-1452). The **Vancouver Public Libraries** have, spread through their various branches, more than 5000 books in French. Please also see our section on bookstores in this chapter. The major French organization is housed with **Maison de la Francophonie**. It's **Féderation des Francophones de CB** (732-1420; fax 732-3236).

The main Francophone newspaper is **Le Soleil de Colombie**, 1645 West 5th Ave (730-9575; fax 730-9576), a weekly that publishes Fridays.

There is, of course, French television **SRC** at 700 Hamilton St (662-6200; newsroom fax 662-6229) and **RDI** (the French equivalent to Newsworld) at the same number. In Vancouver, view SRC on cable channel 7 and RDI on cable 50. French CBC radio is **SRC-CBUF**, FM 97.7 (662-6135).

FESTIVALS & CULTURE

Maison de la Francophonie (in conjunction with the **Centre Culturel Francophone de Vancouver**, at the same address, above, 736-9806; fax 736-4661), hosts an annual summer festival. The festival has always taken place over the third weekend in June, but in 1997 it will spread over an entire week, beginning with an outdoor concert on June 15, and continuing toward conjunction with a French-focussed Jazz Festival event on the 22nd. During the festival, their block of West 16th is closed off, so you'll need to park on a nearby side street. Highlights of the festival include French-Canadian meals, street entertainers and a parade.

Two other *fêtes* are worth exploring. There's one in Maillardville during the summer hosted by the **Societé Biculturelle de Maillardville** at 1010 Alderson Ave (520-6509) and another for children, organized by the **Société Fête Columbienne des Enfants** at 202, 12840 16th Ave, Surrey (535-1311; fax 536-2333 or 535-2280).

Theatrical productions are mounted by **Thêatre la Seizième** at 1551 West 7th Ave (736-2616).

Wherever the French live, it's all to our benefit, and not just for the cuisine (which is no small part of our interest, we might add). With that in mind, let's begin with restaurants.

RESTAURANTS

Fine Dining

Café de Paris
751 Denman St (687-1418)

Famous for his classic *frites* (French fries) and three-course *table d'hôte* (fixed menu), Chef André Bernier also shines in the creative department. Try his orange-glazed salmon, roasted pork in a creamy garlic sauce, or smoked rack of lamb. Good desserts, too, such as an exemplary crème caramel. Excellent wine list.

Le Crocodile
100, 909 Burrard St (669-4298)

French cuisine is for the delicate palatte, where each mouthful is savoured, rather than wolfed down. Crocodile caters to a clientele that understands this. Waiters wear typical long linen aprons, black vests and an air of friendly efficiency. There are cafe curtains on the window, but the room is definitely elegant despite that casual touch.

Have the *frissé and chèvre*, a salad of curly endive and a round of goat's cheese rolled in crumbs then lightly pan-fried. Try the salmon tartar with saffron sauce, and the steamed mussels in wine and scallion sauce. For entrees, you might choose the *gigot d'agneau* (delicate lamb) or venison sided by sea asparagus. For dessert, the house special frozen custard comes with its own open-weave "hat" of caramelized spun sugar. Exceptionally fine wine cellar.

Le Gavroche
1616 Alberni St (685-3924)

The departure of Chef Scott Kidd to Lola's may cause a little blip in their kitchen, but rest assured that Le Gavroche, and its longtime reputation for fine French cuisine, will prevail. New chef is Ewald Oberland, whose credentials are impeccable. There's a peek-a-boo view of the mountains, a romantic fireplace in the winter and a very fine a la carte menu. Choose their lobster bisque, followed by house pate, salmon stuffed with goat cheese, and an entree of smoked breast of pheasant. Impressive wine list.

The Hermitage
115, 1025 Robson St (689-3237)

Chef Hervé Martin guides his French gastronomic domain with grace and finesse. Service is very French, very proper and exacting. Inside the restaurant is elegant and restrained. Out on the patio in fair weather, it's decidedly more casual, sort of a sidewalk bistro atmosphere. Hervé's endive salad is blended with Japanese noodles, a creative addition. His roasted lamb in a mustard and rosemary crust is exceptional, and the roast duck with crackling is tasty, too. Side dishes include cauliflower, red cabbage, string beans, spaghetti squash and new potatoes — whatever's in season, and no skimping on quantity. Hervé's desserts — his home-made sorbets and the chocolate mousse — are worth saving room for. Fine choice of wines.

Moderately-priced

Bouquet
542 West Broadway (876-4232)

Though the chef and his wife are Japanese, the food is so accurately and completely French-countryside, you'd never guess. Start with the *potage billi bi* (a broth with mussels), have the *ris de veau, saut! aux capres* (sweetbreads in a caper sauce) and for your entree, try the *filets de sole Duglise* (sole done in a white wine sauce). The desserts are typically French, too, and service is impeccable.

Country Auberge-style

La Belle Auberge
4856 48th Ave, Ladner (946-7717)

A true country inn, this one is well worth the drive from Vancouver. Select *les escargots de Bourgogne parfumeés au vermouth* (Burgundy snails laced with vermouth, herbs and butter), the decadent *poitrine de canard Muscovie poêlée aux bleuets* (Muscovy duckling breast with blueberry sauce), *le carré d'agneau à la façon du Midi* (rack of lamb roasted in an herb crust) and choose from any number of truly French pastries and desserts. Expensive. Fully licensed (top-grade wine cellar).

La Lorraine
228 Sixth St, New West (521-4212)

For sheer capriciousness, order *l'entrecôte Dijonaise* (a New York steak sauteed with shallots, Dijon mustard and cream), or their fresh and sweet *saumon au basilic* (filet in salmon in fresh basil sauce). When you're done, call for the opulent dessert wagon.

La Toque Blanche
4368 Marine Drive, West Van (926-1006; fax 926-1063)

This cosy, romantic, country inn-style place is the domain of Chef John-Carlo Felicella, whose French food styings combine seamlessly with Continental cuisine. There are filo-wrapped escargots, duck liver terrine, roasted breast of duckling, glazed with Calvados, and inventive fusion-stype dishes like potato gnocchi sauteed in sage brown butter with game hen Bolognaise, or prawn and scallop saute with chanterelle and lemon risotto. A menu note reminds customers that their "seafood is prepared slightly underdone."

Casual, cafe-style

La Cuisine de Saint-Germain
1387 West 7th Ave (731-2324)

Genuine dine-in or take-out French food is available from this cute deli, with its corner-cafe-in-Paris demeanour. The daily special might be *estouffade Bourguignonne* (beef stew with carrots), plus a dessert and coffee for $7.99 (half-portion $4.25), or à la carte selections such as *navarin d'agneau* (French-style lamb stew), *Coq au vin* (chicken simmered in wine) or *lapin à la moutarde* (rabbit in a creamy mustard sauce). Catering services available.

BAKERIES

Bon Ton
874 Granville St (681-3058)

Here's the place for marzipan animals, petit-fours (small dessert squares, almost like candies), and other French pastries. They also operate a cafe at this location and serve deli food, desserts and coffee. Closed Mondays.

Boulangerie la Parisienne
1181 Davie St (662-3151; fax 662-7171)
1221 Franklin St (258-4177; fax 258-4178)

These places (the Franklin Street operation provides a lot of baked goods for hotels) sell pastries such as danish, brioche, *palmier* (a puff pastry cut into strips and twisted to form layers) and croissant (almond, chocolate, cheese or savory), baguettes, sourdough, Parisienne (a wider baguette loaf), French rolls, foccaccia rolls, milk rolls and a variety of Kaisers.

Chãteau Bakery
Lonsdale Quay, 123 Carrie Cates Court, North Van (987-0227)
La Baguette et L'Echalotte
Granville Island, 1680 Johnston St (684-1351; fax 684-1352)

Here's where to buy baguettes — undoubtedly the best (crispy on the outside, dense, moist and sweetly fragrant on the inside) and all kinds of other French baked goods, such as pains au levan and fancy French pastries. Both bakeries are operated by the same people.

Patisserie Bourdeaux
3675 West 10th Ave (731-6551)

An authentic French bakeshop, Patisserie Bordeaux rolls up the best chocolate-filled croissants in town, *sans égal.* You'll also find aromatic baguettes, croque'm'bouche, Paris Brest, St. Honoré, pit'hiviers, mousses, mille feuille, savarin, tourtières, quiches, pastries, gateaux, home-made multi-grain crackers, and of course, an *assortiment des petits-four exquis.*

OTHER FOOD

Far-Met Importers
34 West 7th Ave (876-2241; fax 875-1575)

If you're buying in bulk, or are getting together with friends for cooking classes, you can buy from this wholesaler. Among the offerings are *moustards*, cheeses by the kilo and cider. If they can't sell the small quantity you want, ask them which stores carry their stock.

Lesley Stowe Fine Foods
1780 West 3rd Ave (731-3663)
Here's the only place we know to find *sel gris*, a particular kind of salt used in French cookery.

BOUCHERIE (BUTCHER) & CULINARY CLASSES

Architect and cooking instructor Genévieve Lemarchand insists the very best local butcher is not francaise, but anglaise, being the English butcher at the Robson Public market (see RB's Gourmet Butchers, in our British Isles chapter). Genévieve also claims the cheese shop next to it ("expensive but worth it") sells the best chevre, boursault and other French imports. It's **Robson Gourmet Foods** (683-2862).

If you can't get up to Sechelt for Genévieve's cooking classes (1-604-885-4617, phone or fax), the best ones in Vancouver are at **DuBrulle French Culinary School**, 1522 West 8th Ave (738-3155; fax 738-3205) and at **Caren's Cooking School**, 1856 Pandora St (255-5119). **The CookShop** at City Square, 555 West 12th Ave (873-5683) periodically asks local chefs to teach classes. Call to inquire or to be added to their mailing list.

NEWSPAPER SHOPS, MAGAZINES & BOOKS

Bonjour Books
230, 8711 Beckwith Road, Richmond (271-2665; fax 274-2665)
They carry a large selection of books, with emphasis on children's literature in French.

Manhattan Books & Magazines
1089 Robson St (681-9074; fax 681-8619)
The people at **Maison de la Francophonie** who stock that library

find their French-language books and magazines here. Ask for Marc Fournier, who is in charge of their French titles.

Mayfair News
1535 West Broadway (738-8951)

Though they have a branch in the Royal Centre, this one has the best selection of French-language magazines and newspapers in town.

Vancouver Kidsbooks
3083 West Broadway (738-5335; fax 738-5362)

Former librarian Phyllis Simon, herself once a French-immersion mom, carries an impressive number of French books for children.

LANGUAGE CLASSES

Adult night school classes vary from good to hit-and-miss. If you get a great teacher, you're home-free. For conversational classes that are consistently good, try **Alliance Française** at 6161 Cambie St (327-0201; fax 327-6606).

French immersion for children is governed by **Canadian Parents for French, BC** at 203, 1002 Auckland St, New West (524-0134; fax 524-0135). Closed during the summer. If your query is urgent, call president Donna Archibald at 1-604-864-4917; fax 864-4918).

BELGIAN

Vancouver's Belgian community is quite small — barely 1000 or so — but there is an association representing the group: the **Belgian Canadian Association** at 412, 4001 Mt Seymour Pkwy, North Van (924-2054).

Belgium is world-renowned for its chocolates, ice cream and pastries — of which there are numerous sources in the Lower Mainland.

BAKERIES

D C Duby Patisserie Bruxelles
1463 Hunter St, North Van (980-6776 or 980-6790)

Dominic and Cindy Duby are award-winning pastry chefs who produce fabulous desserts for their hotel and restaurant clients, but they'll sell to the walk-in trade, too. Specialties include chocolate truffle cakes, French pastries and petits-fours, cheese-cakes, tortes and flans.

Van Den Bosch Patisserie Belge
106, 4255 Arbutus St (731-0055)
2567 Granville St (731-0023)
25M Park Royal South, West Van (926-4401; fax 926-2738)
Richmond Public Market, 1370, 8260 Westminster Hwy (244-2230)

Their pastry chef, Marc, is brilliant, especially with fruit cakes and special occasion cakes, so Van de Bosch deserves its long-standing reputation for excellence. For more info, call Talking Yellow Pages at 299-9000, #4401.

CHOCOLATES

Daniel Le Chocolat Belge
1105 Robson St (688-9624)
2820 Granville St (733-1994)
Park Royal South, West Van (925-2213)

Daniel set up shop in Vancouver in 1981. However rich his choco-lates may taste, no preservatives or fat are used. Among his artistic triumphs are a hazelnut paste, creamy caramel, delicious ganache creams and liquor truffles sleekly enrobed in pure, rich chocolate.

House of Brussels Chocolates
1092 Robson St (681-5971)
Cathedral Place, 925 West Georgia St (684-5444)
Factory outlet: 208, 750 Terminal Ave (687-1524)
and some mall locations

Since 1983, House of Brussels Chocolates, a Vancouver-based company, has produced high-quality Belgian-style moulded chocolates, using techniques developed in Brussels almost 100 years ago. Among the exotic temptations are chocolate-coated ginger, manon (hazelnut cream in white chocolate), almond cream Napoleons, Royale (dark chocolate and orange cream), real strawberry cream in dark chocolate, real champagne mixed with milk chocolate truffle filling, and of course their irresistible Hedgehogs — hazelnut cream made from the finest Turkish hazelnut paste and milk chocolate, moulded into the polished shape of little hedgehogs in milk, white or dark chocolate. The added secret is a sprinkling of crushed walnuts in the moulded shell — unequalled anywhere.

DUTCH

Surprisingly, though the Lower Mainland's Dutch population is substantial — some 25,000, many of them in the Fraser Valley — there is very little evidence of traditional Dutch life in commercial operations like restaurants and shops.

According to Albert van der Heide, who publishes **the Windmill Herald:** "Part of the uniqueness of the Dutch community has to do with its own mosaic: The Dutch East Indies contingent, the Netherlands Dutch, Calvinist, Reformed Church, Catholics and many religious factions. For many, the common denominator is the church. When you look for Dutch cultural expression, most of Dutch life — about 70% — is centred around the church." Van der Heide also points out that two of the most authentic Dutch restaurants in the region are not in the Lower Mainland at all, but down in Lynden, Washington. And, he adds, many of the local Indonesian restaurants serve Dutch food, just as the Dutch ones serve Indonesian.

The only daily Dutch-Canadian radio show in Canada emanates from CJVB 1470 AM Vancouver, where Anke Dekker does a show every weekday evening from 9 to 10 pm called **Holland Calling.** Word for Mrs. Dekker may be left at 688-9931; fax 688-6559 (the program is pre-taped).

RESTAURANTS

The Bulldog Vancouver
510 Nelson St (688-4438)

The concept for this boisterous international restaurant chain originated in Amsterdam, and this is the only one in Canada. The menu features only Dutch and Indonesian foods. Fully licensed.

De Dutch Pannekoek House
4441 Boundary Road (430-2223)
1260 Davie St (669-8211)
2622 Granville St (731-0775)
4003 Knight St (876-8221)
1530 Main St (669-4216)
3192 Oak St (732-1915)
1, 1725 Robson St (687-7065)
6651 Hastings St, Burnaby (298-4400)

John Dys founded the first of these restaurants in 1975 (at Knight and 25th); he eventually he brought in partner Bill Waring, who has run these Dutch restaurants for years. A pannekoek is, of course, a Dutch pancake. They're simply huge (12 inches or more across), so one is usually enough for a complete meal. Toppings range from sweet (apple-cinnamon-raisin, peach, strawberry, raspberry, blackberry) with whipped cream and icing sugar or Dutch *stroop* (almost a molasses syrup), to savory (include bacon, mushroom, sausage cheese "salami hash" cooked-inside, or topped with cheese-and-egg). The most substantial meal is the "Boer's pannekoek," which comes with sausage, bacon, ham, bratwurst, and two eggs on top. The "Windmill" comes with smoked salmon. Baby pannekoeks for children are half-sized. Open daily for lunch; the Surrey one is currently open for dinner, and other stores may follow suit.

De Hollandse Coffee Shop
20474 Logan Ave, Langley (534-5111)

Substantial daily soups, Dutch coffee and biscuits are featured here.

Dutch Wooden Shoe Cafe
3292 Cambie St (874-0922)

They boast widest variety of pannekoeks in town — some savory, some sweet, plus *croquettes* (appetizer-sized sausage-shaped minced meat), and some Indonesian foods like *nasi goreng* (fried rice) and *nasi guri* (rice cooked in coconut milk with peanuts and mint).

SHOPPING

Best Bi Foods
4610 Earles St (439-8855)

This is the region's premier Dutch butcher, selling not only the customary horsemeat, but also Dutch croquettes and other meats.

Dollenkamps European Bakery
2778 West Broadway (738-6788)

They do Dutch breads (including wheat-free, sugar-free and yeast-free ryes), special occasion cakes, plus a host of other baked goods for the health- (and diet-) conscious.

Valley Bakery
4058 East Hastings St, Burnaby (291-0674)

A longtime favourite of ours, this place features many authentic Dutch baked goods and particularly good cakes.

Holland Shopping Centre
41 Eighth Ave, New West (522-8333; fax 522-0236)

Biscuits, candies, cookies, canned goods, cheese, Dutch coffee, sweets, some Indonesian foods and other goods are available here. They also offer a mail order catalogue (postal code is V3L 1X6), Christmas gift packs to friends in Holland, and toll-free ordering at 1-800-270-3595.

Holland Shopping Centre Langley
20474 Logan Ave, Langley (534-5111)

No relation to the previous entry, this place — basically a deli — features Dutch groceries, giftware, Delft blue chinaware, CDs and tapes. There's also a small coffee shop on the premises. Best deal is their self-serve bulk candy — many varieties of typically Dutch salted licorice.

BOOKS, NEWSPAPERS & PERIODICALS

Speelman's Bookhouse
Unit 12, 5010 Steeles Ave West, Rexdale, ON M9V 5C6 (416-741-6563; fax 416-748-3062)

Note the Ontario location. Speelman's offers a free catalogue of Dutch-subject and Dutch-language books, plus flags, videos, CDs and cassettes. Many of their materials and books are available through Albert van der Heide, locally (details in next entries).

Vanderheide Publishing
P.O. Bag 9033, Surrey V3T 4X3 (532-1733; fax 532-1734)

Albert van der Heide's company publishes a number of volumes (and videos) on life in the Dutch East Indies, among other themes. A catalogue of over 200 titles is available, too, under the title "The Dutch Heritage Pages." Also available are customized Delft blue plaques, other gift items and books from other publishers, such as "Of Dutch Ways" and "The Backroads of Holland."

Windmill Herald
P.O. Bag 9033, Surrey V3T 4X3 (532-1733; fax 532-1734)

Founded in 1958, the Windmill Herald offers four pages in English with each issue; otherwise it's in Dutch. Publisher Albert van der Heide has been involved with the paper since 1969. A subscription costs $21.90 per year.

BED & BREAKFASTS

Among the local hosts offering "Dutch hospitality" and genteel accommodation are **Der Olde Klok** at 1090 West King Edward

Ave (738-7207); **Peter & Evelyn Scheffelaar's** place at 11040 64A Ave., Delta (591-9264); and **Gerry & Alice van Kessel's** at 325 Pine St, New West (526-0978).

GERMANIC

The Germans were some of the earliest immigrants to British Columbia, attracted by the Fraser Valley gold rush of the mid-19th century. Today, some 60,000 Lower Mainlanders claim German ethnicity, although they celebrate few unifying festivals or religious celebrations. We have listed the most active of the several clubs and organizations in this category. A dozen or so churches — mostly Baptist, Mennonite and Lutheran — conduct German-language services. The largest congregation meets at **St. Mark's Lutheran Church**, 1573 East 18th Ave., Vancouver V5N 2H4 (876-4312, 874-8427); German-language services are held Sunday at 9:30 am.

German-speaking Austrians, Swiss and Germans read the weekly **Deutsche Press** newspaper for news and entertainment information. If you don't find copies at the stores or restaurants listed below, you can pick one up 7, 707 East 21st Ave (877-0305; fax 877-0308). **Pazifische Rundschau** (Pacific Review) is a bi-weekly German-language paper. Mailing address: P.O. 88047, Richmond V6Y 2A6 (270-2923). And **Kanada Kurier** is a German weekly, from 958 West 21st Ave, Vancouver V5Z 1Z1 (731-5220). German-language news from Europe, community news and music can be heard Friday from 8 to 9 pm on **CJVB Radio** (AM 1430; 103.3 FM cable; for details, call 688-9931). The **Rogers Multicultural Channel** offers daily German programming, produced by Richard Weischler. For details, call 669-1325 or fax 669-5250.

CULTURAL ORGANIZATIONS

Austria-Vancouver Club
5851 Westminster Hwy, Richmond (273-4725)

This is the main meeting place for Vancouver's Austrian community.

The Goethe Institute
944 West 8th Ave (732-3966; fax 732-5062)

One of three chapters in Canada (there are more than 150 world-wide), this German government-funded institution promotes German language and culture. The holdings of its extensive library — books, magazines, records and tapes, videos, film scripts and art catalogues — are open to the public free of charge. The institute also hosts numerous lectures, art shows and performances by theatrical troupes. Call for details.

The Vancouver Alpen Club (Deutsches Haus)
4875 Victoria Drive (874-3811)

The Alpen Club was founded in 1935 for the preservation of the German language and culture; its original members met to dance the *Schuhplattler*, a German folkdance that originated in the Bavarian and Tyrolean Alps. (Hence the name Alpen.) Current activities at the centre include choral performances, theatrical productions and athletic team meetings. The building itself is visually distinctive, with its flower-filled window boxes and painted-on shutters; inside, the banquet hall's dance floor was deliberately designed to be springy — harkening back to the club's origins.

Vancouver Westside German School
Carnarvon Community School, 3400 Balaclava St (736-5955)

German-language classes are offered for kids age five and up, leading to the German Language Diploma.

BAKERIES AND DELICATESSENS

Not surprisingly, the German community supports dozens of excellent food shops, where you can find a tremendous array of traditional breads, sausages, wieners, ham, strudel and so on.

Fraser Bakery and Konditorei
6533 Fraser St (325-6612)

Some of the most popular breads, like the ryes and pumpernickles sell out early, so the regulars know to order them in advance. They bake special Easter braided breads, their Black Forest cakes are smothered in cherries, and their Sacher Tortes (named for the Hotel in Vienna where they originated) have little marzipan tags on each section. There's a great variety of strudel, with fillings ranging from apples to blueberries, as well as bags of ground hazelnuts and poppy seeds if you want to try making your own. Excellent kaiser buns — and huge pretzels just crying out for a tankard of beer. Near the door are posters advertising upcoming German-style events in town.

Fraserview Sausage & Delicatessen
6579 Fraser St (325-1814)

As the name suggests, sausage, sausage and more sausage (even blood sausage), Hanover ham, smoked ribs and cheeses. Imported German grocery items include coffee, chocolates, mustards (hot, sweet or spicy), sauerkraut, herb teas, Oetker-brand strudel and cake mixes, and bottled fruit and vegetable juices (including carrot juice and sauerkraut juice), soaps and shampoo. There's also a small selection of children's books, games and greeting cards in German.

Freybe Sausage
716 East Hastings St (255-6922)

You'll hear the staff speaking German to their regular customers here. The meat selection varies from visit to visit due to the outlet nature of the store, but they usually offer such traditional items as bratwurst, weisswurst sausages, steak tartare, rouladen, weiners and frankfurters.

P & G Sausage
4, 190 152nd St, White Rock (535-6776)
108, 20551 Langley By-Pass, Langley (533-1990)

The draw here is the homemade German sausages — without fillers or MSG. They smoke their own meat, and there is a refrigerator full of smoked pork chops, jowls, chickens and other meats, liver dumplings and German potato salad.

Schnees Delicatessen
5492 Salt Lane, Langley (534-1313)

Good one-stop German shopping: cold meats and cheeses, non-alcoholic German beer, marzipan logs (half circles of marzipan covered in chocolate), small Sacher tortes, grocery items, herbal teas for a variety of ailments, cosmetics and magazines.

Victoria Bakery & Delicatessen
5663 Victoria Drive (321-1555)

This combination bakery, deli and grocery store has a German baker on staff who bakes traditional breads — rye bread, light rye, caraway rye and a Russian rye that's so heavy it could double as a door stop; Russian rye goes into the freezer as it has no preservatives — and pastries: strudel, Black Forest cakes (also sold by the slice) and *bomben* (chocolate-covered cone shaped pastries filled with a rum ball mixture). The deli section has a variety of cheese and meats, including double smoked bacon, smoked pork hocks, frankfurters, speckwurst, German butter cheese and Edam. As for groceries: soaps, lotions and cosmetics, herbal teas, pumpkin oil for salads, gummie candies (which originated in Germany), eucalyptus and menthol candy, cherry, blackberry and rosehip fruit syrups. On shelves behind the counter are bottles of bitters that are used as healing remedies and digestive aids; Sechsomtertropfer bitters come in the very attractively shaped brown bottles. Finally, there's a rack of German magazines.

Other fine outlets for any array of German delicacies are **Black Forest Delicatessen** (1001 Park Royal South, West Van, 926-3462), **Bavarian Bakery & Delicatessen** (6471 Victoria Drive, 325-5200), **Country Deli** (Cloverdale Mall, 5738 175th St, Surrey, 574-4944), **Dussa Delicatessen** (4125 Main St, 874-8610), **International Sausage Co** (1846 Gilmore Ave, Burnaby, 294-8248).

RESTAURANTS

Bavaria Restaurant
33233 Walsh Ave, Abbotsford, 859-3154

Lobster, schnitzel, steaks and other local foods prepared Bavarian style. Dinner only.

The Bavaria House Restaurant
233 Sixth St, New West (524-5824)

This charming place, with Bavarian decor inside and out, specializes in 16 types of *schnitzel* — from the traditional Wiener Schnitzel to Black Forest Schnitzel (with wild mushrooms and red wine sauce), Schnitzel Oscar (with crab) and Schnitzel Madagascar (mushrooms and green peppercorn sauce). There's also steak tartare, Spaetzle Jaeger Art (a type of egg pasta with wild mushroom sauce) and *rinds rouladen* (beef rolls stuffed with bacon, mustard, onion and dill pickle).

The Black Forest Restaurant
3140 King George Hwy, White Rock (536-7950)

Again, Bavarian decor, various schnitzels (Oscar, mushroom), Brochette (served with prawns scallops and mushrooms) and roast duckling.

Heidelberg House
1256 Robson St (682-1661)

German specialties include sauerbraten and *spaetzle* (tiny egg dumplings), several different types of schnitzel, and *kassler* (smoked pork chops and potato pancakes with sour cream and apple sauce). Traditional desserts include marble cake and hazelnut cake.

Old Country Inn
20598 Fraser Hwy, Langley (534-8696)

The building looks as if it could have been transported straight from the Austrian countryside — complete with shutters sporting heart-shaped cutouts and paintings over the windows. Among the-Austrian specialties served here are Schnitzel Franz Lehar (with crab) and roast duckling with red cabbage.

The Vancouver Alpen Club Restaurant
4875 Victoria Drive (874-3811)

This moderately priced restaurant, located in the lower level of the club, is open for lunch and dinner, with a menu in English and German. Lunch offerings include wieners or bratwurst with sauerkraut, Schnitzel or veal loaf with egg; dinner includes sauerbraten, rouladen with dumplings, and roast beef with vegetables and spaetzle. Imported German beers: Becks and Warsteiner; there's also schnaps and Gluewein (mulled wine).

SWISS

The **Swiss Society of Vancouver**, with some 600 members, is the parent organization in the Lower Mainland; the mailing address is Box 4468, 349 West Georgia St, Vancouver, V6B 3Z8 (phone & fax: 324-1291 or 322-1807). President is Lilly Senn. Volunteer coordinator is Edith Morton at 278-0608. The Swiss Society also hosts a New Year's brunch on the first Sunday in January at the **William Tell** (you must be a Society member to attend). A open-to-the-public soccer tournament day is usually held in June in the park under the Second Narrows Bridge.

The Swiss Society produces a small magazine about six times a year, called **The Swiss Herald.** For details, contact editor Elisabeth Rechsteiner, 7718 Jensen Place, Burnaby, V5A 2A8 (420-5661; fax 420-5669).

Other organizations include: **Swiss Canadian Athletic Club**, (which provides soccer, outings, and so on — President is Oskar Fluehler at 435-3220); **Swiss Outdoors Club**, which has a cabin at the foot of Mt. Baker and organizes hiking, mountain-climbing and bike trips, c/o membership co-ordinator Trudi Feller at 261-8601 or president Joe Muller at 732-6213); the **Swiss Crossbow Association**, which hosts an annual visitors' day, including a children's competition, c/o president Walter Buerki at 274-2094. (Says longtime member Erwin Doebeli: "No, apples are not a challenge for us...we only use cherries.")

Other active groups are **Swiss Canadian Mountain Range Association**, 4141 Quarry Road, Coquitlam (942-4434), which owns a posh chalet on Burke Mountain. Contact is Rene Zollinger (944-0503); their biggest event draws up to a thousand people to the chalet. It's held on the nearest Saturday to **Swiss National Day**, August 1.

A compass orienteering course is offered by **Othmar Kaegi**. Call 943-5699 for information and deadlines.

The Swiss Society, the William Tell Restaurant and Rotary Clubs may again host a big public event like the one held in mid-July at the Plaza of Nations, which featured yodelling, singing and other performances. Call the Society for details. One of the highlights was **Vancouver Dorfmusik**, a wonderful harmony band. President is Martin Russenberger at 859-4936. The **Swiss Choir**, conducted by Rory Fader, has a stellar reputation; for membership details call chair Annamarie Bellucci at 263-3969, Othmar Kaegi at 943-5699 or Claudette Bell at 942-8058 for info.

Swiss Folk Dancing is introduced to the community via practise sessions each fall. Call Vroni Bernardis at 255-1872 or Judith Chan at 939-1874 for details.

The **Swiss Chamber of Commerce** at Box 2684, 600, 555 West Georgia St, Vancouver V6B 3W8 (688-7947; fax 682-1329) promotes ties between Canada and Switzerland, and very active in local cultural activities, as well. Call Dorothy Smith at the number above for more information.

RESTAURANTS

The William Tell
765 Beatty St (688-3504)

We're mentioning this place out of alphabetical order because Erwin Doebeli's landmark Vancouver restaurant in the Georgian Court Hotel was not just the first Swiss restaurant in Vancouver, it is still undoubtedly the best. Doebeli is constantly revising his outstanding menu, incorporating local produce and game whenever possible; he has one of the best wine cellars in town, offers sumptuous made-on-premises desserts (always a knockout), and on Sunday evening hosts a traditional Swiss farmers' buffet. It's expensive, but positively worth it.

Abercorn Inn
9260 Bridgeport Rd, Richmond (270-7576)

The restaurant at this Best Western Hotel features authentic Swiss specials. Chef Lucien Frauenselder is the former president of the Vancouver Chefs' Association.

Calvin's
2452 Marine Drive, West Van (922-4222; fax 922-0080)

Named after the Calvin the Reformer, this North Shore establishment offers a smattering of Swiss dishes.

Restaurant des Gitans
83 Sixth St, New West (524-6122)

The name means "of the gypsies." Jack Hoppensellar offers a full
menu of Swiss specialties.

The Swiss Gourmet Restaurant
270 Esplanade Ave, Harrison Hot Springs (796-9339)

Swiss music, German draft beer, authentic *raclette* (melted
cheese with boiled potatoes, chopped onions and pickles),
schnitzel and "prawns Geneve" make this a worthy outing.

MISCELLANEOUS FOOD

Gizella's
3436 Lougheed Hwy (253-5220; fax 253-4825)

This former restaurateur now markets more than 200 varieties of
baked goods (especially tortes and cakes) and has branched out
with a full line of fine Swiss chocolates. The bulk of her business
is restaurant supply, but anyone can buy retail from her, as long
as they call ahead and pre-order.

Swiss Bakery
1873 West 4th Ave (736-8785)

Michael, who runs this place, trained with a German baker from
Switzerland. His is the most genuine local source of Swiss baked
goods, such as Swiss rye (without wheat flour), heavy rye bread
(good for extra-thin slicing) and Swiss-German-style "real" pretzels. The breads are characterized by being very moist and having
long keeping quality. Michael also makes a typical Swiss dessert
called Bee-sting cake, which is a sweet dough with custard on
top. He does a splendid mousse cake, too.

CLOCKS & WATCHES

The Swiss are known for their timepieces — many of which can be purchased at reputable jewellery stores — but Vancouver is also home to a few top-notch watchmakers:

Swiss Trade Co
334, 5740 Cambie St (325-2501; fax 325-0024; cel 328-8805)

This is a source of superb antique watches and clocks; by appointment only.

Time & Gold
516 West Pender St (683-1812)
557 West Georgia St (682-4487)

Jean-Jacques Maurer is a Swiss watchmaker who provides sales and service for all fine clocks and watches.

Kurt's Clock Repairs
103, 2423 Bellevue Ave, West Van (922-7593)

Kurt Alleman offers repairs and sells all kinds of timepieces. He's one of the best.

HERBAL REMEDIES

The Alpine obsession with good health dovetails nicely with the West Coast lifestyle. Here are a few enterprises that cater to such vitality.

Laboratoires St. Ives S.A.
1 Place St Gervais, 1211 Geneve, Suisse

St. Ives personal care products are sold throughout the Lower Mainland, principally in supermarkets and drugstores. However, if you write the manufacturer — for any reason — your name is automatically entered into an annual drawing for a free trip to Switzerland. Send your letter (or postcard) to the attention of Maurice Dormond.

Thaler Enterprises
3655 Bonneville Place, Burnaby (420-4229)

This family-run outfit produces the Natural Factor vitamin and supplement line (100% natural-source), and acts as the Canadian distributor for the Swiss Herbal product line.

And every health store carries **Swiss Herbal Remedies** from 8, 2439 Beta Ave, Burnaby (298-4114; fax 298-4119).

EASTERN EUROPEAN

CROATIAN

The Croatian community, numbering approximately 12,000, has kept a generally low profile in Vancouver, with the exception of occasional rallies inspired by current events in the strife-torn former Yugoslavia. The largest residential concentration is in North Burnaby, but there is no "Little Croatia" to speak of. According to Zarko Perko, past president of the Canadian Croatian Business Association, it is difficult to run a business catering solely to Croatians, who while honouring their roots seem committed to assimilation into Canadian society. Croations are well represented in the construction and real estate development industries, and Perko estimates that, next to the First Nations, Croations are the largest stakeholders in B.C.'s commercial fishery.

What visible Croatian social life there is revolves around the **Croatian Cultural Centre** and the **Immaculate Heart of Mary**

Croatian Catholic Church. The two main events of the year are the **Croatian Folk Festival**, held on Victoria Day, and **St. Anthony's Day**, in honour of the patron saint of Croatia, held annually in mid-June. Details on both can be had by calling the cultural centre (3250 Commercial Drive; 879-0154 or 879-2304; fax 879-2308; recorded info 879-6177), which features meetings rooms, a ballroom, a social club and a library, open to the public Mondays from 7 to 9 pm.

The Immaculate Heart of Mary Croatian Catholic Church (3105 East 1st Ave; 253-2089; fax 254-5198) — easily identified by the large red-and-white checkerboard crests as you approach from either direction on 1st Ave — is the religious focus for the community. English-language Mass is conducted Sundays at 9 am, followed by Croatian-language services at 10 and 11. Its choir has recently released its first CD.

A biweekly, bilingual newspaper, **Hrvatski Glas/Voice of Canadian-American Croatians**, is published out of Nanaimo, and provides an interesting insight into the concerns, mostly political, of its emigres. It is available in the stores and delis listed below, or by writing P.O. Box 596, Nanaimo, BC V9R 5K4 (754-8282; fax 753-4303).

FOOD STORES

1st Avenue Deli
3292 East 1st Ave (251-4187)

Just down the street from the Croatian church, Franjo and Yagoda Dejanovic specialize in such authentic meats as *kranske* (garlic sausage), *debricine* (paprika-spiced sausage), Croatian-style smoked bacon, blood sausage and head cheese. There's a wide array of imported canned and prepared goods (fried pickled mushrooms, vegetable spreads, soups, chocolate and biscuits) and pastries, like poppyseed and walnut strudel. A wide selection of up-to-date newspapers and magazines, shipped from Zagreb less than a week before.

Paradise Imports
2463 East Hastings St (253-1720)

From the sidewalk, this looks like a typical fruit-and-vegetables store. In back, though, you'll find myriad Croatian groceries, with an emphasis on chocolates, biscuits, spices, and soup mixes, and at the very back an array of newspapers. Near the cash register is a display of videocassettes for sale, mostly of Croatian movies and musical stars in concert.

GIFT STORES

Zagreb Imports
2497 Nanaimo St (251-4480; fax 254-1169)

Petar and Sena Dolanjski offer the city's best display of Croatian goods, everything from crystal, CDs and audiocassettes, videos for sale or rent, phrasebooks and guidebooks, flags and T-shirts sporting the Croatian crest, current newspapers and magazines, and an array of foodstuffs: chocolate, jams and preserves, pickled goods, hard candy, cookies and stomach bitters. (There are also items from Poland, Hungary and Bulgaria.) Sena also runs the travel agency right next door (Sena Travel, 2499 Nanaimo St; 254-4433; fax 254-1169), specializing, of course, in travel to the former Yugoslavia.

RESTAURANTS

La Barka
2135 West 4th Ave (734-4008)

Surprisingly, there are no cafes or restaurants in all of Vancouver that resemble the ones Croatians remember from the old country. The only Croatian-owned place with a nod to authentic cuisine is this cute place, decorated in West Coast shipyard motif (a *barka* is a small fishing boat), specializing in Italian-influenced cuisine. (Given its geographical location opposite Italy on the

Adriatic, coastal Croatian cuisine greatly resembles Italian fare.) Highlights are the seafood cakes, pasta and paella.

CZECH & SLOVAK

In the aftermath of the Velvet Revolution and the ongoing restitution of private property in the former Czechoslovakia, many of those who fled the country in the decades after the Communist takeover in 1968 are tempted, at least, to return to Europe to see if they can pick up the pieces of their former lives. From a high of about 8000, there are now approximately 3000 Czechs and 4000 Slovaks in the entire Lower Mainland. For information about the remaining Czech community in Vancouver, write **The Czechoslovak Association of Canada** at Box 48863, Bentall Centre, Vancouver V7X 1A8 (922-1445; 681-1093). The mailing address for the **Canadian Slovak League** is 9734, 150A Street, Surrey V3R 7M4 (581-1037).

Religious life for the Slovak community revolves around the **Sts. Cyril and Methodius Roman Catholic Slovak Parish** at 472 East 8th Ave, New Westminster V3L 4L2 (526-7351). Sunday mass is performed in English at 9 am and in Slovakian at 11 am.

RESTAURANTS

U Zavoralu
707 Queensbury Ave, North Van (988-1331)

The area's only thoroughly Czech restaurant is tucked away in a small strip mall on an otherwise residential street on the North Shore. Large but cosy, decorated with Czech art, U Zavoralu is run by Vera Zavoral and her husband, who hail from the town of Liberec, up near the German border. They serve appetizers like smoked garnished cod liver; such soups as goulash with a salt stick and beef bouillon with liver dumplings (all soups can be ordered in bulk to go); and entrees ranging from *vrabec* (roast pork with garlic, dumplings and sauerkraut) to *rostena* (stewed beef with mushroom or gypsy sauce) to *szegedin* (goulash with dumplings and vegetables). The specialty of the house is a dinner-for-two roasted duck with red cabbage and dumplings. The house dessert is warm fruit dumplings, topped with whipped cream and cinnamon. Enough of the fine Czech beer Pilsner Urquell will doubtless send you heading for the restaurant's small dance floor.

Kafe Europa
735 Denman St (683-4982)

Lithographs of Prague Castle and the Charles Bridge identify this as a Czech restaurant, although the menu is generally Eastern European: appetizers like European sausage with horseradish and mustard sauce, or smoked trout with sour cream dill sauce; goulash soup, half a duckling with caraway seeds and red cabbage, chicken schnitzel and beef goulash, roasted pork loin with red cabbage; and such desserts as apple strudel and *palascinta* (crepes).

Slavia
815 Denman St (no phone)

This basement "joint" has the definite air of a real-life Czech working man's bar: smoky atmosphere, mismatched formica tables, posters and pennants from Prague, beer and cheap food. Goulash, tripe or cauliflower soup is less than $3, while main dishes like roast or smoked pork, goulash or cabbage rolls cost less than $6.

HUNGARIAN

Most of Canada's Hungarians arrived as refugees shortly after the Russian invasion of Hungary in 1956; Vancouver initially welcomed several hundred, but now some 7500 Hungarian Canadians live throughout the Lower Mainland

The **Hungarian Cultural Society of Greater Vancouver** is housed at 728 Kingsway in a building that's hard to miss, thanks to the green, red and white bands that decorate the front in honour of the Hungarian flag. The society organizes singing, dancing and social groups for all ages and publishes *Tarogato*, a monthly magazine featuring essays and poetry in Hungarian. Call 876-4720 or 876-1123 for details about upcoming Hungarian activities.

Hungarian-language services are performed at **Our Lady of Hungary (Magyarok Nagyaszonya) Roman Catholic Church** (1810 East 7th Ave, 253-2577) and **Hungarian-Calvin Presbyterian Church** (2791 27th Ave, 438-0349) on Sunday.

STORES

Duna Delicatessen and Gift Shop
5026 Victoria Drive (324-2715)

The staff at this all-purpose Hungarian-oriented store bake their own *toportyus pogacsa* (bacon biscuits), multilayered torts, and strudel filled with walnuts or poppy seeds. There are cold meats (including Hungarian sausage, of course), cheeses, preserved peppers, popular jams (cherry, gooseberry) and all sorts of Hungarian paprika — in bags as powder, or in tubes as paste. The gift-shop side sells cassette tapes and books, handpainted porcelains and pottery, and embroidered blouses and tablecloths, along with the embroidery threads with which to try your own hand.

RESTAURANTS

It is difficult, within the general area of Central and Eastern European cuisine, to identify precisely those restaurants that have purely Hungarian influences. Given the reach of old Austro-Hungarian Empire, which ended only as recently as 1918, you tend to see the same dishes, or at least taste the same flavours, in restaurants claiming Czech, Austrian and German origins. However, the ones listed below do try to serve cuisine you'd find in Hungary.

Bandi's
1427 Howe St (685-3391)

Specialties here include goulash soup or chilled sour-cherry soup. Entrées include veal goulash with dumplings, chicken in a mushroom sour cream and paprika sauce, cabbage rolls with pork, and a platter for two of veal, pork and reindeer meat. There's usually a cake of the day and *gyumolcs hag* (a fruit mousse).

Goulash House Restaurant
1065 Granville St (688-0206)

Start with Hungarian cucumber salad or goulash soup, then Hungarian spinach roll and *langos* (fried bread dough), paprika chicken with *nokedli* (similar to the German spaetzle), and pork sausage with potato. Their baker comes in at 5 am to prepare the fresh sourdough bread that comes with every meal; you can also buy whole loaves to take home with you. There is a wide selection of luscious baked goods.

Kulacs International Restaurant
1345 Kingsway (875-6224)

A classic appetizer is the fried cauliflower, followed by goulash soup or chicken soup. Entrees include a range of schnitzels, Budapest *bakonyi* cutlets (pork with mushroom sauce, sour cream and dumplings), chicken paprikas, and gypsy steak (seasoned pork with fried mushrooms and onions). The quintessential Eastern European dessert is *palascinta* (crepes, stuffed with chocolate and walnuts, jam or cottage cheese).

Szasz Delicatessen and Restaurant
2881 Granville St (738-7925)

This 35-year-old business specializes in goulash soup, *langos* (fried bread dough), veal goulash with dumplings, Hungarian noodles, bakonyi (pork cutlet) and a variety of cakes, like *malakoff torte* (lady fingers and whipped cream). The deli section sells meats, frozen soups and baked goods.

POLISH

The Polish Canadian community numbers approximately 14,000 and actively supports the **Polish Community Centre** at 4015 Fraser St. The building houses a credit union and meeting halls for the Polish Canadian Congress, various social and youth groups, folk-dancing troupes and so on. For information about the centre's activities, call 874-8620. **The Polish Combatants Hall** (at 1134 Kingsway) was founded to assist Polish veterans of World

War Two. It functions primarily like any Legion Hall, but its facilities include a Polish-language library, of interest to anyone studying Polish life in general. Call 873-2821 for open hours.

The Polish community is large enough to support its own telephone directory, a copy of which can be picked up at these two locations or at many of the stores listed below.

St. Casimir's Polish Church (1187 East 27th Ave) is the only Catholic church in the Lower Mainland that offers mass in Polish on Saturday (7 pm) and Sunday (10:15 am, 11:45 am, 5 pm). For details, call 876-3194 or fax 872-8171.

Every September, the **Polish Thanksgiving** celebrations, called *Dozunki*, include a colourful parade from St. Casimir's to the Polish Community Centre, where food and music can be enjoyed with a harvest theme. Call the centre for details.

Western Canada's largest Polish weekly magazine is actually a tabloid-style newspaper called **Gazeta informacyjna**, available at most delis listed below. To arrange a copy, write 3, 804 East 15th Ave, Vancouver V5T 2R9 or call 879-5477; fax 879-5027. The e-mail address is andmanus@wimsey.com.

Or look for **Pacyfik**, a bi-weekly, Polish and multilingual paper from 181D West Broadway, Vancouver V5Y 1P4 (251-3560).

The **Rogers Multicultural Channel** airs *Polish TV Weekly* on Sundays and Wednesdays; producer Jerzy Mrozewski can be reached at 322-8519; fax 683-3455.

FOOD STORES & DELICATESSENS

Danex Polish Delicatessen
2611 Kingsway (432-7795)
4544 Fraser St (876-1355)

Both outlets offer the usual array of smoked and prepared meats (tongue cheese), tinned and pickled goods, juices (blackcurrant and sour cherry), candy and rental video. The Kingsway location is the larger of the two, and also stocks audio cassettes, children's books and Polish handicrafts (especially wooden carvings).

J, Z & N Deli
1729 Commercial Drive (251-4144)

The smoky aroma of preserved meat wafts out the doorway of this tiny shop, luring you in as you stroll the otherwise Italian strip of Commercial Drive. Inside, the place feels vaguely subterranean, like a butcher's basement — with smoked meats hung everywhere: hams, bacon, sausages of very description, all prepared according to traditional Polish methods. There's also a limited selection of imported tinned and pickled goods from Eastern Europe.

Jagoda European Deli
157, 4800 No 3 Road, Richmond (821-0691; fax 241-4635)

In addition to the usual tinned meats, smoked meats and cheeses, cookies, coffee, crackers and candy, there's a wide array of frozen perogies (meat, cheese, meat and sauerkraut, blueberry, potato and cheese). Readers who crave their Harlequin Romances in Polish can get their fix here, along with concert and movie videos for rent.

Mazurek Deli
104 West 3rd St, North Van (987-0440)

Just up the hill from Lonsdale Quay — you can't miss the huge Polish flag in the window — this deli is a big booster of all things Polish; pick up a copy of the Polish phone book here. You can eat at four tables (two inside, two outside), selecting from the cold case (blood sausage, head cheese, Krakow-style dry sausage, *kielbasa* sausage, meat loaf; various cheeses) or a hot meal — anything from cabbage rolls to *flaczki* (meat soup). In the candy department, there's a massive display featuring the delicacies of the E. Wedel company, the Warsaw equivalent of, say, House of Brussels chocolate. In the cooler, next to the soft drinks and waters, you can sometimes find Okocim Pils, the excellent Polish beer.

Polish Deli
5068A Kingsway (435-2773)

Take-out lunch selections included stuffed cabbage rolls, hot sausage and home-made perogies. There is an assortment of deli meats (such as *mysliwska*, a delicious home-style version of hunter sausage), cheeses, grocery items and cakes, and a freezer full of perogies (cheese, potato and onion, meat, meat and sauerkraut) and *Bigos* (meat and sauerkraut simmered for hours). Their bulletin board is covered with flyers and info (mostly in Polish). The deli also sells Polish magazines and rents videos.

Polonia
2434 East Hastings St (251-2239)

This tantalizingly aromatic shop is renowned for its all-natural Polish sausages — which some think are the best in town.

Polish Bakery & Pastry
115, 13320 76th Ave, Surrey (590-7354)

A dependable source for rye breads of every description, buns and pastries.

Terra International Foods Inc.
3902-3904 Fraser St (879-1922; fax 879-9255)

This wholesale/retail enterprise imports many of the goods from Poland and neighbouring countries that you'll find in smaller stores and delis in this and other Eastern European categories, so shopping here will give you a good sense of what to expect elsewhere: pickled peppers and cucumbers, red cabbage with apples, tinned herring in various sauces (paprika, mushroom, tomato), horseradish and mustard, gooseberry jam, chocolate and hard candy, fruit juice syrup and stomach bitters, dried soups like borscht and *kapusniak* (cabbage with mushroom), and Polish gelatin and pudding mixes.

GIFT AND BOOK SHOPS

The Polish Bookstore
183 West Broadway (876-8718)

The stock of this small shop leans toward coffee-table art and photography books, illustrated encyclopedias, attractive children's books, novels (especially science fiction) and Polish translations of the likes of Steinbeck and Kafka.

Zofia Polish Store
3958 Fraser St (874-3338; fax 430-6849)

Barbara and Stelian Kulig can invariably be found chatting with friends around the desk at the back of this small shop, leaving you alone to browse the shelves: lots of books and newspapers, a large selection of video cassettes, dolls, handicrafts, carvings, and a select array of jams, pickled goods, candy and preserves.

UKRAINIAN & RUSSIAN

Ukrainians were, relatively speaking, late-comers to the Lower Mainland, not emigrating here in large numbers until this century. By now, however, there are almost 25,000 Ukrainian Canadians in and around Vancouver.

A good access point for those interested in the community is the **Holy Trinity Ukrainian Orthodox Cathedral**, a designated Heritage building at 154 East 10th Ave. The interior of the church displays spectacular religious iconography, and services in Ukrainian and English can be heard at various times of the day, depending on the season; call 876-4747 or 325-5570 for details. In the church basement is the **Ukrainian Museum of Canada**, which features artifacts of traditional life in the Ukraine (embroidered clothing, baked goods. etc.) The museum's hours are irregular, so call 876-4747, 327-7725 or 299-6764. Finally, there's an authentic Ukrainian feast served in the adjacent auditorium on the first Friday of every month; for menu details and prices, call 432-8287.

Notable among the half-dozen other Ukrainian churches in town is the **Protection of the Blessed Virgin Mary Catholic Church**, whose spectacular golden domes can be seem from miles away; it's located at 550 West 14th Ave (879-5830; fax 874-2727). Like Holy Trinity, it's a magnificent edifice — inside and out. Ukrainian-language mass is heard on Sunday.

There are various organizations of a political nature (like the Ukrainian Canadian Congress), but the most pertinent to this book's theme is the **Ukrainian Community Society of Ivan Franko**, named after a beloved poet and journalist. The hall at 5311 Francis St. in Richmond plays host to various languages classes, dances and other social functions; for details, call 274-4119.

Further information about community activities can be gleaned from the pages of the **Russian-Vancouver Magazine**, a monthly publication with an annual subscription rate of $20; write to 504, 1260 Howe Street, Vancouver V6R 1R5 or call 681-0648.

RESTAURANTS

Babushka's Kitchen
1689 Johnston St (669-4119)

This take-away stall in the Granville Island Market serves *Kolbassa* (a lean ham garlic sausage) on a bun, *piroshki* (rolls stuffed with savory fillings), and Ukrainian cabbage salad with homemade sauce, *pelmeni* (mini beef dumplings), cabbage rolls, borscht soup and blintzes (crepes filled with beef and rice, or cottage cheese with raisins).

Hunky Bill's House of Perogies
957 Denman St (689-3100)
1613 Nanaimo St (251-1185; fax 254-7917)

Ukrainian fast food, take-out only, is the name of the game here: perogies (with or without sausage), cabbage rolls and Ukrainian sausage.

Lala's Perogy Express
8031 Park Rd, Richmond (273-0121)

Lala's, a Richmond institution for almost 25 years, is hard to find but definitely worth the effort; it's in the rear lane between the Royal Bank and Time Square. Specialties include borscht soup and goulash, perogies, cabbage rolls, kolbassa (best enjoyed with *burachky*, a beet-and-horseradish relish), *pyrizhky* (baked buckweat buns with dill sauce), *nalysnyky* (cabbage-filled crepes) and *zrazy* (meatballs in a mushroom sauce). Fresh or frozen perogies can be taken away, complete with heating or storage instructions.

Perogy's Perogies
1941 Cornwall Ave (733-8802)

This tiny take-out or dine-in spot serves a great variety of tender Russian-style perogies (slightly larger than Ukrainian).

The Russian & Ukrainian Restaurant
3124 Main St (876-5810)

The perogy is also the big draw at this elegant but comfortable restaurant: cottage cheese perogies, potato and onion perogies, sauerkraut perogies, and so on. There's Ukrainian borscht soup, *pelmeny* (filled with minced meat and onion, garnished with tomato sauce and chives). Desserts include — guess what? — perogies (fruit-filled, usually blueberry and raspberry) and an excellent unbaked cheesecake.

Kavkas
1696 Robson St (662-8777)

This tiny Russian cafe offers honest-to-goodness *peroshkis* (perogies), plus cabbage rolls and an excellent borscht.

STORES

Perestroika Products Limited
8626-A Joffre Ave, Burnaby (451-0808, fax 451-1849 or 271-6800)

Here's a wonderful source for fresh, all-natural perogies, *vareniki* (mini-perogies), pelmeni and borscht right from the people who make them for Superstore, Costco and others. This is a true wholesale operation, but Inessa Tsemakhovich and her family will even serve you samples of their great products if they're not too busy. Piroshki cost about 80 cents each; vareniki (mini-perogies) are about $3/lb; pelmeni are about $3.30/lb; and Russian breads (each loaf weighing about one kilo, white or whole wheat) cost $2/loaf. A new product, Anushka's Russian Borscht, is now available. Perfect if you're planning on entertaining a large party.

Skazska Gallery
3632 West 4th Ave (731-9968)

At press time, the owner of this store was relocating from her old

4th Ave location to larger premises. Call 689-8881 (fax 689-8589) to learn the new location. Store inventory included those classic wooden stacking Russian dolls, books, fine platters, china, hangings and art.

Ukrainian Gift Shop
124 East Broadway (876-5489)

Its decorative arts section dominates the store — everything from Russian stacking dolls to traditionally patterned ceramics, crystal, embroidered linen and carved wooden model ships. There are also cook books and Ukrainian/English dictionaries. Free parking at rear.

Ukrainian Gift Shop
5151 Blundell Rd, Richmond

This is a somewhat different operation from that mentioned directly above. Here, Pete Lycky sells embroidered tablecloths, painted eggs, table runners, ceramics and various engraved plaques that he has collected on trips to the Ukraine; the cash he raises goes back to aid the children of the Chernobyl region on his next scouting trip. Naturally, Lycky's stock is ever-changing, depending on what he finds.

MEDITERRANEAN

PORTUGUESE

The majority of the Lower Mainland's 9000 or so Portuguese Canadians emigrated from the Azores, off the coast of Portugal, so they came to this country as experts in fishing and agriculture. The community is large enough to support a telephone directory, which includes Brazilian Canadians. To arrange a copy of **Lista Telefonico Portuguese/Brazileira**, call 250-2094.

The **Portuguese Club of Vancouver** is the community's recreational and social centre. One section is reserved for members, but visitors are welcome to visit a common area to partake of a snack — a beer, coffee or perhaps pork steak in a Portuguese bun. Meanwhile, the **Portuguese Canadian Seniors Foundation** meets every Friday at the Trout Lake Community Centre to enjoy refreshments and light meals, games, music and dancing. For details, write 5162 Joyce St, Vancouver V5R 4H1, or call 430-6633.

The Portuguese community's main place of worship is **Nossa Sehora de Fatima (Our Lady of Fatima) Roman Catholic Church**, where Portuguese-language mass is held on Saturday evening and Sunday morning (1423 East 13th Ave, 879-0729). Bilingual English-and-Portuguese services are held at **Good News Foreign Nations Baptist Church** on Sunday evenings (4580 Gothard St, 435-1103).

The bilingual **Periodico News**, published monthly (2628 East 21st Ave, 430-4330; fax 430-8737), serves Portuguese and Brazilian readers. On television, **Rogers Multicultural Channel** airs *Voz Portuguesa* four days per week; for details, call producer Maria Medeiros at 251-6410.

FOOD STORES

Carmelo's Bakery
1399 Commercial Drive (254-7024)
Harbour Centre, 555 West Hastings St (no phone)

Traditional Portuguese baked goods and monumental special occasions cakes are the highlights here. Also: good Portuguese buns, which resemble Kaisers but are softer and dusted with flour.

John's Meats & Groceries
5453 Victoria Drive (321-3567)

One-stop Portuguese shopping: deli and baked goods, groceries, housewares and gifts. The Portuguese buns are delivered fresh daily; in the cheese section, there's *quejo tip serra* (a sheep's milk cheese similar in texture to a Brie), St George (a mountain- style cheese made from a mix of cream and goat's milk, available in strong, medium and mild) and sometimes a fresh cheese that's similar to ricotta. In meats: a smoked ham called *presunto*, the popular sausage called *chourico*, and *morcela* (a blood sausage similar to England's blood pudding). The freezer at the back of the store is filled with quail, rabbit, small sardines, squid and stickleback fish. John's also imports bottled water and orange or pineapple soda, pottery and cookware. Portuguese videos for rent.

Latin Supermarket
1680 East 13th Ave (874-8618)

A good source of fish, either fresh, frozen or salted. There's some produce, a selection of olives and cheeses, juice for making wine, imported ceramics and Portuguese music tapes.

Portugal Meats & Groceries
2147 Kingsway (438-3022)

This is a relatively new store with a wide range of Portuguese products: bulk olives, nuts and dried lupini beans; frozen fish (sardines — which taste nothing like the canned variety — smelts, mackerel and bonita) and dried fish (like *bacalhau*, a salted cod that comes in board stiff slabs); cheeses, meats and Portuguese sausages; juice for winemaking; large bags of spices; canned goods (especially fava beans); dessert mixes for puddings and flan (creme caramel) and even tubes of caramel, so you don't have to bother caramelizing your own sugar. In the gift section, you'll find T-shirts, tapes and other items from Portugal.

Union Food Market
810 Union St (255-5025)

Formerly Gomes Bakery, this small corner store in the Strathcona area is recommended for its terrific baked goods (but come early, as by the end of the day the selection is very limited); they bake all their own corn bread, cheese bread, sweet bread, Portuguese buns and custard cakes. There's also a warming oven near the cash register where they keep the warm sausage buns, codfish balls (made from bacalhau), fritters and shrimp croquets. Also available are bulk olives, pine nuts, frozen imported fish and winemaking juice.

Dependable sources of excellent Portuguese buns are **Calabria Bakery** at 5036 Victoria Drive (324-1337; fax 324-1330); **Fortuna Bakery**, 4240 Hastings St, Burnaby (298-9611); the **Lisbon Bakery** (2454 East Hastings St, 253-0234) and the **Strawberry Bakery** (100, 1641 Commercial Drive, 254-5191).

RESTAURANTS

Adega Restaurant
1022 Main St (685-7818)

The menu offers a sampling of foods from the different regions of Portugal: *capapaus fritos* (grilled stickleback with potatoes and vegetables), *carne alentejana* (a classic Portuguese beef dish), pork served over baby clams, *sardinhas assada* (char-broiled sardines, which are abundant in Portuguese waters—and fresh ones are a national favourite), and *chourico frito* (homemade Azorean sausage). For dessert: *pudim flan*, pudding floating in a caramelized sugar sauce.

Cinco Estrelas Restaurant
2268 Kingsway (439-1124)

Having ordered your breakfast, lunch or dinner, peruse the postcards pinned to the walls from different areas of Portugal and the Portuguese ornaments on the shelves. For breakfast, try the Portuguese omelette (with Portuguese sausage, onion and parsley). Appetizers include marinated quail in wine sauce, Portuguese sausage, deep fried stickleback fish, and *prawns la planche* (sauteed in a white wine and garlic sauce). House specialties are pork and clams (marinated pork and fresh clams in a white wine and lemon sauce), *rojoes a casa* (marinated pork and potatoes in a white wine sauce), Portuguese steak (served with fried potatoes and fried egg in a garlic and wine sauce) and dry cod (boiled and served with potatoes, vegetables and egg). The wine list includes Portuguese favourites.

Nando's Chickenland
8231 Ackroyd Road (278-2727; fax 278-2803)
Lonsdale at 13th St, North Van (phone unavailable at press time)

This international chain restaurant — with locations from South Africa to Israel, Portugal and England — serves nothing but chicken (with accompanying rice, potatoes, cole slaw, salad, etc.) based on an authentic, spicy Portuguese recipe. A recent winner in the Best Chicken Restaurant in *The Province* newspaper,

Nando's marinates its birds for 24 hours in its own spicy "peri-peri" sauce, which it also sells bottled for home cooking in various styles: mild, hot, extra-hot, garlic, and wild herb.

Santos Tapas
1191 Commercial Drive (253-0444)

Tapas were originally small morsels of food that were given away to people drinking in bars (possibly to help absorb the alcohol, so they could carry on drinking). Here it's fun to bring a crowd and share a selection of tapas. There's *sopa do dia* (soup of the day), *chourico assado* (BBQ portuguese sausage), *sardinhas assadas* (grilled Portuguese sardines); *lulas grelhadas* (squid) and clams Algarve (in a garlic and wine sauce) — all of it accompanied by live music.

Sporting Restaurant Cafe
3532 Commercial Drive (876-7646)

The new management says that even more Portuguese dishes will soon be added to the menu. Already, you can sample *caldo verde* (kale soup), *frango grelhado* (grilled chicken seasoned with garlic, paprika and red hot peppers) and lulas grelhadas.

SPANISH

Although the Spanish can lay claim to having one of their own be the first European to set foot on the West Coast — in July of 1791 — Vancouver's Spanish community today is neither large (numbering perhaps 5000) nor very visible. (Central and South American Canadians of Hispanic origin seem more prominent; see that chapter for details.)

There is a **Spanish Cultural Centre** at 759 Carnarvon St in New Westminster (524-2506), which is involved in language classes, but as of late 1995, Spanish religious and cultural life will primarily revolve around the **Spanish Catholic Mission** in its new headquarters at 125 East 12th Ave; for details, contact Father Eduardo Diaz at 261-4804. Spanish language mass can be heard Sundays at **Holy Family Church** at 4851 Beatrice St (875-8414).

Mundo and Familia is a locally published biweekly Spanish magazine with a dual focus — educating Spanish Canadians about this country and introducing Canadians to the best of Spanish literature and culture; write 73, 8415 Granville St, Vancouver V6P 4Z9 (or call 322-0285). **El Contacto Directo** is a monthly newspaper with a greater focus on current Hispanic activities in Vancouver; write 2827 East 14th Ave or call 438-4864.

RESTAURANTS

Andale's
1175 Davie St (682-8820)
3211 West Broadway (738-9782)

This place features good, reliable family fare, with emphasis on the Spanish influence in Mexican cuisine. Specialties include a fine *paella* (Spanish-style fish stew), *mole poblano* (a stew combining the flavours of chocolate and ancho chilies), and an outstanding *zarzuela de mariscos* (shellfish stew).

Cielo's
15069 Marine Drive, White Rock (538-8152)

This truly Mediterranean atmosphere offers a patio and view over the water — even the washroom makes you feel like you're outside. Foodwise, it's an authentic Spanish tapas bar (though they do offer some seafood and meat entrees, as well). Among the special tapas available are chicken, seafood, sausages and various pastas (with tomato or saffron sauce), roast garlic (a guilty pleasure) and a particularly good seafood risotto. Good wine list. It's right next door to Wolfie's (same owner), a well-known White Rock landmark restaurant for fine European dining.

Las Tapas
760 Cambie St (669-1624)

A great hangout for producers and personalities from the CBC, this place was the first tapas bar in Vancouver — launched by a pair of world-weary travellers who had dined in places like this in

Spain, and who fairly accurately translated what they'd experienced when they returned to Vancouver. The food is still fine; try the *sopo do porro* (chicken soup with chickpeas) or sample several tapas in small, medium or large sizes. Perfect for after-theatre at the Queen Elizabeth.

Mediterranean Maza Bar
11h, 777 Dunsmuir St (683-5660)

This crowded and busy restaurant offers foods from Italy, Greece, Spain — all Mediterranean foodstyles.

Pepitas
180 West Esplanade Ave, North Van (980-2405)
1170 Robson St (669-4736)
2043 West 4th Ave (732-8884)

Fabulous fajitas (soft tortilla rolled with grilled meats, lettuce, tomatoes, green onion and grated cheese and topped with sour cream), a superior paella (saffron rice with seafood, simmered with veggies in olive oil and water), a party atmosphere and live entertainment combine to make this a memorable dining experience, with an authentic Spanish flavour.

MARKETS & BAKERIES

Mediterranean Bakery & Cafe
523 Park Royal South, West Van (925-5184; fax 925-9184)

Here they make 20 types of cakes and Spanish-style fruit flans in sizes from six to 12 inches (the latter is enough for a party dessert to feed 20 to 24).

Mediterranean Market
7498 Edmonds St (520-1411)

The expected olive oil is here (in many sizes and qualities), as well as several full shelves of spices. For instance, they sell a number of kinds of saffron.

ITALIAN

Vancouver's 30,000-strong Italian community is large enough to support two Little Italy's — the older, main one along Commercial Drive from 3rd Avenue to Napier, the other in the 2500 and 2600 blocks of East Hastings. Both areas offer numerous food shops and delicatessens, coffee bars and some clothing stores, and Commercial Drive particularly gives off a true neighbourhood feel. Another demi-area is along the 6500 block of East Hastings in Burnaby. Meanwhile, Italian food has enjoyed such universal acceptance that fine dining and specialty food shops can be found throughout the Lower Mainland.

The hub of Italian cultural life can be found at the **Italian Cultural Centre** at 3075 Slocan Street (430-3337), just off Grandview Highway. ICC Society membership entitles you to free use of its covered bocci courts and its cafe Osteria, a 15% discount on dinners at the on-site restaurant, La Piazza, access to the Italian-language library, and advance information on upcoming events. The highlight of the year is Italian Week, usually held at the centre in early July. Typical events are Italian Market Day, art exhibits, folk performances, musical variety, an opera evening, and dinner-and-dance events. Throughout the year, the centre acts as a hub for such activities as the Italian-Canadian Winemakers Club (call Angelo Veschini, 980-1029), the ICC Youth Choir, a Ladies' Club, an Over 50 Club, and Sunday bingo games.

For up-to-date information on Italian life throughout the Lower Mainland, pick up **L'Eco D'Italia**, the 5000-circulation weekly newspaper, published Tuesdays. Listen to Italian segments on CHMB radio (AM 1030) or watch *Telitalia* on the **Rogers Multicultural Channel**; for details and program schedules on either radio or TV, call 299-0866; fax 299-9661). As well, radio station **CJVB** (AM 1470) airs an hour of Italian programming weekdays at 6 pm, and for five hours on Sunday, beginning at 11:30 am; call 688-9931 or fax 688-6559. A surprisingly good source for pre-recorded Italian videos — primarily movies and popular TV shows, opera and other programming — is **La Grotta del Formaggio** (see details below).

RESTAURANTS

Fine Dining

Alabaster
1168 Hamilton St (687-1758; fax 687-1785)

Northern Italian food is the theme here, where Chef Markus Wieland has carved out a name for himself among Vancouver gourmets. Wieland's cuisine is "food of the people," replying heavily on such staples as risotto, polenta, osso bucco, and simple soups and salads. Presentation is stunning. The polenta, for instance, arrives in an attractive display of concentric circles and dots of pesto sauce. The herb-crusted rack of lamb is top-notch, as is the saltimbocco. Desserts run the gamut from panacotta to tira misu. A carefully managed wine cellar starring many fine Italian and French wines.

Bianco Nero
475 West Georgia St (682-6376)

Elegant black-and-white decor and Northern Italian cuisine, with an extensive fresh sheet including as many of three dozen new items, in addition to the regular menu. Highlights include an impressive sole in aquavit with Danish caviar, tortellini in a light mustard cream sauce, a perfect osso bucco and a stop-the-presses penne gorgonzola. Great desserts (a superior tira misu, for example), if you've saved room. Excellent cappuccino, by the way. Impeccable and exhaustive wine list.

Café il Nido
780 Thurlow St (685-6436)

The atmosphere is reminiscent of Tuscany, the food is fine, and the service impeccable. The butternut squash soup (filled with fresh crabmeat and sided with zucchini scones) is a sensation. And who could resist the linguine Gorgonzola with cream, chicken and walnuts? They also prepare a flawless veal with three peppercorn and brandy sauce. Save room for dessert: The Belgian chocolate mousse is served with creme fraiche, or the light touch of fresh, homemade sorbets.

Cincin Ristorante
1154 Robson St (688-7338)

A popular hangout for visiting Hollywood royalty, this downtown trattoria specializes in wood-oven pizza and carpaccios like the smoked beef one, or the *carpaccio d'agnello* (peppered lamb loin, charred rare with mint and chives). Their roasted garlic soup is superb. Pasta choices range from fettucine with asparagus and olives in a smoked salmon cream to *risotto con funghi* (mushroom risotto). How about a pizza with wood-spit-roasted chicken or another with pesto, shitake mushrooms and roasted garlic. Entrees (from their alderwood-fired grill) include chicken, salmon, pork and marlin. Some 200 labels of wine are stocked — 24 by the glass. Their balcony-patio is heated, so you can overlook the crowds on Robson even in cool weather.

Il Giardino
1382 Hornby St (669-2422)

Vancouver's high-rollers — real and wanna-be — congregate here, attracted by the open garden atmosphere and Umberto Menghi's cuisine. Lots of fresh fish, veal and excellent pasta. Arguably the best antipasto in town. Try the *penne Arrabiata* (with chilies and tomato sauce), the osso bucco Milanese with risotto, or get really wild with quail in a grape-brandy sauce, or braised breast of pheasant and polenta. They're not kidding when they say they specialize in game and fowl. Substantial wine list. Dress to see and be seen.

Villa del Lupo
869 Hamilton St (688-7436; fax: 688-3058)

The youthful energy of the owners shines through with a truly inventive menu — a taste of fusion that owes much of its inspiration to Northern Italian cuisine — like rigatoni in a tomato-basil sauce, accompanied by grilled scallops. One of the soups is *pasta e fagioli alla Venetta* (Venetian bean and pasta soup). Many of the dishes are faithfully reproduced from old family recipes, including the crowd-pleasing Lamb Osso Bucco. Another choice is the grilled lamb loin with pear William and cinnamon sauce. Desserts include a tart apple flan, a creme brulee and a white chocolate mousse with mango puree. An impressive wine list and perfect service.

Mid-range

Moustache Cafe
1265 Marine Dr, North Van (987-8461)
1812 West Broadway (730-1467)

Both restaurants occupy beautifully restored Heritage homes, with tasteful decor and even tastier food. Try any of the pastas (carbonara is one they do well), or settle for a subtle veal *picatta* (lemon and fine herbs) or *scaloppine al limone* (veal with lemon and white wine sauce). Good dessert selection. Sophisticated wine list. Cosy atmosphere at both locations, but at the West Broadway one there's also an upstairs cigar-and-port room, which tends to keep the main room downstairs pleasantly smoke-free.

Papi's Ristorante Italiano
12251 No 1 Road, Steveston (275-8355)

This restaurant in the sleepy fishing village of Steveston is the only place we've been able to find special kinds of the imported cake known as *pannetone* at Christmas. Overall, the menu is as good as any you'll find at a high-end joint downtown — *vongole alla marinara* (fresh local clams in a garlic, chilies, white wine and tomato sauce) or a lingeringly spicy linguine al pesto — but at two-thirds of the price.

Spumante's Cafe Ristorante
1736 Commercial Drive (253-8899)

The neat thing about this restaurant is that you get the chance to "customize" your meal by determining your own combinations from a menu that offers 38 different "pasta and..." choices, all at the same price of $9.95 at lunch or $24.95 at dinner. We go for the spaghetti carbonara paired with veal. If you want pasta alone, at dinner it's a moderate $9.95. Lunch specials are a great bargain, too. The family running the place is friendly and welcoming, the room is elegant without being intimidating, and the food is well-priced. Clearly a neighbourhood favourite.

Zeppo's Trattoria
1967 West Broadway (737-7444)
6451 Buswell St, Richmond (278-8084)

Owner Urs Fricker runs these locations of Zeppo's with Swiss precision, yet the atmosphere is so authentically Italian, it's uncanny. Daily lunch specials are priced from just $6.95. Pizzas from Zeppo's wood-burning ovens start at $7.95 (for the *Margherita* (tomatoes, Mozzarella and basil) and most of the pastas (like penne puttanesca — fresh tomatoes, olives, capers, garlic and white wine) hover around the $9 mark.

Budget

Without sacrificing a pleasant (and sometimes authentic) ambiance, the following restaurants offer simple, excellent Italian fare at very reasonable prices.

Aldo's Pasta Bar & Italian Restaurant
441 Columbia St, New West (525-3473)

Aldo Zenone offers a varied and very cost-efficient menu in his new restaurant. Pasta dishes start at $6.95 for a generous serving; $9.95 for extra-large. There are soups (a very good *stracciatella* or egg-swirl soup included), antipasto, salads and a variety of pizzas (crusts made with home-made dough).

Anton's Pasta Bar
4260 Hastings St, Burnaby (299-6636)

Immense portions of solid Italian fare explain the number of diners we've seen leaving with doggie-bags — past a lineup of customers waiting to get in. Excellent value for money.

Cipriano's Ristorante & Pizzeria
3995 Main St (879-0020)

This tiny storefront-style operation is an award-winner for its addictive garlic bread, veal, chicken and ribs, Leonardo Da Vinci pizzas ("create your own masterpiece") and six pastas that can be matched with the sauce of your choice.

Da Pasta Bar
1232 Robson St (688-1288; fax: 688-2675)
Da Pasta Bar on Yew
2201 West 1st Ave (738-6515)

There are in excess of 100 possible combinations of pasta shape and sauce available at both these locations. Their secret to success is building the dish from scratch each time — no pre-prepared elements. Good and inexpensive wine list.

Spargo's Restaurant
1796 Nanaimo St (253-5525, 253-4211)

For $7.49, you can get garlic bread, a traditional pasta (spaghetti, lasagna, ravioli) and a salad. (No wonder reservations are a good idea: they're packed at night.) Lo-dough ambiance.

Take-out and Delivery

Although virtually every Italian restaurant in town will prepare food to go, two centrally located establishments deserve their award-winning reputation for fast service and authentic fare.

Lombardo's Ristorante & Pizzeria
#120, 1641 Commercial Drive (251-2240)

Owners Patty and Marcello serve award-winning pizza and calzone, although they don't deliver. The regular menu of pastas and daily specials are served in full or half-portions.

Martini's
151 West Broadway (873-0021, 873-2037, 873-9225)

Famous for their whole-wheat pizza crust and 27 regular and 14 vegetarian choices. Other excellent take-out ranges from pasta to veal Parmesan, all with green salad and garlic bread.

COFFEE BARS, CAFES & COFFEE ROASTING

Three liquids rank in highest esteem in the eyes of Italians: wine, olive oil and coffee. In Little Italy, the little black bean is offered up as both a refreshment and a social lubricant -- whether in a coffee roasting store, a hangout cafe or a combination of the two. Some of these establishments, notably Caffe Roma and Continental Coffee, also make their own Italian-style ice cream on the premises. The Calabria and Caffe Roma, with their gilded mirrors, statuary, faux waterfalls and marble-topped tables could have been transported intact straight from the old country.

For a taste of Italian coffee life, have an espresso and something sweet at one of the following: **Cafe Calabria** (1745 Commercial Drive, 253-7017); **Caffe Roma** (1510 Commercial Drive, 251-7084); **Continental Coffee** (1806 Commercial Drive, 255-0712); **Il Caffe di Milano** (1437 Commercial Drive, 255-5220); **Joe's** (1150 Commercial Drive, 253-9919); and **Torrefazione Coliera** (2206 Commercial Drive, 254-3723).

FOOD STORES

A Bosa & Co
562 Victoria Drive (253-5578; fax: 253-5656)

A wholesale-retail operation, offering everything from food to restaurant equipment. Specializes in bulk quantities of fine extra virgin olive oil, balsamic vinegar and winemaking juice, and several exclusive lines of imported Italian pasta.

Bianca Maria
2469 East Hastings St (253-9626)

Owner Susan Renzullo, who hails from Vicenza, runs this tiny but densely packed store—with a small but select range of goods in every Italian category imaginable.

Cioffi's Meat Market & Deli
4152 Hastings St, Burnaby (291-9373)

Their big, red awning says "Macelleria & Salumeria," and there are the Italian sausages in the window, all right, with large cheeses. Inside, there's a vast assortment of deli meats, cheeses and packaged goods.

Duso's Italian
Granville Island, 1689 Johnson St (685-5921; fax 685-5919)
Lonsdale Quay, 116, 123 Carrie Cates Court, North Van (987-0511)

These two excellent public-market stalls specialize in fresh and dried pasta, dozens of bottled olive oils, fresh sauces and prepared meats.

La Grotta del Formaggio
1791 Commercial Drive (255-3911)

Cheeses, mostly Italian, of every imaginable variety —everything from *caciocavallo* (smoky, cheddar-like), to mozzarella, gorgonzola and Parmesan, sold in rounds, wedges or grated. As well, vinegar, oil, cold meats, pasta, cookies and the seasonal cake pannetone. At the back of the store is a remarkably large collection of Italian videos for rent.

Olivieri Foods
1900 Commercial Drive (255-8844)

Opened in 1957 when Commercial Drive had yet to become little Italy, this is now the humble headquarters of an empire for pasta-maker Peter Olivieri. Great selection of oil, fresh and dried pasta, Parmesan cheese and marinated vegetables.

Falcone Bros Meat Market
1810 Commercial Drive (253-6131)

Established in 1967, this outlet sells fresh and cured meats, sausages and rounds of cheese.

Tosi Italian Food Import Co
624 Main St (681-5740)

This long narrow store (in Chinatown, of all places) carries an extraordinary range of bulk olive oil, whole cheeses, a wide selection of biscuits, biscotti and Baci cookies, and lots of imported, tinned espresso.

Ugo & Joe's Market
2404 East Hastings St (253-6844)

An Italian supermarket with the expected array of oils, cheeses and pastas; also features a large in-store butcher shop (sausage made on the premises) and an espresso bar.

BAKERIES

Ecco Il Pane
1780 West 3rd Ave (731-1814)
238 West 5th Ave (873-6888)
2563 West Broadway (739-1314)

Christopher Brown and Pamela Gaudreault are the hard-working force behind this bread operation. They bake the most wonderful and wholesome Italian country breads you've ever tasted. Their *pane alle oliva* combines the subtlety of Manzanilla and calamata olives in a dense, fragrant, round loaf. *Ficelle*, a small cousin to the French baguette, has a crunchy crust and moist, porous interior. A popular choice is the *dolce mio*, a buttery and fragrant version of raisin bread with orange zest, anise, Marsala, currants and walnuts.

There are numerous shops catering to the Italian sweet tooth with everything from ornate cakes to cream filled tarts, plus, of course, classic breads. Plunk your *lire* down at **Bon Bon Bakery** (where fresh fruit cakes, cream puff cakes and biscotti are tops at 5807 Victoria Drive, 325-3612); tira misu, bread, buns and take-out pizza at **Italia Pasticeria Bakery & Deli** (2828 East Hastings St, 251-6800); and **Renato Pastry Shop** (1795 Commercial Drive, 255-8921).

ITALIAN-STYLE ICE CREAM

Rich, creamy Italian ice cream is a sweet treat, even though many of its makers now accommodate health-conscious devotees with low-fat versions. Most of the outlets listed here do a brisk retail and wholesale business, and make their wares on-site: **Ital Cream** (829

Bute St, 687-0829), with more than 40 flavours, creamy and sher-
bet-style, guaranteed no more than 24 hours old; **La Casa Gelato** at
1033 Venables (251-3211); **Mario's Gelati** (235 East 5th Ave, 879-
9411; fax: 879-0435); **Valentino's Ice Cream Corner** (8646
Granville St, 263-3310), the city's first Italian ice cream maker and
vendor; and **Venezia Ice Cream** (5752 Victoria Drive, 327-8614).

APPAREL

Shoes

Vancouver has three locations for fabulous Italian footwear, generally regarded as the finest in the world. It can seen prohibitively
expensive, but it's often said that the old adage "You get what
you pay for" was first coined about shoes: **Rino's Italian Shoe
Centre** (4172 Fraser St, 876-5316); **Salvatore Ferragamo** (918
Robson St, 669-4495, 669-2218); and **Melonari Custom Made
Shoes** (1165 William St, 255-4459).

High Fashion

Chevalier Creations
2756 Granville St (731-8746)

Moroccan-born Gabriel Kalfon tailors men's and women's
Italian-style custom suits here. Expensive.

Leone
757 West Hastings St (683-1133)

Imported men's and women's attire from Armani, Versace and
Leone's own lines. Expensive.

ENTERTAINMENT

Video Rentals

24-Hour Video
2496 East Hastings St (254-7164)

About 50 titles in Italian are available.

Videomatica
1185 West 4th Ave (734-0411)

Graham Peet carries a wide array of recent-release and classic Italian films; some are available for purchase at Videomatica Sales next door.

GREEK

The Greek community, now numbering some 6500, laid down its earliest roots in East Vancouver in the mid-19th century but soon established a business centre along West Broadway, near its church of the day, which was at West 7th Ave and Vine; by the time a new church was built at 4500 Arbutus in the early '70s, the commercial district between 2900 and 3200 West Broadway was a sufficiently thriving part of the city's life as to earn the nickname "Greektown."

There are two centres of Greek cultural life in the metropolitan area. **The Hellenic Centre**, established in 1977 by the 70-year-old Hellenic Community of Vancouver, is an impressive white complex at 4500 Arbutus St (266-7148; fax 266-7140). It houses a Greek-language school, provides meeting facilities for a variety of youth, social, musical and sporting clubs, and is the headquarters of the **Hellenic Canadian Congress of B.C.**, which represents organizations province-wide and publishes a Greek telephone directory. (The Hellenic Canadian Congress can be contacted at 733-3736; fax 738-7101). **The Greek Community of East Vancouver** (4541 Boundary Rd, 438-6432) is responsible for, among other activities, the annual Greek festival (details below). Note that both the Hellenic Centre and East Vancouver groups are adjuncts — geographically and doubtless spiritually — of the city's two Greek Orthodox churches.

The **Kitsilano branch** of the Vancouver Public Library has extensive holdings devoted to Greek literature and the visual arts.

St. George's Greek Orthodox Cathedral (4500 Arbutus St, 266-7148), with its ornate gilt religious artifacts and paintings, is not just a religious centre for the Greek community but virtually an ecclesiastical museum worth a visit from a visual standpoint alone. In recognition of the numbers of tourists who visit, St. George's has published *A Personal Welcome*, a guidebook that explains the church's architectural, artistic and religious significance. Greek-language services begin Sunday at 10 am. **St. Nicholas-Demetrios Greek Orthodox Church** (4641 Boundary Rd, 438-6432) has services beginning Sunday at 9 am.

Greek Summer Fest, which began in 1974, is now an annual mid-July celebration organized by the Greek Community of East Vancouver adjacent to the St. Nicholas-Demetrios church; the festival runs for 10 days and attracts upwards of 40,000 revellers. There are performances by musical groups and school dance troupes (the Socrates Greek School, the Pythagoras Greek School, etc.), slide shows, church tours and food galore at rock-bottom prices.

The **Greek Canadian Voice** is a weekly bilingual newspaper, a good source for restaurant and retail information through its advertisements, not all of which are in Greek. **Opinion** is a biweekly newspaper. **Patrides** is a monthly continent-wide newspaper with a Vancouver edition — and thus some local news and ads. All of these publications can usually be found at Greek stores and restaurants.

CJVB Radio (AM 1470, cable 103.3 FM) broadcasts two hours of Greek news and music every Sunday afternoon. The subscriber-based **HRN** (**67 FM**), a division of Hellenic Radio and Television Media, prides itself on "broadcasting to the Greek community in the official language of Greece every minute of every day since 1987." (For details, call 325-1292; fax 327-9703.)

FOOD STORES

Whether in Greektown or elsewhere in the city, a Greek food store worthy of the name will stock a seemingly endless variety of olives — purple, black and green, available by the scoop — and there'll be entire aisles of tinned and bottled olive oil. In the deli section, you'll find tubs of yogurt, anchovies, a pork sausage called *loukania*, and usually such prepared delicacies as *dolmathes* (grape leaves stuffed with rice and ground meat) and *spanakopita* (cheese and spinach wrapped in filo pastry). The most famous Greek cheese is, of course, the crumbly goat cheese called *feta*, but almost as popular are *kasseri* (soft, oily), *kefalotyri* (salty, somewhat parmesan-like), and *mizithra* (mild and dry). The grocery section will stock tinned tomato paste, pickled goods (like the pink onions known as *volvi*), dried beans, sultana raisins, coffee, bulk spices and Greek honey (*meli*), the key sweetener in the famous *baklava* dessert.

Bread, fish and fresh meat in any great variety are usually purchased in stores exclusively devoted to such fare.

With all of that in mind, we've found the following outlets to be the most dependable and fun to explore.

Broadway Bakery & Pastries
3273 West Broadway (733-1422)

Greek pastries, pita bread and light but substantial Greek loaves.

Minerva Imports
2924 West 4th Ave (733-3956)
Minerva's Mediterranean Deli
3207 West Broadway (733-3954; fax 732-7113)

A wide array of Greek foodstuffs (particularly spices, much of it packaged under their own label), citrus and orange blossom waters, frozen filo pastry, biscuits, preserves, olives, oils and figs. Also: a selection of decorative artworks, and cassette tapes and videos for sale or rent.

Parthenon Wholesale and Retail Food
2968 West Broadway (733-4191)

If you're hooked on those steamed almond milks that cost far more at the cappuccino bars, buy the almond syrup — it's the same. Food-service people may be able to get further discounts here, but only for bulk purchases. Parthenon sells all kinds of feta cheeses, and if you're browsing for olives, they'll let you sample to find ones you like. Meanwhile, enjoy the Greek music on the sound system.

Serano Greek Pastry
3185 West Broadway (739-3181)

This small shop is a dependable source of pita bread, *spanako-pita*, *tiropita* and *baklava*. Try the *rox*, a honey-sweet confection resembling a cinnamon bun.

Zorba's Bakery & Foods Ltd
7173 Buller Ave, Burnaby (439-7731, fax: 439-0525)

Wholesale prices on Greek foods such as pitas, homous, tzatziki and Greek pastries at this factory/bakery, which also carries some imported Greek specialty foods. All their products are wholesome, made without artificial flavours, additives or colours. If there's no one at the counter when you arrive, just ring the cowbell for service.

RESTAURANTS

Greek cuisine is one of the most affordable, delicious and widely enjoyed of the city's many international dining experiences. Restaurant ambiance is invariable cheerful (if not boisterous) and genuinely reminiscent of the *tavernas* in Greece. Classic Greek meals start with *mezethes* (hors d'oeuvres) like *dolmathes* (grape leaves stuffed with rice and ground meat), *kalamari* (deep-fried squid), *keftedes* (meatballs), *sikotakia* (sauteed chicken livers), *spanakopita* (cheese and spinach wrapped in filo). The famous Greek salad is called *horiatiki*, while *avgolemono* is the ever-popular egg-and-chicken-broth soup. Entrees range from *souvlaki* (meat — usually lamb — charcoaled on a skewer) to *moussaka* (like an eggplant lasagna) to *pasticio* (pasta with ground beef or lamb). The most famous dessert is *baklava*, an exquisitely sweet combination of filo pastry, nuts and honey. Ouzo, an anise-flavoured liquor, is the national after-dinner drink.

Following are places to enjoy an authentic Greek meal — always accompanied by music, sometimes performed live. Most are licensed.

Joudy's
122 Kingsway (874-3800)

Stated simply, this is our favourite Greek restaurant in town. The avgolemono soup is always perfect — and chock full of fresh, tender chicken (not the usual boiling fowl). That, and all the rest of the excellent fare, is prepared by Joudy Jarwe himself, a former a ship's cook — until he jumped ship to settle here. His new location is upstairs and around the corner from where he used to be — look for his large blue and white striped awning; free parking in the back after 6 pm. New menu items include escargots, fillet of sole or exquisite prawns and scallops.

Kalamata
487 West Broadway (872-7050)

A place that really doesn't get nearly the amount of recognition it deserves, Kalamata is a charming, bright, clean and spacious environment with tile floors, comfy wooden chairs and a varied and affordable menu.

Le Grec
1447 Commercial Drive (253-1253)

Sun-splashed walls and real plants trailing down plaster arches provide a backdrop for the splendid menu of upmarket Greek cuisine. This is a nice place to take a client for lunch, or stop for a solid meal while shopping on The Drive.

Martini's
151 West Broadway (873-0021/2307/9225)

Known largely for its pizza, Martini's has such excellent dishes as prawns "a la Greek" (baked with onions, spinach, tomatoes, feta and white wine); and marinated, breaded and deep-fried kalamari.

Meli's Taverna
1905 West Broadway (736-8330, 736-8345)

In this spotless, light and airy room with nicely spaced tables you can enjoy impeccably prepared food at extremely inexpensive prices: Greek salads made to order, avgolemono soup, rack-of-lamb dinner specials, pan-fried chicken livers.

Vasillis Greek Taverna
2884 West Broadway (733-3231)

Reliably good food in a family-run, large-yet-cosy environment. The pizza is good, the moussaka exceptional.

Other excellent Greek restaurants include **Acropol** (2946 West Broadway, 733-2412); **Maria's Taverna** at 2324 West 4th Ave (731-4722); **Rodos Taverna & Souvlaki House** (2217 East Hastings St, 255-6040); **Romios Greek Taverna** (2272 West 4th Ave, 736-2118, 736-9442); **Santorini Taverna** (345 North Road, Coquitlam, 931-5500, fax 931-5501); **Socrates Greek Taverna** (6633 East Hastings, Burnaby, 299-3777 or 20691 Lougheed Hwy, Maple Ridge, 465-1393); **Stepho's Souvlaki Greek Taverna** at 1124 Davie St (683-2555); **Vassilis Souvlaki Greek Taverna** (no relation to the West Broadway one) at 6558 Kingsway, Burnaby (434-0626); and **The Vine Yard Restaurant** (2296 West 4th Ave, 733-2420).

Adjacent to Lonsdale Quay in North Vancouver are two Greek restaurants worth a visit; both offer charming decor and the standard delicacies: **Anatoli Souvlaki** (5 Lonsdale Ave, 985-9853/7345; fax 985-0277); and **Your Place or Mine** (107 West Esplanade, 986-6211). Nearby is **Pasparos Taverna** (132 West 3rd Ave, North Vancouver, 980-0331).

STORES

Vicky's Children's Wear
2618 West Broadway (731-8919)

Owner John Ferelos designs Greek costumes for festival and ceremonial wear; although he might take as long as two weeks to make a single outfit, the prices can be as low as $200 for a beautiful handmade embroidered vest.

AFRICAN

We have grouped all African nations — and tagged in some Indian foods with an East African flair — because they share a common land base, even though the cultures are so diverse and distinct.

There are almost 6,500 people of African heritage living in the Vancouver region. Among the local organizations are **African Canadian Assn of BC** at 206, 111 West Broadway (875-1763); **Africa-Canada Development & Information Services Assn**, 4, 4926 Imperial St, Burnaby (431-9503; fax 431-9503); **African National Congress** 2705 West 42nd Ave (263-8508); **Ethiopian Community of BC** at P.O. Box 3394, Vancouver V6B 3Y4 (687-6530); **Ghanaian Cultural Association of BC**, P.O. Box 42004, Vancouver V5S 4G3 (583-9847; fax 684-3255); **Guyanese Canadian Assn of BC**, Box 2869, M P O, Vancouver V6B 3W5 (421-0629); **Nigeria Cultural Assn of BC**, 331, 810 West Broadway (publishes quarterly newsletter, The Gong, 228-9068); **Oromo Community Assn**, P.O. Box 2328, M P O, Vancouver V6B 3W5 (872-5124); **Thamil Cultural Society of BC**, Box 2869, MPO, Vancouver V6B 3W5 (language classes for children, cultural activities, 222-3550); and **Uganda Cultural Assn of BC**, 4478 West 13th Ave (228-9241).

Locally, a multicultural festival is held in July in celebration of **Africa Day**, including food, drumming, arts and crafts and membership drives. It's organized by the African Canadian Assn (as above).

RESTAURANTS

In Ethiopian cuisine, the *injera* (or bread) is made from a dough fermented for two or three days before baking. The thin dough is then cooked like a pancake and served in a size about 14 inches in diameter. This is usually accompanied by thin strips of injera, rolled up to be used to scoop and soak up sauces. The texture of the bread is visually not unlike thin, spongy foam padding, yet to the mouth it is remarkably light and tasty.

Afro Canadian Restaurant
324 Cambie St (682-2646)

This Gastown restaurant offers classic Abbysinian/Ethiopian cuisine, where various stews and curries are served on injera. You scoop portions of the food into your mouth with the injera and your hands. Open for lunch and dinner.

Fassil Ethiopian Restaurant
5, 736 East Broadway (879-2001)

As is true in other Ethiopian restaurants, food here is served directly onto the crepe-like injera bread and eaten with the hands. Owner Moges Said explains that the Ethiopian kitchen is a woman's domain. In fact, men aren't even allowed in there. Said's wife, naturally, does all the cooking. A delicious choice is the *atakilt*, sauteed cabbage, potatoes and carrots in a mild sauce. Another is *yedero wot*, a spicy chicken dish with whole, hard-cooked eggs, onions, and fiery berbere sauce.

Nyala Restaurant
2930 West 4th Ave (731-7899)

Aggressive marketing has placed Nyala in the forefront in the Ethiopian restaurant scene (which is growing) in Vancouver. They are very active in the community at festivals, Taste of the Nation, and so on. They also provide cooking classes periodically (call to inquire) and often show photos, such as the recent exhibition of images from Ethiopia, from the Rift Valley to the Spice Markets. Food is characteristic of that country: curries, stews and injera bread. The Nyala's vegetarian buffet is offered Wednesday and Sunday from 5 to 10 pm at a cost of $10 per person (children dine for $6).

Queen Sheba Ethiopian Restaurant
382 West Broadway (877-0189)

The most recent of Vancouver's Ethiopian restaurants offers homemade-style dishes from lamb, beef, chicken and fish, plus many vegetarian choices, all slow-simmered in pure filtered butter or olive oil. Among the offerings are *assa tibs wet* (shrimp and fish in curry), *yebeg alecha* (a mild lamb stew), *doro wet* (a fiery hot chicken stew) and vegetarian items with lentils, chick peas or greens. All are served on injera bread.

EAST AFRICAN

Kilimanjaro
200, 332 Water St (681-9913)

Owners Amyn and Nargis Sunderji dressed their restaurant like a stage set with African masks and batiks and languid ceiling fans. The Zanzibar coconut fish soup is praiseworthy, as is a Swahili specialty of curried goat and a Zairean blending of chicken and ho-ho peppers, palm oil and garlic. The house specialty is Burning Spear, or lamb served flaming on a sword. A cafe operation downstairs (The Safari Bistro) echoes the main restaurant's theme.

Pyasa
3229 Kingsway (437-9272)

Amin Charania, an Ismaili from East Africa, opened this restaurant in December, 1994. They offer good food, karaoke (on selected days) and the unique inducement of free babysitting, while you dine (reserve ahead). Enjoy *bhajia la pyasa* (potatoes, chopped onion, green chilies mixed with flour and deep fried), *mogo* (slices of casava dipped in eggs and chana flour and deep fried), various samosas, many entrees (*karai* lamb, for instance is lamb curry cooked in a special wok), *chapatis* (soft, unleavened, grilled bread) or *papadum* (crispy lentil wafers). Their are novel items like Indian-style French toast (sweet and hot) or an omelette with *paratha* (unleavened bread), *puri* (deep-fried rounds of unleavened bread), and *roti* (Tandoor-bakcd bread). Desserts include various sweets like *ras malai* (homemade cheese patty served cold with pistachio.

Zeenaz Restaurant
6460 Main St (324-9344)

Sadrubin Pisani and his chef-wife Dolly offer a respectable menu with an interesting, East African flair. Casava root, which grows in Fiji, Africa and Costa Rica, plays a large role. Most of the food is East Indian-based, except they use more ginger and garlic and very little tumeric. There's no butter, *ghee* (made from butter) or cheese — only pure vegetable oil in the cooking. They feature an all-you-can-eat buffet that changes daily ($8.95 lunch; $10.95 dinner) of two meat curries, two veggie curries, the "best lentil soup in town," chappatis, papadums, the "best samosas in town," homemade carrot or lemon pickles, med-hot, strong-hot chutneys and a medium-sweet dessert. All cooking is mild to medium (with hot stuff on the side).

STORES

African Market
2258 West 4th Ave (739-1280)
2665 West Broadway (732-7480)

Nick & Sigi Bhangi run these places where you can find Kenyan *kilimbas* ("thumb pianos"), carved ebony figures (from the Makone people of Tanzania), wooden snakes and bracelets, Ugandan drums, purses, shirts, jackets and loose-fitting, colourful cotton pants.

Flavors
2054 Commercial Drive (258-0016; fax 258-4046)

This dine-in, take-out deli has everything from Ethiopian groceries to cheesecake, falafel, spices and bread. They also sell African tapes and CDs.

Out of Africa Global Culture
Lonsdale Quay, 201, 123 Carrie Cates Court, North Van (986-4113)

This "global culture" shop on the building's second floor has cast its net far beyond the so-called Dark Continent. You'll find Indonesian sarongs, Guatemalan cotton tops, Burmese pots and trays, Tibetan stone jewellery, Thai silver earrings, and "unisex vests" from Thailand, Nepal and Guatemala. Consistent with their name, though, are masks from Mali and the Ivory Coast, carved wooden animals and ebony from Kenya, and South African pottery and marimbas.

Touch of Africa
737K, 4567 Lougheed Hwy, Burnaby (291-0606)
130, 810 Quayside Drive, New West (524-8822)

A very nice collection of Kenyan carvings, wooden puzzles, drums, bright clothing, pots and decor items. The small wooden "hairpick" carvings of African animals are good value for a couple of dollars.

DRUM & DANCE

Drum and Dance workshops are held periodically (usually in the summer) at various venues and community colleges. The best way to find out about them is to scan Commercial Drive for posters.

The **First African Diaspora Dance Workshop** (three days of African dance) was held in the fall of 1995 at Main Dance Studio, 828 East Hastings St, featuring native drummers from Brazil, Nigeria and Caribe. For details on the next one, call 436-9221.

MIDDLE EASTERN

ARABIC

As reported recently in the *Courier* newspaper, Vancouver's 12,000 Arabs are committed to assimilation in Canada and thus have tended not to foster community associations based on nationality — partly because they have come from as many as 22 countries, ranging from Morocco in the west to Afghanistan in the east. What few clubs do exist (the Lebanese club, the Egyptian club, etc.) have no official buildings, and members are inclined to meet at one another's homes. Still, there is hope, in the form of the **Arab Community Centre Association**, that a permanent meeting place may be built someday. For details about the association's activities and fundraising plans, write P.O. Box 27060, 1395 Marine Drive, West Vancouver V7T 1H0 or call 421-1217.

Until an Arab-Canadian centre is erected, the Muslim majority can be counted on to congregate at any one of three Lower Mainland mosques: at 12300 Bundell Road in Richmond, also the location of the B.C. Muslim Association (call 270-2522 for details about both);

12407, 72nd Ave in Surrey; and 655 West 8th Ave in Vancouver.

Meanwhile, some stores and cafes do exist to cater to a middle Eastern clientele. **101 Yek O Yek Deli & Bulk Food** at 3046 Main St (877-0139) offers a full roster of spices, groceries and foods imported from the Mediterranean, Mid-East and even Far East, as well as falafel, samosas and deli take-out. The store plans to have videos for rent in various mid-Eastern languages.

Then there's Shlomo Cohen's **Deserts Middle East Vegetarian Restaurant**, a hidden gem across at 322 West Hastings St (669-0042), which does catering and festivals, as well as providing a full range of Moroccan and other middle Eastern cuisine at rock-bottom prices. Try the *falafel* (chopped, spiced chickpeas) or *latke* (potato pancake) at only $3, the lentil soup at $2 or a veggie samosa and chutney for a mere $1.25. Falafel, by the way was supposed to have originated in Egypt (in Cairo it's called *ta'amia*), where it's made instead with broad beans. The chickpea version is popular in Syria, Lebanon, Israel — and here.

Also consider **Elmasu Food Importers** at 3477 Commercial St (873-2244; fax 873-2262). (Yes, that's Commercial Street, not Drive.) This importer specializes in Mediterranean foods, and has — since 1977 — supplied the Arab community with top quality comestibles. Though they call themselves wholesalers, they will sell retail. Check them out for olives, cheese, spices, bulk olive oil, bulgur wheat, falafel, deli meats and lentils. The bakery section (called **Jerusalem Bakery**) features Arabic and Mid-Eastern pastries.

There's also **B.C. Market** at 930 Twelfth St, New West (522-3733) with Arabic video rentals, foods (Koura olive oil, cous cous, *halabi* (a spice mix of thyme, crushed sumac, sesame seed and salt), pickled wild cucumbers and an entire wall of spices.

The **Voice of Palestine** (Box 3003, Vancouver V6B 3X5) at 102.7 FM (684-8494) broadcasts to our Arab community.

HALAL MEATS

Halal is a Muslim religious tradition where the animal (beef, chicken, goat, lamb) is blessed when slaughtered or cut and is prepared in a particularly hygienic fashion. *Halal* is food permitted by the doctrines of the Koran.

Only certain Lower Mainland butchers specialize in Halal

meats. Among them is **The Mad Butcher** at 6489 Victoria Dr (327-5884), which specializes in lamb chops, fine cuts of beef, fresh local goat, New Zealand lamb, fresh stewing chicken, plus an assortment of East Indian sweets, plus samosas, *idli* (a steamed round bread made of rice and lentils, usually flavoured with coconut), chutneys and more.

Also check out **Al-Aqsa Specialty Foods** at 4879 Main St (877-2243); **Al Halal Meats** at 5022 Victoria Drive (322-9781); **Fraser Halal Meats** at 4283 Fraser St (874-4014); **Halal Meats & Deli**, 4413 Main St (879-5518); **Kohinoor Grocery**, specializing in lamb and goat at 195 East 26th Ave (872-7399); **Madina Halal Meats & Delicatessen** at 4971 Victoria Drive (321-5552); **Richmond Halal Meats** 6390 No 3 Road, Richmond (279-0332), which also stocks Adhan clocks, Islamic books and tapes; and **Zodiak Fast Foods** at 151 East Hastings St (683-9632).

LEBANESE

The **Lebanese Canadian Society of B.C.** is a non-political organization committed simply to preserving social and cultural connections. It is the driving force behind the annual Lebanese Cultural Day, famous for performances by its Dabke Dancers troupe. For information, write P.O. Box 31075, 8 - 2929 St. John's Street, Port Moody V3H 2C0 or call/fax 520-1346.

A substantial minority of Lebanese are Christian, who have a choice of worshipping at two Vancouver churches: **St. Elias Orthodox Church** (1308 Ewen Ave, New Westminster, 433-5674) holds services in Arabic and English Sunday at 10:30 am; **St. George's Melkite Greek Catholic Mission** (6610 Balmoral St, 434-0279; fax 434-4798) has services in Arabic three Sundays per month.

RESTAURANTS

Cedars of Lebanon Restaurant
818 Howe St (683-7972)

At this mostly-takeout restaurant (there's a small eating area), you order from a 10-item menu, refreshing your memory with the food photographs on the wall. The house specialty is the chicken or beef *shawarma*, which is similar to a Greek donair: The meat is cooked in a conical mass on a vertical spit that rotates in front of a special grill; thin slices are cut off as the outer layers of meat cook. There's also a vegetable platter and *tabouleh*, a Lebanese salad made with parsley, bulgar wheat, tomatoes, olive oil and lemon.

El Caravan
809 Seymour St (682-7000)
805 West Broadway (875-8338)

The owner is Egyptian here, but the cooks are Lebanese; together they serve a cuisine that you'll find throughout the Middle East and Mediterranean: falafel (chick pea patties in pita), *houmous* (chick peas, a sesame paste called *tahini*, lemon and garlic) and *baba ghannoj* (a dip made from eggplant and tahini). An all-inclusive price on Saturday night gets you dinner and live Arabic music and dancing.

The Falafel King
1110 Denman St (669-7278)

Again, photographs of the dishes help you decide whether you want a falafel sandwich, tabouleh, shawarma, houmous, kabob or a vegetarian plate (which includes most of the above). The main dessert, *baklava* (walnuts and honey wrapped in paper thin layers of filo pastry) is found throughout Greece and the Middle East.

IRANIAN

The North Shore — particularly around the 900 block of Marine Drive — has become a popular residential and commercial centre for the city's Iranian Canadians, who number approximately 6500.

Shahrvand-E-Vancouver bills itself as "a weekly newspaper published for the Persian Speaking Community in Western Canada" (and that's the extent of the English you'll read in this paper.

For a copy, write P.O. Box 78084, Port Coquitlam V3B 7H5 or call 469-1808.

Then there's the **Persian Moslem Foundation** at 1668 Lloyd Ave, North Van (980-9422).

Rogers Multicultural Channel airs *Beyad-E-Iran*, an arts, entertainment and news package in Farsi, daily. Producer is Ladan Bahramnia (294-4384; fax 294-4354).

FOOD STORES

Bijan Specialty Foods
1451 Clyde Ave, West Van (925-1055)

This grocery store offers mixes for making yogurt dip and *kooko sabzi* (a type of vegetable omelette); seasonings for chicken kabobs; packets of spices — like sumac, a dried, ground red berry from the sumach tree that has a lemony taste and is used in soups and salads and is often sprinkled on top of rice or kebabs; a large selection of jams, including some made from carrots; cans of flavoured yogurt soda; bulk pistachios and dried fruit as well as olives and feta cheese; and *halva*, a confection made from ground nuts. Bijan also rents Iranian videos and sells tapes and CDs.

Iran Super
987 Marine Dr, North Van (987-0987)

Just inside the door of this grocery store are sacks of snack foods — everything from watermelon and pumpkin seeds to pistachio nuts and green raisins. Other imported Iranian delicacies sold in bulk are figs, dates, olives and feta cheese. You'll find a dozen types of rice; fava beans (dried, tinned and even frozen); and packages of herbs, spices and dried fruit and vegetables, like leeks and whole limes (*limu omani*) that are used to flavour soups and stews. There are such tinned items as green tomato salad and fried eggplant, and bottles of syrups (mint, rose water and orange blossom) used for flavouring drinks and desserts. Also tapes and CDs.

Pars Deli Mart
1801 Lonsdale Ave, North Van (988-3515)

You'll find Iranian food imports, bulk olives and cheese, and some foodstuffs from other middle Eastern countries. There's a particularly large selection of rental videos, plus music tapes and books in Persian for sale.

BAKERIES

The **Rose Bakery** at 1537 Lonsdale Ave, North Van (980-2649) and the **Laleh Bakery** at 130 West 15th St, North Van (986-6364) offer pretty much the same sort of wares and supply other Iranian stores in the area: a variety of Arabic *sheriny* (pastries and cookies) and *nan* (bread). They specialize in almond and walnut cookies, *lavash* (squares of thin crispy bread), *barbari* (long flat loaves of bread some with a sprinkle of sesame seeds on top), *bomia* (doughnut-like batter is deep-fried and then dipped in honey), Turkish delight sold by the gram, and a shortbread-style cookie with the name of the store stamped right onto the cookie.

RESTAURANTS

Caspian Restaurant
1495 Marine Dr, West Van (922-0101)

This upscale Persian dining experience, complete with live entertainment on weekends, features such dishes as a variety of mildly spiced *Khoresh* (stewed meat in sauce — a mainstay of Iranian cuisine, always served with rice); various kids of *kebabs* (which literally means cooked on a grill); a mint flavoured yogurt drink called *doogh*; and *faloodeh*, a uniquely Iranian dessert of vermicelli noodles in a lemon ice (sounds odd, but it's very good). Ice cream, incidentally, is believed to have been invented in the Middle East, so it's worth trying some here.

Kababsara Restaurant
1533 Lonsdale Ave, North Van (985-5321)

The menu is limited to three different types of kabobs — ground beef, boneless chicken, or bone-in chicken — with yogurt and cucumber sauce, and soft drinks or special *kababsara doogh*, a drink made from yogurt, water, mint, salt and pepper. Each dish comes with pita bread and a mound of parsley, lemon and grilled tomatoes. This is the type of food sold in roadside stands all over Iran and is the equivalent of our hamburger.

Kolbeh Deli & Restaurant
731 Lonsdale Ave, North Van (990-0062)

Owner Rahim Farokhi dishes up family recipes at a small eating area or for takeout; photographs on the wall help identify items on the menu. There's *aashe reshteh* (vegetable soup with noodle) or *kolbeh* soup (lamb, vegetables and rice); *falafel* (deep fried ground chickpeas) and kebabs served in pita bread with your choice of tabooli salad, tahini sauce, hot peppers and dill pickle; *kooko sabzi* (a type of omelette jampacked with vegetables); and the *bandari* hot dog (a wiener in hot sauce served on pita). For dessert, try *sholezard* (a kind of rice pudding made with rosewater, saffron and cinnamon, topped with ground pistachios), *jelubia* (a doughnut batter deep fried in a circular pattern and then soaked in rosewater); and *palootah* (or *faloodeh*, which is noodles in frozen sweetened lemon).

Soody's Cuisine
203, 1610 Robson St (687-7475)

Located in the Robson Market, they offer a different soup daily, and rotate their entree specials every two weeks — like *badenjon atew* (eggplant and meat in a tomato sauce), *albaloo polo* (black cherries with meat and rice) and *fesenjune stew*, which contains walnuts and pomegranate juice.

Other restaurants with Iranian food on their menus are **Cazba Restaurant** at 1352 Lonsdale Ave, North Van (984-7311); and **Zagros** at 1326 Davie St (689-1683).

CARPET STORES

Persian carpets are probably the best-known Iranian export.

Sizes vary from one-square-foot squares to room-sized carpets. Most are 100% wool, but there are some silk carpets, which are popular for their clarity of colour and sheen. A good carpet store will have stacks of carpets, each clearly marked with the type of carpet as well as the country and city of origin. Here are a few of the city's many carpet dealers.

Minaret Oriental Carpets
3003 Granville St (733-6414)

Watch for the partially completed rug on a loom in the window, along with the chart that explains the process.

Shensai Carpet Ltd
1165 West 15th, North Van (986-8514)
1446 Marine Drive, West Van (925-1446)

Both stores have miniature looms in the window with half-finished rugs, so you can see how they're hand-knotted. The West Vancouver outlet, which is the much smaller of the two, has a selection of shoes and handbags made from handwoven fabric.

Vancouver Rug Import
101 Water St (688-6787)

They sell round Tabriz carpets, which are much less common than the usual rectangular ones. Be sure to pick up their pamphlet on the story of handmade Persian rugs.

BOOKS

Furugh Books
244 Lonsdale Ave, North Van (988-2236)

They carry books for adults and children in Parsi and in English.

S. Eskandani
2003 West 35th Ave, Vancouver V6M 1J1 (266-4553)

Not a retail operation, this supplier instead takes orders for books for Iranian children's literature, and for fiction.

AFGHANISTAN

Immigrants from Afghanistan use **The Afghan Association of B.C.** (101, 6955 Kingsway, 522-2340) as a central clearinghouse for information on cultural events; as well, they can avail themselves of lessons in their native language, which is called *Dari*. Afghan television can be sampled on the **Rogers** multicultural channel, Sunday from 1 pm to 1:30, with rebroadcasts Monday 3 to 3:30 and Wednesday 4 to 4:30.

RESTAURANTS AND FOOD STORES

Afghan Fast Foods
1167 Granville St (685-7771)

There's a small area for those who wish to eat in, but most of the traffic at this shop is takeout. Specialties include *aash* (a vegetable soup with meat), *bolani* (potato, tomato and onion), *chapali kebab* (ground beef cooked on a skewer and served in Afghani bread) and goat stew.

Afghan Horseman Restaurant
445 West Broadway (873-5923)

The best way to get a taste of a number of different items is to order the appetizer platter or the Horseman platter for two. Specialties are *sabzi maast* (a spinach and yogurt dip), a lentil stew called *dahl palav*, *aushak* (the Afghan equivalent of ravioli) and kebabs made with chicken, lamb or ground beef.

CARPETS

Afghanistan's main exports are sheepskins and carpets. (Note that carpet stores listed in our Iran section also carry Afghan rugs.) Another attractive handicraft is the camel bag, which features carpet on one side and plain weaving on the other.

Ararat Oriental Rug Co
2221 Granville St (733-5616)

Ararat has been operating from the same South Granville location since 1930. Owner Mohammed carries carpets like Tabriz
(from Iran), Hamadan or Boukhara (both from Pakistan) and
Afhgani carpets, at prices from $300 to $15,000. Ararat also provides reliable repairs and cleaning.

JEWISH

The Jewish community in B.C. has roots in the province that ex-
tend as far back as the 1850s, though the first tiny synagogue,
B'nai Yehudah (later to become Schara Tzedeck), wasn't built until 1912. By that time, there were some 1,300 Jews in Vancouver
— mainly downtown in what is now Strathcona and Chinatown.
Today, Vancouver's Jewish population numbers some 30,000,
with the largest communities concentrated in the Oakridge area
and in Richmond.

The Jewish faith is based on a strong sense of family and community. Consequently, synagogues (*shuls*, or temples, as they are
sometimes called) are as often a nexus for social life as a place for
religious observance. According to Leo Rosten's excellent and
highly entertaining **The Joys of Yiddish**, "The *shul* was the cen-
ter, the 'courthouse square,' the forum of Jewish communal life."
Throughout the Lower Mainland, in fact, even organizations calling themselves "community centres" function in a quasi-spiri-
tual manner. Such is the case with the **White Rock/South Surrey
Jewish Community Centre** (mentioned below) and the **Jewish
Community Centre** on West 41st Avenue. Certainly the oldest —
and likely the largest Jewish congregation is at **Schara Tzedeck**,
the synagogue at 3476 Oak St (736-7607). **Beth Israel's** congregation is attracting lots of younger Jewish families at 4350 Oak St
(731-4161). Smaller temples, such as the progressive and egalitar-
ian **Or Shalom** at 710 East 10th Ave (872-1614) attract a growing
number of Jews who may have felt out of place attending services
in larger places of worship.

Festivals are celebrated for *Chanukah* (the Festival of Lights),
Purim (the Feast of Esther) and *Simcha Torah* (the date when the

holy book's scroll is rolled back to the beginning, so the reading can start anew). A minor festival honours the harvest as *Succot,* when free-standing structures are built and decorated with wheat, corn, squash and other harvested foods.

CULTURAL LIFE

As already noted, the **Jewish Community Centre at** 950 West 41th Ave (257-5111; fax 257-5121) is the hub of much of Jewish cultural life in Vancouver. It houses various organizations and provides support for immigrants, via the **Jewish Family Service Agency** at 257-5151 (fax 263-2264). A greeting service for newcomers to the community is operated by **Shalom Vancouver** at the JCC.

Jewish music events and plays are held throughout the year at various venues, ranging from the Vancouver East Cultural Centre to Firehall Theatre. Information about most of these upcoming events, as well as recitals, lectures and art shows, can usually be obtained from the JCC.

The annual **Jewish Film Festival** runs in May and June, sponsored by the Jewish Festival of the Arts Society (266-0245). Some screenings are at the Pacific Cinematheque; others are in the Norman Rothstein Theatre in the JCC. Call for details.

The **Jewish Arts Festival** was a two-day event held for the first time in 1995 at Performance Works on Granville Island, and there are plans to make it an annual event. This year's festival included musical performances (jazz through klezmer), choirs, arts & crafts, storytelling, comedy, a craft market, a juried art exhibit and children's entertainers. For details, write c/o 305, 950 West 41st Ave, Vancouver, V5Z 2N7 (266-0245; fax: 266-0247).

The **Jewish Beaux Arts** is a show and sale of Jewish fine art, held in the fall at the Sidney and Gertrude Zack Gallery, 950 West 41st Ave (257-5111).

On a musical note, the **Jewish Folk Choir,** founded by Searle Friedman, combines haunting harmonies with stirring music. For bookings, call 325-1812. Another traditional Jewish singing group available for party engagements is **Simchaphonics;** contact Gordon or Joyce Cherry at 261-5454. The **Tzimmes Musical Ensemble** derives its name from a traditional Jewish dish made with stewed carrots, honey, raisins and prunes; its music is known as *klezmer* (mid-Eastern Sephardic mixed with North American folk music). The group sings in Hebrew, Yiddish, Ladino and English. For booking information, write c/o 12, 719 East 31st Ave, or call Moe at 879-8415; fax 873-0501).

A popular community-participation event is the yearly **Walk with Israel**, usually held the last weekend of May. For details, call the **Canadian Zionist Federation** at 257-5140.

Interested in Jewish genealogy and research? The **Jewish Genealogical Institute of B.C.**, c/o 206, 950 West 41st Ave, V5Z 2N7 (321-9870, 257-5199; fax 257-5110), delves into some previously inaccessible regions of Eastern Europe, and has made great strides in helping interested parties seek their ancestors. Periodically, guest speakers and experts are brought in for seminars. Membership costs $30 per year ($45 family; $20 out-of-town).

The **White Rock/South Surrey Jewish Community Centre** organization can be contacted c/o Box 75186, White Rock, V4A 9N4 (541-9995); Ted Gerstl is president. (The Centre is so far without a building, but there's already an active membership of about 400.) In June of 1995, the group held its first "Blintzes, Bagels and Bargains Bazaar" at Centennial Park. The majority of the participation families consist of mixed marriages, so the Centre is deemed "Reform-Conservative" in religious orientation, attracting many who have drifted away from Judaism and previously felt somewhat disenfranchised. A newsletter is being published 10 times a year (call for details).

Two publications are of particular note. The **Jewish Western Bulletin** is a weekly, English-language paper with a readership of about 2500; it lists events, news of particular interest to the Jewish community, and some obits and memorial notices. A subscription for 52 issues costs $48.15 — you may mail in your subscription to 203, 873 Beatty St, Vancouver V6B 2M6 or call 689-1520; fax 689-1525. The e-mail address is 6441175@mcimail.com. **Keren Or** is a bi-monthly newsletter focussing on the Or Shalom community; it offers unique perspectives on Jewish holidays, issues and events. Subscriptions cost $25 a year and can be arranged by writing 710 East 10th Ave, Vancouver V5T 2A7 or calling 872-1614.

On Sunday mornings, **Co-op Radio** (102.7 FM) airs the *Anthology of Jewish Music*, a one-hour weekly program highlighting events in the Jewish community and featuring Ladino, Israeli and Yiddish music. For details, call (263-8498)

Now, here's a little-known tale of Vancouver Jewish lore: A local tailor and synagogue president, David Marks, decided to invite a visiting performer playing at the Orpheum to join his family's Passover *seder*. The performer, Benny Kubelsky of Chicago, and Marks's daughter Sadie fell in love at first sight, and soon married. In time, the couple were better known to their legions of radio and movie fans by their stage names: Jack Benny and Mary Livingstone. The apartment block where the couple met, by the way, still stands, though nowadays it's in a pretty run-down area. It's Ferrera Court, at 504 East Hastings St. Naturally, their love was born over dinner, which brings us to the subject of food.

FOOD & WINE

Jewish people love food that *schmecks*. And that means lip-smacking good. Though celebrated Jewish delicatessens have come and (mostly) gone in Vancouver, there are still a few great places to get bona fide Jewish food and baked goods.

Aviv Kosher Meats
3710 Oak St (736-5888; fax 821-0076)

Here they sell "Israeli-style" falafel with salad, potatoes and a dynamite hot sauce, plus the usual array of vegetarian products, Kosher meats (including Chai brand free-range Kosher poultry) and take-out, as well as giant-sized *challah* (a delicious braided egg bread) for special occasions, *Shabbat* (Sabbath) and other ceremonies. Also various prepared deli and baked goods.

Benny's Bagels
2505 West Broadway (736-4686; orders 731-9730; fax 736-6202)
1095 Hamilton St (688-8018; fax 688-8078)

Granted, original owners Michael Hallatt and Colin Gareau are not (and never were) Jewish, but at least they know how to make an authentic, Toronto-style bagel, already! Purists may dispute our choice, but we prefer Benny's version: crusty on the outside, light and fragrant on the inside.

Golda's Delicatessen
101, 10151 No 3 Road, Richmond (241-5632)

Owner Glenda Saitowitz decided to *cease* featuring a strictly Kosher menu in July of 1995, though she does still carry Kosher dry goods and cheeses. In any case, she has developed a loyal following in Richmond since she first opened her doors at the beginning of the year. For those wishing to locate a source for Kosher meat in Richmond, call the Orthodox Rabbinical Council of B.C. (BCK) at 275-0042.

I Love Bagels
105 East 12th St, North Van (986-3578)

An excellent source of those chewy, Montreal-style, hearth-baked bagels.

J Beethoven's Pizza Gourmet
4, 2909 Bainbridge Ave, Burnaby (421-7735)

Yes, it's an unlikely name and location, but owner and former New Yorker Mike Vitow does indeed serve the best corned-beef-on-rye sandwich in town — corned beef he cures himself in the age-old, time-consuming fashion required to create this food of the gods. Dine-in or take-out.

Kaplan's Deli
5775 Oak St (263-2625)

Serge Haber makes excellent chicken matzo ball soup and kosher dill pickles, as well as many authentic (and delicious) bakery goods, like *mandelbroit* (hard almond biscuits), *kichel* (poppy seed puffs) and *taiglach* (honey and citron confections).

Max's Bakery & Delicatessen
3105 Oak St (733-4838, 733-1737; fax 733-0871)
523 West 8th Ave (873-6297)

Home to a really authentic bagel-maker in Vancouver, these places now do a thriving take-out and deli business, offering fresh meats, sausage, mixes, pastries, dips, spreads, olives, cheeses, and many foods imported from the Middle East. This is where we usually buy our *challah*.

Pita Plus Deli
2967 West Broadway (733-9900)

Even a competitor, Susan Mendelson, swears by the pita and other Mid-East fare at this take-out deli. They've got great falafel, 20 kinds of Mediterranean salads (many of their own creation), two daily soups, 15 kinds of pita bread, and an exceptional homous.

Popovers Plus
3211 Oak St (731-0799, 733-9686)

Hand-rolled bagels, smoked salmon spread, sandwiches, cakes and knishes. A half-price bin offers bargains just outside the front door. Under new management; dine in or take-out.

Rosie's on Robson at the Rosedale Hotel
838 Hamilton St (689-4499)

Owned by the same family that brought you the Elephant & Castle chain (Jeffrey, Hildy, Peter and Shirley Barnett), this New York- style deli and gathering place recently opened and is already a hit. Try their "ultimate chicken soup," complete with *lockshen* noodles (Kosher egg noodles), *kreplach* (triangular dumplings, similar to perogies) and matzo balls. Other specialties are *gefilte* fish (minced whitefish in jelly), chopped liver and great cheese *blintzes* (kind of like egg rolls except they contain sweetened cottage cheese). The Barnetts sent Chef Anne Milne off to study delis in New York and L.A.

Sabra Kosher Bakery & Deli
3844 Oak St (733-4912)

Both dairy and *pareveh* (neither animal nor dairy, thus can be eaten with either) foods are sold here for take-out, as are special bagels and a killer falafel. The atmosphere at Sabra's deserves mention: a good Jewish hangout, particularly if you find the aroma of great food a comfort. Catering available.

Siegel's Bagels
1883 Cornwall Ave (737-8151)
5671 No 3 Road, Richmond (821-0151)

Joel Siegel went to great pains to construct his wood-burning oven to guarantee the right temperature and flavour for his authentic "Montreal" bagels. Siegel and his bakers have won award after award for their top-notch creations; celebrated Canadian author Peter C. Newman declares them his favourite bagels *in the world* — and that's saying a mouthful.

Solly's Bagelry
189 East 28th Ave (872-1821)

Joe Markovitch runs this great family-run hangout-cum-deli. In addition to his *genuine* Montreal-style bagels, there are massive cinnamon rolls, three varieties of *rugoleh* (like tiny cinnamon rolls), Gina's apple slice (wonderfully moist cake), Bubba's cheesecake (made with cottage cheese instead of cream cheese, served warm with sour cream and strawberries), poppy and chocolate swirls, cheese pockets, cottage cheese muffins (light and delicious, and unique to this shop), three varieties of *knishes*, wonderful *blintzes, mon* (poppyseed) cookies, and superlative smoked salmon pate or dill spread.

Star Catering Inc
8320 Heather St, Richmond (272-9560)

Stacey Kettleman provides in-home and special event Kosher catering for b'nei mitzvot, weddings, unveilings, Seders, or even a *bris* (circumcision).

Tele-Kosher
873-0703; fax 873-0102

Yes, Kosher food is only as far away as your telephone. You may also pick up order-by-fax forms (charge to your Visa) at a variety of local stops, including Sabra's and La Page d'Or.

CHEESECAKE

We've put cheesecake into a separate category, so that those who are watching their waistlines can simply skip to the book section. Great Jewish cheesecake is dense-yet-light and it tastes so good you know it's bad for you. There are some "diet" versions available, and many are Kosher. Here are the best: **Cakes To Go** Kosher and reasonably priced. Each arrives frozen for storage and can be defrosted in a couple of hours (266-7727 (or fax 261-9685); **Cheesecake Etc** 2141 Granville St (734-7704); **Classic Cakes** 2385 Burrard St (736-3760); **Lazy Gourmet** 1595 West 6th Ave (734-2507; fax 734-5877); and **Rosie's on Robson at the Rosedale Hotel**: a must is their "Ely" cheesecake from Chicago at 838 Hamilton St (689-4499).

BOOKS

Jewish people are well-known for their scholarship, yet a book called *The Jewish Traveller* notes that "The Jewish novel of Vancouver has yet to be written." Sadly, Shalom Books is no more, but in its place is **La Page d'Or**, at 3756 Oak St (731-3756; fax 731-3705), with a vast inventory of Jewish authors' works and every form of reading material in English, Yiddish and Hebrew. A great source for *bar mitzvah* gifts, as well as for obscure volumes on Jewish mysticism and ritual. They also offer a B'nei Mitzvah registry service to help you avoid gift duplication.

The **Isaac Waldman Jewish Public Library** is still in its infancy. Friends of the Library chairperson is Rita Weintraub (266-9830), if you wish to donate books or money for library acquisitions.

Another source of reading material is the annual book sale, usually held in September at the JCC (257-5111; fax 257-5121). Included are story-telling sessions, author signings and usually a food component, should stirring your brain cells also stir your appetite.

LANGUAGE STUDIES

The **Vancouver Peretz School** at 325-1812 or 324-5101 focusses on Yiddish literature. Those interested in studying Yiddish should contact **Hillel Foundation B'nai Brith**, 1882 East Mall, UBC (224-4748). Most of the city's synagogues offer Hebrew classes. The **University of B.C.** maintains a library of Judaica, as does the JCC.

CHOTCHKES (ALSO CALLED CHATCHKAS)

Chotchkes are knick-knacks. What to buy for that bar mitzvah boy (or bat mitzvah girl) whom you've been invited to honour? Why worry? There are many places to shop for the right gift, and ample encouragement (and free advice) from knowledgable sales-people. Among the best sources are synagogue gift shops, usually run by the sisterhood and staffed by volunteers.

The first and most comprehensive of these is at **Temple Sholom**, 7190 Oak St (266-7190; fax 266-7126), which sometimes also hosts a craft and giftware show (the first such event was held last June — call to find out if they're doing it again). Other synagogue giftshops include ones in **Beth Tikvah** at 9711 Geall Road, Richmond (271-6262) and **Beth Israel** at 4350 Oak St (731-4161; fax 731-4989).

Hadassah Bazaar
PNE Colliseum (Fay Riback at 279-0065)

Held annually, usually during the first week of November, this giant rummage and bake sale offers a golden opportunity to purchase food, gifts, bric-a-brac and "junque" — all at bargain prices. Current chairperson is Daniella Givon (264-8950).

Yerushalem Imports
2375 West 41st Ave (266-0662)

This is an amply stocked shop of high-calibre goods originating from the Holy Land. There are baby gifts (hand-made, embroidered alphabet — or *alef-bet* — felt hangings), stationery supplies, nativity scenes, art, pottery and a fine selection of silver or gold Jewish stars on well-crafted chains.

INDO-ASIAN

EAST INDIAN

The East Indian population of the Lower Mainland is vast — almost 70,000 according to the 1991 census, almost double what it was 10 years earlier. The Indo-Canadian community in the Lower Mainland is also diverse, encompassing Punjabi Sikhs, Hindus, East African Ismailis, Indo-Fijians and Malaysian Sikhs, among others.

Rogers Multicultural Channel offers several airings of Indian language programming: *Indradhanush* (in Hindi, Hindustani, Punjabi, Gujarati and Urdu) and *Rung Punjabi* (Punjabi), produced by Sushma Datt (299-1727; fax 299-3088). Fijian programming is also available in Kaiviti and Hindi languages (see Fijian section for details). On **CJVB Radio** (AM 1470, cable 103.3 FM)

On **CHEK 6 TV**, *Apni Boli, Apna Desh* is a Punjabi-language program of music, dance and entertainment airing Saturday mornings. It is produced in the Lower Mainland at Unit 202, 12837 76th Ave, Surrey (572-1030; fax 572-1031).

The Indo Canadian Business Pages is published by Kranti Enterprises, #31, 8212 128th St, Surrey, V3W 4G2 (599-6560; fax 599-6579). Call to find out where to pick up a copy if you need one. Included are community access pages listing places of worship, wedding tips, theatre and movie info and events like the Indo Canadian Golf Tournament.

FESTIVALS

The birth of Sikhism is celebrated in a New Year festival known as *Baisakhi*, usually held around mid-April. There is a parade with wondrous costumes, symbolic dress and ornate floats, involving thousands of East Indians. The procession culminates at the headquarters of the **Khalsa Diwan Society** at 8000 Ross St (324-2010; fax 322-5610), where spectators and participants alike are invited to share a free vegetarian buffet. You need not be a Sikh to attend.

In August, *Raksha Bandhan* is held, followed by the *Janmastami Festival* (commemorating the appearance day of Lord Krishna). This festival is sponsored by the Hare Krishna Temple. At midnight, there is the traditional *Arotika* ceremony. The next festival observed is *Rathayatra*, or Festival of the Chariots, sponsored jointly by the Hare Krishna Temple and the Festival of India. A chariot race usually takes place at Sunset Beach in the West End.

Diwali is another important festival, observed by most Indo-Canadians, but most important to the Hindu members of that population. Traditions of this autumn festival include exchanging sweets such as *gulab jamun* (similar to *baba au rhum*, or rum baba), and setting off firecrackers.

SHOPPING

The stretch of Main Street from about 49th to 53rd Ave has become known as "Little India," although there are also large concentrations of immigrants from India and Pakistan in Surrey, Delta and Abbotsford. Many stores on the Little India strip are closed Tuesday — or operate with eccentric hours; it seems some owner-operated shops will close whenever they feel like it if business is slow, so if you want to visit one in particular, you're advised to call in advance.

Punjabi Market, also known as **Pabla Trade Centre**, at 6569 Main and 49th is an Indian mini-mall with gift shops, sari shops, jewellers and outlets selling Indian music tapes and videos.

Fabric and Sari Shops

Fabric and clothing stores abound, some selling material by the entire bolt or in sari lengths (also known as "saree lengths" — approximately 6 yards), which are often beaded or extravagantly embroidered in silver or gold. Other fabrics are sold in *shilvar kamis* (Pubjabi trouser suit) lengths of about 3 yards. Many shops stocking yard goods carry a wide selection of raw silk and some unique woven patterned silk or jacquards.

Frontier Cloth House
6695 Main St (325-3515)

The window displays a variety of saris and suits. This large, busy and always bustling store also sells bedspreads and blankets, shoes and fabrics — in an ambiance less boutique-y than many of its neighbours.

Memsaab Boutique
6437 Main St (322-0250)

Given new larger premises, this shop has really gone "upmarket," featuring the latest fashions in designer wear, salwar kameez, saris and duppattas, plus lots of shoes.

Mohan Cloth House
6545 Main St (321-4211)

The sign says "artificial jewellery", but there's also plenty of women's and children's clothing, trims, yard goods and hats. This is a crowded little shop just like one you'd find in India itself.

Riwaaz Exclusif
6415 Main St (325-1607)

This store is not to be missed. Absolutely gorgeous designer sal-waar-kameez from India are featured here, some in dazzling reds with lavish gold embroidery.

Rokko Saree & Fabrics
6201 Fraser St (327-3033)

Over 6,500 square feet of fabrics — silks, polyesters, cottons, nylons wools — are sold here, some pre-cut to saree length but most are by the yard (not meter). Their motto: "At Rokko's all you require is good taste — not a fat purse".

Shahnoor Designer Wear
6505 Main St (322-5411)

For years one of the most chic stores in the area, this one recently relocated to these larger premises. It's part of a famous chain of boutiques that leads the fashion market in India, so naturally their elegant ladies' apparel is different from the traditional saris you'll find elsewhere on Main. There are lovely hand-painted silk dresses and saris, dupattas, shawls, novel earrings, and many choices of golden trims and braids. There are numerous variations on the unusual *bindi* charms (the dots that Indian women often wear on their foreheads).

Costume Jewellery, Giftware, Shoes & Bridal items

Ashoka
6621 Main St (324-7521)
Ashoka Boutique
6502 Main St (322-1113)

Bangles, fabric, trims and other costume jewellery. Closed Tuesday. The boutique operation offers "high-class fashions, bridal wear and jewellery."

The Bride & Groom Shop
216 East 50th Ave (324-5662)

This shop has everything from tacky car decorations to ritzy wedding accessories. There are small bridal gifts for Indian-style weddings, too. Across the street, don't miss the **Wedding & Party** store at 205 East 50th Ave (much the same, lots of glitter).

Flying Fashion
6647 Main St (327-9444)

This bright store sells saris, children's suits and many sparkly trims, purses, bangles, gold belts and garlands.

Quality Shoes & Gifts
215 East 50th Ave (322-1494)

This shop sells toys and gifts, shoes, children's clothing and brassware.

Shingaar Emporium
6610 Main St (322-6756)

Bangles galore, hairpieces, unique musical instruments, footwear, decorations and other costume jewellery.

Fine Jewellery

Most Indian jewellery is wrought in 22K and 24K. Places like **Shubh Laxmi Jewellers** (6510 Main St, 322-7371) have precision scales to weigh gold content; a design fee is then added on for custom work. Costume jewellery is everywhere, in almost every shop, so you should comparison-shop for the best deal.

Among the top high-end jewellers in Little India are: **A Golden Star Jewellery**, 6596 Main St (325-3434); **Bharti Art Jewellers**, ear pins, nose pins, bangles, diamond-cutting, at 6612 Main St (327-8711); **Bhatti's Bombay Jewellers**, considered one of the best in town, at 6566 Main St (327-1616); **Damini Jewellers** at 103, 8434 120th St, Surrey (590-1240); **Steven Sadurah's Fancy Jewellers**, 6524 Main St (327-9200); **Hari Om's Jewellers**, 6604 Main St (324-1067); **Main Jewellers**, 6672 Main St (325-1335 or 325-7734); and **Nanda Jewellers**, 6632 Main St (327-9316).

Lamps

Crystal chandeliers are prized in East Indian homes. One of the top sources is **Ayalamp** with locations at 13979 104th Ave, Surrey (589-8012), 3738 Parker St, Burnaby (294-5523), and 11500 Bridgeport Road, Richmond (231-0643).

FILMS

The top local theatre playing Indian language films is the **Regal Theatre** at 3215 Kingsway (436-1511, 433-7117, or info line 299-6525). First-run Indian movies also show at **Dolphin Cinemas** at 4555 East Hastings St, Burnaby (293-0321).

VIDEO STORES

The film industry in India, based in Bombay (and thus nicknamed "Bollywood"), is astonishing productive, releasing some 2000 movies per year, so it's not surprising that Vancouver has numerous East Indian video outlets offering rentals in Punjabi, Hindi Pakistani and Urdu. Many video stores do PAL transfers to NTSC (and vice versa) and sell cassettes and CDs.

The most comprehensive rental place in town is run by a fellow called Sharma, whose store is called **Kamal's Video Palace**, 5095 Victoria Drive (325-4888; fax 325-7800). Sharma himself does a TV program and knows as much about old and new Indian movies as anyone in Vancouver.

Other reliable video shops are: **Asian Video**, 9329 Scott Road, Delta (589-3553); **Green Market**, 15278 Fraser Hwy, Surrey (583-7576); **India Video & Gift Shop**, 3157 Kingsway (432-6073); **Jeet Video & Food Market** at 1110, 7330 137th St, Surrey (594-3755); **Joyal Import-Export**, 4156 Fraser St (877-7778); **Mann Bros. Meat Shop & Video Store**, 8615 120th St (594-9233); **Sandhu's Video**, 7285 Fraser St (324-1455); **Shaan Video & Gifts**, 102, 8434 120th St. Surrey 543-9669; **Shaz Video & Snack House**, 3710 Canada Way, Burnaby (439-0463); **Tasleem's Video & Gifts**, 6438 Main St (325-9110 or 324-9496); and **The Video Shop** at 6669 Main St (321-1333).

FOOD

Sweet Shops

Sweet shops, often a section of a larger restaurant, are of special interest to the East Indian community, and are crowded any time of day with people there are much for socializing as for shopping. Sweets are often exchanged for special festivals or reserved as treats for honoured guests. Here are some of the top places in Lower Mainland to buy them.

All India Sweets
6507 Main St (327-0891)

Various confections and a warm and hospitable sit-down cafe. A special offers samosas (deep-fried pastries filled with meat or vegetable mixtures) at two-for-$1.

Bhaia Sweet Shop & Restaurant
7585 6th Street, Burnaby (522-5211)

Mixed sweets sell for $4.99/lb, and two samosas cost 99 cents. Bhaia also offers catering.

Bombay Sweets Cash & Carry
6556 Main St (874-5722)

Both the divine and the dreadful of Indian sweets (a matter of personal taste, we think) are sold here. (At the very least it's an interesting experience.) Western palates will probably favour the *gulab jamun*, the Indian equivalent of *baba au rhum*. The charming and personable owner, Nick Shukla, also operates a very successful restaurant and grocery store at this address.

Doaba Sweets
9381 Scott Road, Delta (583-9203)

Manjit Singh offers a full roster of home-made Indian sweets, and also provides catering for all occasions. For catering, call 583-9207.

Guru Lucky Sweets
7898 6th St, Burnaby (525-9300)

This place sells East Indian spices, sweets, condiments and other food items, plus Fiji treats — all at low prices.

Hardawar Sweet Shop & Restaurant
6673 Fraser St (325-9444)

The usual assortment of East Indian sweets, and take-out samosas and other foods.

Jagga Sweets & Cuisine
9243 120th St, Delta (583-1324)

Catering to the burgeoning Surrey-Delta East Indian population, this shop is a favourite for traditional and special occasion sweets.

Shan-E-Punjab Restaurant & Sweet Shop
6591 Fraser St (327-7020)

A recent addition to the sweet shop scene, this one sometimes offers specials, such as mixed *barfi* (dessert squares with a fudge-like consistency, flavoured with coconut, rosewater, nuts or cocoa) at $4.50/lb. They also sell savories like samosas, pakoras and Punjabi toast.

Surat Sweet
6665 Fraser St (322-9544)

Surat is famous for its *shrikhand*, a yogurt dessert made with saffron, cardamom and pistachio. There's a tiny restaurant as well, offering a full range of East Indian favourites.

FOOD STORES

At a good East Indian food store, you'll find fresh produce such as the long skinny purple eggplants, okra and many varieties of chilies — rangingfrom hot to lethal. You can buy bulk spices, legumes and nuts, canned and bottled specialties such as mango juice, rose water and chutneys. Milk, a staple in many recipes, is usually bargain-priced. There can also be very good values in stainless steel cookware and serving trays.

A & S Meats
105, 12827 76th Ave, Surrey (599-7345)

The featured meats here are chicken, pork, lamb, goat, quail, pigeons, pheasant, and goat or pork *achar* (marinated and barbecued).

Ajay Food Store
9245 120th St, Delta (584-8887)

In addition to the usual groceries, Ajay stocks organic items from the Khalistan Dairy Co-op in 150 Mile House.

All India Foods
6517 Main St (324-2195; fax 324-2195)

Karnail Singh's popular food store stocks bulk items, fresh produce, Indian spices and specialty items — and unusual names of otherwise familiar products. For example, *dnaniya* means cilantro, which of course is also known as coriander and Chinese parsley. Supermarket-sized, yet with narrow aisles crowding as much stuff into the space as possible, this is surely the widest stock of East Indian specialty foods and seasonings in all of North America. (And rightly so — in that Vancouver's East Indian population is, in fact, the largest anywhere in the world outside India.) You'll find curry powders, chutneys, cardamon seed, saffron, chilies, and other specialty spices in more varieties, sizes and forms than anywhere else in town.

J & B Foods
6607 Main St (321-0224)

They sell cookware, pots, woks, and food items like Uganda toast.

Patel's Discount Bulk Foods
2210 Commercial Drive (255-6729)

Established for almost 25 years in this primarily Italian area, this East Indian store carries natural foods, spices and many Asian specialties, most at bulk-food prices. Free parking in the back, while you shop.

Punjab Food Centre
6635 Main St (322-5502)

You'll be entranced by the wonderful smell of spices and incense, exotic foods like *urad* (lentils) and *dal* (beans, peas, lentils), Indian radio playing in the background and low prices on housewares, bulk foods, produce and dairy foods.

Quality Foods
5481 No 3 Road, Richmond (273-1712)

This large establishment combines a grocery store, restaurant (273-1728) and Misha Video (278-3261) to provide rice, flour, lentils, spices, take-out foods (like roti, naan, curries and sweets), and the latest Indian movies, cassettes and CDs.

Singh Foods
6684 Main St (327-4911)

Huge bags of rice flour, bulk spices, produce (out front, as well as inside), cookware and pots.

Spiceland Cash & Carry
9336 120th St, Surrey (951-0566)

This place combines both East and West Indian foods in a grocery store setting: spices and grains (both packaged and bulk), fresh produce, bulk Indian snacks (like candy-coated fennel seeds) and an assortment of imported vegetables.

Trufoods (Satnam Foods)
10119 136A St, Surrey (584-7011)

This large grocery store carries meat and dairy products, Indian sweets and spices. They grind their own pure ginger powder, hot chili powder, *garam masala* (a spice blend of cardamon, cinnamon, cloves, coriander, cumin and black pepper) and *haldi* (tumeric). Also video rentals.

RESTAURANTS

Vancouver's East Indian restaurants offer styles ranging from elegant to deli, from Tandoori (baked in a large Tandoor oven) to Punjabi, to a new version of fusion cuisine that rivals the best in town.

Fine Dining

Akbar's Own Dining Room
3629 West Broadway (739-8411)

Interesting Kashmiri and Muglai cuisine, with many items deep-fried in a delicate sesame seed batter. Start with a selection of spicy *pakoras* (fritters of chick-pea flour, onion and spices), then the prawn Kashmiri, the lamb biryani and the *alu gobi* (a curry of spiced cauliflower and potato). Excellent food in a comfortable, family-run environment.

Dawat
5976 Victoria Drive (322-3550)

This is the authors' favourite high-tone Indian restaurant in Vancouver. In fact, every time the name "Dawat" is mentioned, we exchange a glance and sigh: "curried mussels." This dish is exceptional, but there are many other tempting items on their full dinner menu — like lamb vindaloo and chicken tikka — all elegantly served with candle warmers in portions that look small until you try to finish them all. Fully licensed. Owners Kamal and Davinder Maroke also run a twin restaurant in Bellevue/Seattle that gleans awards right and left.

India Fine Cuisine Punjab
796 Main St (688-5236)

The house specialty is a dessert of milk cakes with cream sauce, but first, try the goat curry, lamb spinach, prawn mukhani or *kofta malai* (spicy meat balls). A long-established, consistently good place.

India Village
308 Water St (681-0678)

Though it's situated in touristy Gastown, the food is very good here. Try the butter chicken or chicken tikka-masala. Many dishes are cooked in traditional tandoor ovens.

Natraj
5656 Fraser St (327-6141)

Minimal decor, but excellent food characterize this spot. Try the chicken Shahjahni Biriyani (a rich curry served with saffron basmati rice) or their outstanding *malai kofta* (patties of potato, veggies and cheese). Fully licensed. Easy street parking.

Nirvana
2313 Main St (872-8779)

This is another always-dependable family dining establishment on the site of the old Himalaya Restaurant. Owner Davinder Singh Dhani always greets customers and gives each individual his personal attention. Recommended are the lamb *vindaloo* and the chicken tandoori. The sweet mango chutney is perfect, as is the mango shake, which you'll require to neutralize the heat effects of the curries. Nirvana also provides take-out, catering and delivery.

Moderately expensive

Ethnic Food at South Vancouver Neighbourhood House
6470 Victoria Drive (324-6212; fax 324-6116)

The SVNH provides an ethnic lunch on the last Friday of every month except June, July, August and December, consisting of food from India. A typical lunch includes *pilau* (basmati rice), *sabzi* (curried vegetables), a curried meat dish, *raita* (dip), *chapati* (bread), chutney, salad, *chai* (tea) and a dessert, such as mango ice cream. Mrs. Hundle and Mrs. Shokar are the veteran volunteers. Call the SVNH for details on the next lunch offered (reservations required). Cost is $6 per person for the whole buffet.

The SVNH also operates a food booth at the Vancouver Folk

Festival every summer, where Sujeet's *pakoras* (vegetables in a spicy batter and deep-fried) are legendary.

Heaven & Earth India Curry House
1754 West 4th Ave (732-5313)

This 30-year-old institution has an extensive vegetarian menu, as well as regular fare. Try the *sabji* and *rogan josh* (both curries).

Inexpensive

Noor Mahal
4354 Fraser St (873-9263)

Try the *dosas*, a crepe-like pancake made from lentil flour, rice and wheat flours, and filled with chicken, shrimp or vegetables. Dosas come with *sambar*, a soothing lentil stew, sided with *chatni* (coconut chutney). The decor is jarring, to say the least, but everything is inexpensive, so you can dine like a pasha for mere rupees.

Tandoori-style

Ashiana Tandoori Restaurant & Sweet Shop
1440 Kingsway (874-5060; fax 951-4522)
Ashiana Tandoori
6560 Main St (325-3031)

Rick and Sonia Takhar have run these top-rated places for years and years. Food here is family fare (the Takhars have five kids themselves) in an elegant and tranquil setting. Licensed; sweets to take out. The Main Street location is a small take-out or dine-in deli version, featuring two-for-99-cents samosas.

India Gate
616 Robson St (684-4617 or 682-1000)

Featuring many curries and fine Tandoori specialties, this place has been here since 1978 and is still going strong.

Rubina Tandoori Lazeez Cuisine of India
1962 Kingsway (874-3621)

This place isn't quite sure whether it wants to be a restaurant, a bistro or a club, but the food is consistently good, so we'll allow them their identity crisis.

Tandoori King
8015 Fraser St (327-3355)

Our introduction to tandoor-style cooking took place here, with coaching by chef/owner Sharnjit. There's a varied menu, and you can choose to have your choices extra spicy or toned-down; the breads are baked in the traditional clay oven. The room is small but cosy, a comforting place on a chilly winter day.

Tandoori Taj
2189 Kingsway (439-8902)

Elegant pink and burgundy decor and subdued music greet you here. This is a classic tandoori restaurant, where many items — all excellent — are cooked in a giant tandoor oven. There's a large catering hall and free parking at the rear.

Vegetarian

Annapurna
1812 West 4th Ave (736-5959)

One of the few East Indian restaurants specializing in vegetarian cooking.

Govinda's
5464 S E Marine Drive, Burnaby (433-2454, 431-0165 or 433-9728)

This place, next to the Hare Krishna Temple, offers an all-you-can eat vegetarian buffet lunch for $4.95, including rice, soup, dahl, curried vegetables and salad. Dinner is similar, plus sweet and a savoury course, all for $5.95. Individual items may be purchased a la carte, or for take-out. A cosy environment; no smoking. Always lots of parking out front.

Vij's
1453 West Broadway (736-6664)

This relatively new establishment serves dishes that seem to marry the best of French and East Indian cuisine. The menu is written on boards (the board to the left as you enter is appetizers; board to the right is entrees). The chef, formerly of Bishop's and Star Anise, offers personal attention to each guest. The cauliflower rice with mustard seed is sensational. Mainly vegetarian.

HEALTH

Homeopathy is widely thought to be more effective than Western medicine in India; its practitioners claim success with many 20th century problems we can't seem to eliminate. The **Pacific Homeopathic Clinic**, with offices at #1, 6648 Main St (322-4020) and in Surrey at #204, 7028 120th St (572-7765; fax 572-8879) promises relief from migraines, allergies, warts and joint pain, to name a few afflictions. Owner Ararjeet Singh Ahluwalia has 40 years' experience, and speaks Punjabi, Hindi and English.

BOOKS AND NEWSPAPERS

Looking for out-of-town newspapers, or magazines from India? Try **Noorali's International News & Magazines** at 133 Alderbridge Place, 4940 No 3 Road, Richmond (278-5714). Books about Indo-Canadians in English, Punjabi, Hindi and Urdu are available at **Asian Publications** at 7495 Hurdle Cres, Surrey (597-5837; fax 594-8514). They also have volumes on language acquisition in Punjabi, Hindi, Gujrati, Bengali and Urdu, plus fiction in each of those languages.

A number of newspapers serve the Indo Canadian community, such as **Indo Canadian Voice** 201, 4580 Main St (874-1550; fax 874-1561) and **The Link** 201, 225 East 17th Ave (876-9300; 897-8500). Magazines include **Awaaz** (same address as Indo Canadian Voice, 879-0054), **Mehfil** 301, 1334 West 6th Ave (254-9015; fax 731-2965) and the increasingly slick and well designed **Rungh**, a South Asian quarterly of culture, comment and criticism, from Rungh Cultural Society, Station F, Box 66019, Vancouver V5N 5L4 (254-0320; fax 662-7466).

FIJIAN

The Fijian community in Vancouver currently numbers almost 5000. The top newspaper is **The Fiji Sun**, 5552 Victoria Drive (323-1759). The Rogers multicultural channel show *Visions of Fiji* is produced by Indar Narayan (327-5002; fax 874-3560) in both Kaiviti and Hindi; it airs on Sundays and is rebroadcast Wednesdays. *Fiji Today*, an English, Hindi and Kaiviti-language variety and news program, also airs on Rogers; It is produced by Fiji Commonwealth Forum Society, 2419 East 34th Ave (437-0852; fax 876-1717).

The **Fiji Canada Association** is the principal social club for Fijians of Indian descent. It's at 1791 Douglas St, Burnaby (299-8887). Otherwise, there's the **Sangam Education & Cultural Society**, at 8920 Charles St, Richmond (mailing address: P.O. Box 76773, Station S, Vancouver V5R 5S7, 278-0958).

The primary place of worship for Vancouver Fijians is **Shiv Mandir** at 1795 Napier St (254-2624); services in Hindi are held on Monday and Tuesday evenings.

HALAL MEATS

Halal is a Muslim religious tradition where the animal (beef, chicken, goat, lamb) is blessed when slaughtered or cut and is prepared in a particularly hygienic fashion. *Halal* is food permitted by the doctrines of the Koran. Please see our section on the Middle East for Halal butchers.

MISCELLANEOUS FOOD SHOPPING

Fiji Fresh
110, 8910 120th St, Surrey (586-6400)

Operated by Mukesh Dewar and family, this produce and meat shop sells New Zealand and Australian lamb, fresh local chicken, idli, samosas and chutney. The on-premises cafe serves vegetarian meals and provide catering for all occasions.

Fiji Islands Guru Lucky Sweets
7521 Sixth St, Burnaby (525-9370)

A typical sweet shop, this time with focus on Fijian foods. Also operates as a small cafe and provides take-out.

Indo Fiji Supermarket
5157 Victoria Drive (324-3264)

Featured here are fresh vegetables, groceries and kitchenwares, and such hard-to-find items as mackerel, pilchard, sardines, corned mutton, lemon grass, plantain and imported Fijian cosmetics.

Vita Meats & Seafood
12045 88th St, Surrey (599-4552)

Fiji groceries are the focus here, including bulk prices on mango pickles, green mangoes (and other fresh produce) and frozen lamb and duck.

SRI LANKAN

There are fewer than 600 Sri Lankan residents in Vancouver, yet the community offers a few fascinating glimpses of life in the former country of Ceylon.

TRADE & CULTURE

Sri Lankan Gem Museum
150, 925 West Georgia St (662-7768)

This place, owner Shelton De Silva's ambitious undertaking at Cathedral Place, sends half its proceeds to Vancouver cultural operations. De Silva's wife, Lanka, says it was his long-time dream to open a museum and teach people about gems.

The entrance is plated with 24 karat hammered gold, the floor is inlaid with 9000 pieces of polished agate slabs, the ceiling and parts of the walls are covered with hand-painted, enamelled plaques plated with 24 karat gold, and the collection comes not just from Sri Lanka, but worldwide. There are circa 1800 Ching dynasty carved jade artifacts (one valued at $600,000), large natural (not cultured, that is) South Sea pearls, dinosaur bones and fossils, tourmaline chunks, sapphires, garnets (including a rare green garnet), two kilograms of emeralds and Burmese rubies.

It's a sensational tour ($3.50 for adults; less for children and seniors), which runs every half hour, Monday through Saturday. The de Silvas operate a fine jewellery store near the museum, which helps to support the project.

FOOD STORES

Lucky Foods
5190 Victoria Drive (325-1148)

This little shop offers Sri Lankan groceries and video movie rentals in Tamil.

Luxmiis
4301 Main St (874-3400)

The main Vancouver source for Sri Lankan (and Indian) groceries, such as *gingelly oil* (spiced oil), *rasam* mix (coriander, cumin, curry leaf and other spices), mulligatawny mix, buriyani mix, Nanesh brand yellow curry powder, lime pickle, Kashmiri *masala* (curry), *nelli* juice (similar to berry), *Kurakkan* (lentil) flour, mango cordial, jackfruit in syrup, sambal rice and *asafoetida* (spice). They also do rent videos from a large stock and provide video transfers.

Na di Lanka Impexco
2074 Kingsway (874-7322)

Another grocery store featuring Sri Lankan foods, this one also sells gifts, clothing and "pure Ceylon tea," many packages of spices at low prices, and lots of canned goods, imported from Sri Lanka.

SOUTHEAST ASIAN

VIETNAMESE & CAMBODIAN

We've combined these two groups mainly because their food-styles are so similar. There are approximately 10,000 Vietnamese residents in Vancouver; just under 1000 from Cambodia.

Vietnamese restaurants are of several general types: There are full-menu family-style restaurants, there are glorified coffee bars (each with a particularly wonderful version of French roast), there are *pho* or soup-and-noodle cafes, and there are karaoke or classic night clubs.

RESTAURANTS

Full & family-style

At these restaurants, we expect tablecloths, attentive service and an assortment of entrees, in addition to soups and rice dishes. Here are a few notable examples.

Casablanca
535 East Hastings St (254-6270)

Don't be put off by the seedy neighbourhood; the food here is good — and cheap. A typical Vietnamese combo meal costs $4.95. Karaoke in the evenings.

Hai Kee Cambodian & Vietnamese Restaurant
2702 Main St (875-8915)

Self-described as the "legendary noodle soup house," this place makes good on that claim with a menu offering almost 50 choices of soup, noodles, rice, spring rolls, a few curries and some bargain-priced combinations (three different dinner-for-one combos each cost only $7.50). Dine-in or take-out.

Phnom Penh Restaurant
955 West Broadway (734-8898 or 734-8988)
244 East Georgia St (682-5777)

Phnom Penh Restaurant has two locations (we prefer the Chinatown one), amply displaying their award-winning Cambodian cuisine.

Pho Thai Hoa
789 Kingsway (874-5667)

Not as fancy as some of the other sit-down-style restaurants, this little place is one step up from a pho house because they do serve a full range of complete meals — at very modest prices, we might add. This is one of the few places we have been able to find really vegetarian spring rolls (made with shrimp, not chicken), and the cosy, family-run atmosphere always makes us feel welcome. A nice neighbourhood restaurant. They do speedy take-out, too.

Saigon Restaurant
950 West Broadway (732-7608)
1500 Robson St (682-8020)
2394 West 4th Ave (731-1217)
302, 403 North Road, Coquitlam (939-2288)
Lonsdale Quay, 123 Carrie Cates Court, North Van (984-3055)

The Lonsdale Quay location is a take-out, but the others are comfortable dining establishments featuring items like Vietnamese roll dip and Supreme prawn Royale citron.

Van Lang Vietnamese Restaurant
258 Sixth St, New West (525-5055)

"Unpretentious" was the first word that leapt to mind, until we saw the crisp, white tablecloths and comfy wooden chairs. Among the many fine dishes are beef brochette (very BBQ-tasting, like sate), *so hap* (steamed clams with garlic — note the French influence), an assortment of *pho* treatments, *xup bap* (sweet corn and crab soup), and the delectable *chuoi chien* (deep-fried banana) for dessert.

Vietnam City
2122 East Hastings St (254-8094 or 254-8098)

A rack of lamb lunch special for only $8.95 caught our attention initially (it's delicious), but we were further delighted to discover classic Vietnamese dishes like spring rolls, rice noodles and other great lunch specials, all at modest prices. The specials are the best bet, priced from only $6.95 — for Vietnamese crepes, Vietnamese roll dip (like an egg roll, sliced) and pork brochette.

Good family dining

Other family restaurants include **Chez Lin**, 960 Kingsway (877-1377); **Cuu Long**, 3911 Knight St (873-6926); **Happy Vietnam Family Restaurant**, 6236 Fraser St (324-8855); and **Que Huong**, 1356 Kingsway (876-3360).

Pho places

Pho basically means "soup," though the way these places serve it is often with dumplings, noodles or other additions. Please note: If you're vegetarian, you must usually ask if the stock is made from chicken or beef. In our experience, many Vietnamese pho joints don't make the distinction, and feel if all they've added to the beef stock is vegetable matter, then it's "vegetarian."

Bun Bo Hue
646 Kingsway (874-0073)

They call themselves the "king of noodle soups," and they certainly do a great job of what they do. We like the steamy, welcoming atmosphere, and their soups are delicious. Many choices. Parking at rear.

Kim Dinh Oriental Noodle House
3980 Fraser St (879-7813; fax 879-4686)

They offer a selection of salad rolls, *bun* (vermicelli), and other classic Vietnamese dishes, but where they really shine is in the beverage line. There are avocado shakes, beverages made from durian, jack fruit, star fruit and more.

Pho Hoa
2257 Kingsway (432-6022)
1909 West 4th Ave (732-6129)

Describing their fare as "a delicious one-dish meal for your breakfast, lunch or even dinner," these places are typical of the many soup-and-noodle places we enjoy. There are simple versions with noodles and a little meat, meatballs or brisket with a light covering of fat (*pho tai gau*), or tripe (*pho nam gan sach*). And there are rice plates, egg rolls, vermicelli, and a hearty beef stew (*banh mi pho bo kho*). Finish with homemade desserts, like red bean pudding, jelly-and-tapioca or longan in syrup.

Pho Nam
Fraser Plaza, 4, 3345 Fraser St (872-0455)

A really large room always jammed with customers, this place offers a take-away menu (*thuc an*) which explains how you can choose your own cuts of meat from a list of items like *tal* (rare steak), *gau* (fat brisket), *sach* (beef tripe), or *ga vien* (chicken meat balls), for endless noodle and combinations. Their dinner combos cost $7.95 or $8.95 (eg. Spring roll, beef brochette, prawn supreme on sugar cane).

Miscellaneous pho & noodle places

Other pho-and-noodle places worth finding are: **Beef Bowl Restaurant** at 3775 Main St (876-8611); **Cafe Thanh Loan**, 663 East 15th Ave (good French coffee, 872-8056); **Pho Dong Phuong**, 1188 Kingsway (side parking, 873-6666); **Pho Hoang** absolutely packed all day at 3610 Main St (874-0810) or 238 East Georgia St (682-5666 or 682-3308); **Pho My Xuan** at 714 Main St (free parking, 688-6169); **Pho Ngu Binh** at 398 Kingsway (air conditioned; free parking in front, 876-5575); **Pho Thai Hoa** (no relation to the family restaurant of identical name) at 1303 Kingsway (873-3468); **Pho Quyen** at 720 East Broadway (871-9187); **Pho Thanhg Long**, 3710 Main St (872-4872); **Pho Van** 3370 Fraser St (parking at rear, 872-2879) or at 220, 633 Main St (682-7844); **Sing Sing Restaurant**, 2173 Kingsway (parking at rear, 439-7894); and **Thanh Thanh**, 775 Kingsway (free parking at rear, 873-0775).

Coffee Bars & Sandwich Cafes

Vietnamese and Cambodian cafes — largely due to the influence of the French in that part of Asia — usually serve the most exquisite sandwiches and fresh, deeply flavourful French roast coffees, filter-brewed at your table. The coffee-making ritual is quite different from what you'll see at Starbucks or any typical cappuccino bar. Here are some of the ones we like best:

Pho Kim Saigon Chinese & Vietnamese Restaurant
2925 Cambie St (876-1277)

It's a bit of a misnomer because this restaurant serves so much more than pho. They offer off-premises catering, free delivery (10% discount on pick-up orders) and a menu of some 70 or so items. Combination dinners run about $7.25 per person, while family combos are a little higher, but there's more variety. There's also a full selection of those famous Vietnamese sandwiches on French bread slathered with mayonnaise, plus meat, vegetables, carrot pickle, onion and parsley.

Great Vietnamese coffee & sandwiches

Other cafes: Kerrisdale's carriage trade now has an excellent family restaurant/cafe called **Lemon Grass Vietnamese Cafe**, 2143 West 41st Ave (261-0688). A hole-in-the-wall with great sandwiches is **Tuong Lai Vietnamese** at 547 East Hastings St (255-5105). Other little cafes worth finding are **Bach Dang Ice Cream Cafe**, at 661 East 15th Ave (876-0052); **Cafe Anh Kong**, 10539 King George Hwy, Surrey (582-2001); **Cheo Leo Banh Mi & Cafe**, 1330 Kingsway (pho, coffee, deli, take-out, 874-6969); and **Tan Cang**, 1707 Kingsway (licensed, strong french coffee, 874-8858).

Specialty spring rolls

Don't overlook the **Bao Chao Spring Roll Specialty House** at 2717 East Hastings (251-6956).

Delicatessens

For a full range of Vietnamese take out and deli foods, there's **Kim Chau Delicatessen**, at 1, 711 East Hastings St (255-8385), **Kim Chee Oriental Deli** at 3, 1022 Kingsway (876-3372); and for fresh meats, groceries, vegetables and take-out deli foods, there's **Nhon Hoa BBQ House** at 5, 701 Kingsway (872-0690). A bulletin board outside the latter advertises apartment rentals and other neighbourhood notices.

SUPERMARKETS

Saigon Supermarket
1172 Kingsway (873-3193, fax: 873-3192)

Specializing in Vietnamese items, this place sells fresh meat, live seafood, bulk eggs, Asian baked goods and produce. We found a 20-Kg bag of jasmine fragrant rice for $20.99, which on a special came with a free bottle of "Lucky" fish sauce. There are also some deli items and fast food take-out.

Viet Hoa Market
724 Kingsway, Vancouver (876-6350)

Friendly people and really low prices are the attraction at this unassuming neighbourhood Vietnamese market. Check out the fresh greens (cilantro, bok choi) and tins of miniature corn and water chestnuts at the cheapest prices in town. Parking next door (behind the chain link fence to the East).

KARAOKE BARS & NIGHT CLUBS

Cafe Diem Hua
635 East 15th Ave (876-2078)

Thumping into the wee hours with hot music and dance, this place (formerly Cafe Mimosa) thrives on nightlife; it doesn't even open until evening. Licensed, of course.

Luquan Vietnamese Restaurant
1086 Kingsway (875-8522)

This place is nightclubby in atmosphere, but it's really a coffee bar with excellent sandwiches on incredibly fresh French baguettes. Try the pork floss, for a spicy treat. This is also where we were first introduced to the exotic flavours of sour sop juice (*sinh to mang cau*), and an unusual version of iced coffee called *ca phe sua da*. Espresso is made at your table and poured through your own little strainer, accompanied, Vietnam fashion, by sweetened, condensed milk. Luquan has added karaoke in the evenings.

JEWELLERY

The Vietnamese, like many Asian peoples, are particular about fine jewellery, and as a consequence, many of Vancouver's best (and most off-the-beaten-track) sources of gold jewellery and fine chains are run by the Vietnamese. Note: Many require that you ring for entry. They size you up from inside, then buzz you in.

Here are some top ones: **Kim Hai/Tiem Vang** (same owners as next location) at 329 Gore St (688-4094); and **Tiem Vang Jewellers** (a fancier location) at 539 East Hastings St (254-0735). Another branch is **West Lake Jewellery** (also known as Tiem Vang), at 1281 Kingsway (30-50% off sale items and custom designs, 876-0820).

Then there's **Kim's Jewellers**, 5618 Victoria Drive (324-0053); **Minh Dan Jewellery**, 253 Main St (873-5727); **Minh Nhut Jewellery & Gifts**, 13, 701 Kingsway (874-0711); and **Sun Yin Gems**, custom-design and manufacture at 1259 Kingsway (873-4763).

MUSIC

Here are two finds: **Hai Au Music Centre** for CDs, cassettes and recordings at 1948 Kingsway (874-9504) and music lessons at **Lau's Musical Association** at 1445 West Broadway (730-8338).

BOOKS, VIDEOS & PERIODICALS

We found several, including **Ha Do Video**, 588 East 15th Ave (874-4566); **Han Kook Video & Book Centre** also known as **Kien Giang Video Rental**, 2, 1022 Kingsway (874-6755); **Lang Van Video & Book Store**, 1439 Kingsway (876-3855); **Saigon Book Store & Video Rental** — mostly kids' books at 255 East Georgia St (662-3716); and **Sunrise Videos & Coin Laundry** at 1324/1326 Kingsway (877-0566).

There are a number of monthly publications including **Nang Moi** 5816 Fraser St (321-2636); **Thoi Su**, P.O. Box 39166, Point Grey RPO, Vancouver V6R 4P1 (pager 643-9335); **Tu Do**, P.O. Box 74054, Hillcrest RPO, Vancouver V5V 5C8 (pager 252-5821); and **Viet Nam Thoi Bao** at 2496 East 41st Ave, Vancouver V5R 2W5 (434-8716).

HEALTH PRODUCTS

Thien Dia Nhan
6252 Fraser St (322-0338)

This place offers Chinese Natural Herbs and Health Foods, the services of a traditional herbalist, and items like bee pollen. We were fascinated by the "U-fit slimming pill" and the "Flecks removing cream," meant to banish pimples and freckles alike. The **Saigon Pharmacy** also offers conventional Vietnamese medications, at 1080 Kingsway (872-6708).

THAI, SINGAPOREAN, MALAYSIAN & INDONESIAN

We've grouped these countries together since they share so much in the way of food and culture.

FOOD STYLES COMMON TO THIS REGION

Food styles from Thailand, Singapore, Malaysia, and Indonesia share much common ground. Generally, the food is highly spiced (though you can always request a toned-down version), with lemon grass a recurrent ingredient. Sauces — though sometimes suggesting curries — are thinner, and the flavours more distinct, less blended. *Sambal*, a thick, fiery mixture of chilies and spices, is a frequent ingredient.

Some elements have been adapted and integrated into the cuisines from still other ethnic groups. *Nonya*, for example, is a Malay variation on a Chinese cooking technique in which packets of chicken are fried in parchment. *Nasi goreng*, which is found throughout Indonesia, also creeps onto menus in Singaporean and Malaysian restaurants.

As with Chinese food, dishes from these countries may contain MSG (monosodium glutamate), which is also known as *aji-no-moto*. If you don't like MSG, remember to ask if it's used, when you order. (Since meals should be prepared individually, MSG can *always* be omitted.)

MULTINATIONAL RESTAURANTS

Lotus Eaters is a take-out, dine-in and catering outfit that offers each of these cuisines. Find them at 1399 West 7th Ave (736-6679; fax 739-3369).

In Gastown, the brand new **Paloma** at 108 Cambie St (684-0688) offers such dishes as Indonesian roast lamb shoulder, Singapore steamed sea bass, grills, soups, salads, rice dishes, homemade desserts and exotic beverages. Fully licensed. Open daily.

THAI

The main social and cultural organization for the Thai community is the **Thai Cultural Association of Vancouver**, 6925 Main St (322-5929), which promotes Thai culture and organizes community activities in our area. There are fewer than 400 Thai-Canadians in the city of Vancouver, yet Thai food is so popular, it may well be that most of them have entered the food industry.

RESTAURANTS

Fine Thai cuisine typically involves elaborate food presentation with carefully considered garnishes, herbs and occasionally, flowers. The Chinese influence is apparent in the omnipresent noodle, whether fashioned from wheat or rice flour or bean starch. Much of the Thai menu is stir-fried, yet it is rarely oily; the curved *ka-tha* cooking pans — much like Chinese woks, but usually fashioned from brass instead of steel — require little oil to cook the food.

The popular flavouring in Thai cookery is a fish sauce called *nam pla*, which, despite its name, adds a salty, rather than a fishy taste. For dishes requiring a seafood flavour, *kapi* (a strong paste made from dried shrimp) is used. Almost every Thai menu item will include at least some rice, usually the long-grain and perfume-y jasmine variety. Components are usually *khao* (rice), *kaeng* (dishes with sauces) and *kaeng chud* (soup).

Most of Vancouver's Thai restaurants adhere to these general principles of Thai cuisine. Here are the top choices.

Boua Thai
7090 Kingsway, Burnaby (526-3712)

A delightful room and full Thai menu. Easy parking at Metrotown.

Chili Club
1018 Beach Ave (681-6000; fax 681-2890)

Its twin is in Hong Kong, and the menus are identical — and wonderful. This is gourmet Thai cuisine, served in a shimmering water-blue-and-etched-glass room, overlooking False Creek. Food and service are impeccable.

Malinee's Thai Food
2153 West 4th Ave (737-0097)

Authentic, friendly, clean. A fine place for a filling lunch at reasonable prices.

Nakornthai
1157 Davie St (683-6621)

Another smallish restaurant with a lot of heart, this one offers good Thai food, reasonably priced. Buffet lunch Thursday and Friday.

Salathai
3364 Cambie St (875-6999)

Always reliably good food, served promptly and by cordial staff. Banquet facilities available.

Sawasdee
4250 Main St (876-4030)
2146 Granville St (737-8222)

This was Vancouver's first Thai restaurant. Remarkably authentic Thai food at affordable prices. Try their *choo-chee talay*, a seafood curry with prawns and squid. For dessert, try deep-fried banana fritters — decadent, with ice cream. A comfortable ambience, too.

Thai House
1766 West 7th Ave (737-0088)
129, 4940 No 3 Road, Richmond (278-7373)
115, 4600 Kingsway (438-2288)

When you want it "hot," they don't wimp out. Excellent cuisine, and if you're in the mood for karaoke, you'll find it evenings at the West 7th location.

Tuk Tuk Thai Restaurant
10861 No 4 Road, Richmond (275-8709)

Hostess Nina Chareonmitra helps run this new Thai restaurant, which takes its name from the tiny taxis (little more than a motorcycle with a big back seat) that run tourists all around Bangkok. Excellent, authentic food (by chef Patcharin), good-natured, friendly staff.

SHOPPING

The best food store we've found for Thai imports and groceries also stocks Vietnamese and Filipino goods. It's **Thuan Phat Enterprises** at 747/749 Gore St (688-8235; fax 689-1818). The vast majority of proprietor Tan's stock however, is from Thailand. Tan is so knowledgeable and helpful that he'll even offer recipes and advice for the foodstuffs you purchase.

SINGAPOREAN

The main group for Vancouver Singaporeans is the **Vancouver Singapore Club**, Box 137, 103-9040 Blundell Road, Richmond (273-0117; 273-0530). This is the first Singapore Club in Canada. Its purpose is to act as trade liaison, and to organize social events for its members.

SHOPPING

About the only store with goods exclusively from Singapore is **Singapore Arts & Crafts** in Gastown at 466 West Cordova St (687-2342), where you'll find batik clothing, tapestries, pewter ware, antiques, wood carvings and jewellery.

In the food line, try **Bee Kim Heng Beef & Pork Jerky Ltd** at 2532 Main St (875-8688) for the real thing for take-home. It's all in the name.

RESTAURANTS

Cafe D'Lite
2817 West Broadway (733-8882)

You'd never guess it from the name, but Betty and David Chin's tiny cafe offers genuine Singaporean and Malaysian foods, and their own specialty, Hainanese chicken rice, which hits the spot on a chilly day. Also: curry-chicken and potato with rice, Malaysian curry, *laksa* (noodle soup) and *nasi lemak*. Try the D'Lite fresh soya drink for instant energy.

Prata-Man Restaurant
180, 9020 Capstan Way, Richmond (278-1348)

This Singaporean-Malaysian restaurant has a special on sate sticks — at 10 for $5. They also serve mutton *masala* (a spicy lamb curry), *bo-piah* (spring roll), *char kway teow* (noodles with sausage, clams or fishcakes), *sate ayam* (BBQ skewered chicken, served with peanut sauce), *mee goreng* (fried noodles), *congee* (rice porridge), *rojak* (bean curd, sprouts, cucumbers and peanut sauce), and *rotia perata* (that's the Singaporean name. In Malaysia it's *roti canai*. In either language, they're light wheat flour and egg pancakes tossed in the air like pizza dough to stretch it, then heated on a hot plate and served with gravy).

Rasasayang Singapore Restaurant
2430 East Hastings St (255-3733)

Jinmin Shen's new restaurant at Hastings and Nanaimo is already a hit. A special of 50% off satays is in effect weekdays (chicken, pork, beef or lamb). Otherwise, try one of the combination dinners, or the *udang sambal* (a spicy dish with prawn paste), *curry laksa*, *ikan chili padas* (another hot dish), *gado gado Singapura* (salad with peanut sauce), and to finish: Singapore *chendol* (a pudding). Lunch specials are priced from just $4.25.

Singapore Restaurant
546 West Broadway (874-6161)

Many curries and an interesting, diverse menu mark this little cafe. Try the sambal prawns (sambal is a spice made from fish paste), *choi tow kuey* (Singapore-style radish cake), *hontong* (mixed vegetables, eggs, tofu, coconut rice in a spicy curry), or the Singapore sweet-and-sour ribs. For dessert, there's fried pineapple with vanilla ice cream, among other temptations. Open daily. Free parking in the back (evenings only).

Super 8 Restaurant
7538 Royal Oak Ave, Burnaby (438-8247)

You'd never guess this was a Singapore/Malaysian restaurant, either, but there it is, near the Royal Oak SkyTrain station. They offer the requisite Singapore-style Hainanese chicken rice dish, various BBQ satays and all kinds of modestly priced combinations for singles, or to share. Try the deep-fried sambal tofu for a healthy jolt, or a nice steaming bowl of *assam laksa*, which will sure open your sinuses. This place is surprisingly affordable, compared to many others of its type.

Towkay Singapore Seafood
525 West Broadway (872-0328)

A nicely appointed room complements a varied seafood-focussed menu: There are sambal clams, black pepper crab and the traditional Hainanese chicken-with-rice. Or try the classic Singapore-style sweet-and-sour spareribs.

MALAYSIAN

A number of social and cultural groups have sprung up within the Malaysian community. As is their inclination (the Malaysians are a very open and welcoming people), their clubs and organizations usually invite many different ethnic people to participate. **The Malaysian Singapore Brunei Cultural Association** is comprised mainly of Bruneians and ethnic Chinese from Malaysia and Singapore; for information, write c/o P.O. Box 4171, Vancouver V6B 3Z6 or call 623-2422. The contact for **MASSAC: The Malaysia Singapore Sikh Association of Canada** is Andy Sidhu at 852-1827.

Members are usually of Malaysian, Singaporean, Indonesian or Thai origin, but their seasonal events are open to everyone.

There's usually a *pasar malam* — or night market, incorporating a food fair — held in late August or early September. MASSAC also usually hosts a big public event near Christmas or New Year. Try their *kueh kueh* (desserts), including a spicy and deep-fried Malaysian version of peanut brittle or the *sago kueh*, a kind of coconut tapioca pudding.

RESTAURANTS

Banana Leaf Malaysian Cuisine
1016 West Broadway (731-6333)

Just opened in the summer of 1995, this place invites you to "come and enjoy the warmth and taste of Malaysia," with a different dinner special each night (Monday *doary pisang padas*, Tuesday *roti canai*, etc.). A killer Hainanese boneless chicken and a full roster of tropical desserts, such as *bo bo cha cha* — coconut milk stewed with sweet potato yam, sago seeds (tapioca) and cooked with pandan leaves. Daily lunch specials are a good value.

Malaysia Cuisine
12043 88th Ave, Surrey (599-8242)

Authentic Malaysian cuisine in a friendly atmosphere. Dishes such as *mee goreng* (fried noodle with shrimp, tofu, vegetables), *tahu goreng* (deep fried tofu on lettuce, with stay sauce), and a *gado gado* (green salad with cucumbers and peanut sauce). Closed Monday; open Tuesday for lunch only; other days open 11 to 9.

Tropika Malaysian Cuisine
3105 West Broadway (737-6002)
1096 Denman St (682-1887)
Unit 21, 8280 Lansdowne Road, Richmond (278-6002)

Enjoy *nasi goreng* (fried rice), mee goreng, *rendang lembu* (spicy beef curry), and other well-known Malaysian specialties in these elegant restaurants. If you're brave, try the *chendol*, a traditional Malay village dessert made with red beans, green bean flour, palm sugar and coconut milk over shaved ice. Imported beer.

INDONESIAN

Our tiny Indonesian population (fewer than 500) worships at the **Indonesian Evangelical Church** at 29, 7240 Moffatt Road, Richmond (279-1565).

RESTAURANTS

Rich Cafe
538 Seymour St (682-9850)

Another of those "hole-in-the-wall" cafes, but this one offers excellent, genuine *Herlina* Indonesian food. Cheaply, too.

Rumah Bali
2420 Main St (872-2908)

Their superb 14-dish Indonesian rice table is legendary (if pricey), and their menu is filled with appealing vegetarian fare, if you prefer. Lunch specials are better value. Closed Sunday and Monday.

Tak Sangha Indonesian Restaurant
3916 Main St (876-0121)

They've been in this location for more than 30 years. Try their famous rice table (a combination feast of many courses) in their traditional Java Room.

FOODS

Bali House
883 Heritage Blvd., North Van (986-4547)

Bali House was started about 13 years ago by Anak Agung Oka Suparmi and partners. Suparmi is a native of the Indonesian island of Bali and has been in Vancouver about 22 years. Bali House Foods offers catering to private parties, and will serve authentic Indonesian cuisine anywhere, and to any number of guests. Suparmi's peanut sauce has become famous in its own right, and now she is making it available through Sunrise Market in

Chinatown (and soon in specialty food stores throughout the Lower Mainland). By the way, Suparmi is an accomplished Balinese dancer and has performed at SFU, UBC, the Pan Pacific, and on U.TV.

SHOPPING

Bali Bali
4462 West 10th (224-2347)
Bali Bali Galleria
3598 West 4th Ave (736-2172)

Vivid colours and rich textures are the hallmark of this distinctive collection of third-world costumes, clothing and artifacts. From the bamboo-fronted window box crowded with blooms outside to the Balinese prints at the back, peripatetic owner Mooh has assembled enough browsing amusement for any shopper. We've found Tibetan treasures, temple drums from India, spin drums and gourd rattles from Kenya, frog-motif jewellery in exotic, hammered designs. The Galleria operation focusses on must-have art, hangings, baskets and gifts.

FILIPINO

The more than 20,000 Filipino Canadians in the Greater Vancouver area are enthusiastic supporters of the **Philippine Community Centre Society**, a good place to call if you're interested in the many Filipino activities throughout the year; the society is located at 140, 11780 River Rd, Richmond (270-7227).

Anyone interested in Filipino culture is also invited to contact **The Filipino Association in B.C.** (mailing address: 1871 Coleman Ave, Coquitlam V3K 1B5; call 525-6687) and **The Filipino Canadian Cultural Society** (mailing address: 8030 Oak St, V6P 4A7; call 325-5248). For information about the business community, call to acquire a copy of **The Filipino Canadian Business Directory** (1851 Bowser Ave, North Vancouver, V7P 2Y8, 980-3218), which lists Filipino enterprises in the Lower Mainland.

There are seven local churches attended by Filipino congregations; services in English and Tagalog, the indigenous language, can be heard at **Grace International Baptist Church** (7650 Jasper Cres, Burnaby, 321-3525), **Iglesio Ni Cristo** (5060 Marine Drive, 436-1416, 436-1417), and **Saint Joseph's Roman Catholic Church** (3271 Fleming St, 876-7826).

The community supports a variety of publications, most of which are available at the stores listed below. **The Philippine Chronicle** (P.O. Box 41081 Shaughnessey Outlet, Port Coquitlam, Code V3C 3W4, 631-1780) is a biweekly newspaper and the largest of its kind in Canada. Other sources of news, entertainment listings and retail advertisements are **Amapola Magasin** (2934 Wiggins Pl, Langley, V2Y 1E9, 530-0677), **Newstar Tribune** (230, 12611 Vickers Way, Richmond, V6V 1H9, 244-2377), **Philippine News Canada** (94, 3180 East 58th Ave, V5S 3S8, 451-9181) and **Philipinyana Magasin** (11631 Aztec St, Richmond, V6X 1H9, 276-8623).

The **Rogers Multicultural Channel** offers two programs with a Filipino focus: *Filipiniana*, a mix of news items, folklore, legends and cultural programs from the Philippines, in both English and Tagalog; and *Pionoy Telecine*, featuring locally produced programs and travelogs in both languages. The shows are produced by Marilen Dela Cruz (594-5061, fax 594-5061).

One of the highlights of the year is the **Philippine Day Festival**, usually the second weekend in June or as close possible to June 12th, which is Independence Day in the Philippines. (Freedom from Spanish rule was gained on June 12, 1898.) The two-day event is held at the Plaza of Nations, with booths for traditional foods and singing and dancing groups; the children's groups usually perform on the Sunday. For details, contact organizer Rene Bahena (cel 671-6839).

FOOD STORES

All of the grocery stores have chest or upright freezers — the kind found in the home — full of frozen fish, Philippine sausages, vegetables and tropical flavoured ice cream. Some have the content listed on the outside of each freezer, while with others you have to peek for yourself — but the effort's worth it when you discover the exotic treasures inside. Many of the stores also sell takeout food and rent Filipino videos.

Aling Pining Foods and Video Rentals
4245 Fraser St (873-0519 or 872-4489; fax 873-5498)

Here you'll find mixes to make your own steamed rice cake or chocolate rice sponge. Their many freezers contain such items as cassava, young coconut, glutinous cake wrapped in bamboo leaves with dip, sausages, numerous varieties of fish, and ice cream made from jackfruit, corn and cheese, coconut and purple yams.

There's fresh produce and a large section of canned and bottled goods, such as purple yam jam, sweet mung beans, white beans and hot peppers. Takeout food; for the daily specials, consult the menu board outside the store. Videos in Tagalog.

Goldilocks Bake Shop
1606 West Broadway (736-7744)

This is part of a chain of stores located all over the Philippines; you'll also find their baked items in most of the other Lower Mainland stores that sell Filipino food. The windows are full of ornate wedding cakes, and inside you'll find all manner of baked goods — coconut buns and village cakes that are glazed in yellow, red and purple (the purple colour is from powdered purple yams) and cream-filled log cakes. There are also music tapes in Tagalog.

Kapit Bahay
4853 Main St (874-3635)

This is a combination food store and restaurant. The grocery section at the front offers banana catsup (similar to regular catsup, but made from bananas), canned jackfruit pulp, a variety of fish sauces (made from salty fish), and Mama Sita's mixes for making *menudo* (tripe soup) and *kare-kare* (oxtail stew in a peanut sauce) and *adobo*. The restaurant section is comprised of a mere few tables and chairs, with a menu hand-written on a white board. Item include kare-kare, *juron* (bananas in an egg roll wrapper), *ginataang langka* (jackfruit cooked in coconut milk) and *leche flane* (creme caramel).

Manila Food Mart
12039 88th Ave, Surrey (597-8108)

Virtually all of the grocery items here are imported from the Philippines — like violet rice, which you can get at a fraction of the price you'd pay in gourmet stores. Owners Jimmy and Arlene Castillo rent videos and carry lots of snack items, such as cracker nuts, peanuts coated in a crackerlike shell (try the garlic flavour), and candy made from jackfruit or purple yam.

Pilipinas Specialty Foods
Evergreen Mall, 8920 152nd St, Surrey (930-2438)

This full service fast food outlet and grocery run by the Avendano family features such Filipino specialties as lechon (with home-made sauce), BBQ pork (Pilipinas style), *mami* (noodle soup) & *siopao* (pork bun), *puto* (rice cake) and *dinuguan* (blood pudding), *lugaw with towa't baboy* (congee with pork), menudo, *embutido* (Spanish-style sausage with pork and pickles), *la-ing* (taro root), *lumpiang sariwa* (very fine chopped salad), and *merienda* (desserts) such as *halo-halo* (mixed tropical fruit covered with crushed ice, cream and ice cream), magnolia ice cream, *sago't gulaman* (fruit cooked with cream), *ginatan* (coconut, coconut milk, yam cold soup) *biko* (sweet rice with coconut milk), *bibingka* (rice cake with egg and coconut), *suman* (steamed rice wrapped in banana leaves and slow-cooked, topped with special brown rice syrup), and *kitsinta* (a special flour cake, so much in demand they can hardly keep it in stock).

Presyong Palengke
3994 Fraser St (879-2834)

You can pick up tiny finger bananas or plantains from their selection of fresh produce, there are fresh baked buns from the New Town Bakery, and packages of dried shrimp and banana blossoms (the matchlike flowers found inside a banana pod). Near the front of the store is a bulletin board for Filipino community notices. At the back of the store, **Pinoy Video** both sells and rents movies.

Sari Sari Store
5191 Joyce St (436-0146)

Located several doors down from the Joyce Sky Train Station, this new store sells food and a line of cosmetics imported from the Philippines: imported biscuits and crackers in metal tins (which protects them from the Philippines' humidity); Knorr soup mixes (although they're a Swiss company, these are packaged in the Philippines), including guava and tamarind soup bases; powdered purple yams and dried honeyed tamarind. They sell jars of sweetened beans, which are used in desserts, and the ice-shaving machines to make the slush over which the beans are often poured. The freezer has a good selection of Filipino ice cream.

Other typical Filipino food stores are **Auring** (3298 Main St, 872-1842); **Fraser BBQ & Fresh Meat** with whole *lechon* (roasted piglet) and a variety of Filipino groceries at 6340 Fraser St (324-3738); **Jak en Poy**, Impact Plaza, 113, 15277 100 Ave, Surrey (589-8221); **Josie's Specialty Foods** at 7011 Fraser St (321-1229 or 324-8746), where owner Josie E. Taboada stocks all kinds of Filipino foods; **Kabayan** at 580 Powell St (255-8510); **Manila Food Market** (4443 Hastings St, Burnaby, 298-9122); **Mini Mart Plus** (2096 Kingsway, 876-1639); **Philippine Tropic Express & Food Store** at 114 West Broadway (879-8441); and **Supreme Meat**, which offers Filipino favourites like beef and pork offal — *dugo ng baboy* (pig's blood), pork ears and more, at 1725 Macdonald Ave, Burnaby (299-0541; fax 299-0500).

RESTAURANTS

Alex's Restaurant
641 Powell St (254-8383)

They offer a complete Filipino menu, plus karaoke every night. Weekends, live entertainment is added. Alex's cel phone (for reservations): 341-1748.

Boracay Cafe
826 Renfrew St (255-5795)

This is one of those tiny hole-in-the-wall establishments that really come up with the authentic goods: fine Filipino cuisine at low prices.

Rene's on Broadway
567 West Broadway (876-8785)

Although this a cafeteria-style place with the offerings listed on a chalkboard, the staff are very helpful with the identification of dishes: *pancit guisado* (noodles with mixed vegetables and meats), *adobong pusit* (squid cooked adobo-style—in vinegar, soya sauce and garlic), *caldereta* (beef stew), *sinigang na baka* (beef short ribs) and deep-fried *lumpia* (similar to an egg roll). Beverages include mango and coconut juices.

Galing-galing Restaurant
1606 West Broadway (736-8877)

You'll find it in the same building as Goldilocks Bakery. It, too, is cafeteria-style; items are listed on a board above the food, but there are no English translations, so just point to anything that you fancy. Authentic dishes include lumpia Shanghai (fried egg rolls, Shanghai-style), *laing* (shrimp cooked in coconut milk), *pinakbet* (similar to the French ratatouille, this is vegetables with shrimp paste), *apritadang manok* (a type of chicken stew) and *adobong manok* (chicken adobo-style, as close as anything to being the national dish).

Pacific Breeze
566 Powell St (253-0931)

Another of those diamonds-in-the-rough, this tiny place is in a seedy area, yet the local Philippines crowd seems to have discovered it, since it's always packed; maybe because the food is authentic — and cheap.

ENTERTAINMENT

Filipino Diamonds Society of B.C.
842 Powell St (253-2624)

Visitors are welcome at this social club, where you can watch — or if you know the rules, play — *mah-jong* (the Chinese cross between dominoes and gin) or *pares pares*, a Filipino card game.

VIDEO STORES

Filipinas Video
4873 Main St (875-0983)

There's an extensive selection of videos in Tagalog and English, along with a small grocery section where you can stock up on munchies — like the deep-fried pork rinds known as *chicaron*.

Manila Mini Mart
453 Powell St (phone unavailable)

This place carries lots of clothing and a good assortment of Filipino videos for rent and audio cassettes to buy.

R P Market & Video
7101 Victoria Drive (327-0373; fax 327-0384)

Owner Don Nieveras has just opened this store with a wide selection of Filipino specialty food items, plus many new-release Philippines videos.

CHINESE

TAIWANESE AND MAINLAND

The first of Vancouver's Chinese immigrants were "imported" from China to help build Canada's national railroad. They were treated like indentured slaves and were not even permitted to become Canadian citizens until the 1920s; nor were they allowed to work as accountants or lawyers. And it wasn't until 1946 that Chinese Canadians were allowed to vote. Notwithstanding these (and other) severe restrictions, Vancouver's Chinese community flourished. Today, our Chinese district thrives in our midst, as probably the oldest (and largely most intact) neighbourhood to which we can lay claim. Vancouver's Chinatown is the largest in Canada, and second in North America only to San Francisco's. Accordingly, this is deservedly the largest chapter in the book.

By the way, while in your tours, don't miss the world's thinnest building (according to the Guinness Book of Records), the **Sam Kee Building** at 2, 4, 6, 8, 10 and 12 West Pender St, which today houses the offices of well-known insurance agent Jack Chow. Chow paid for restoration of the heritage structure and the 128-foot glass sidewalk in front, under which public baths were once located.

As well as Vancouver's original Chinatown, other pockets of Chinese settlement have evolved over the years, principally in the Oakridge area (41st Avenue and Cambie/Oak), in Richmond and now Coquitlam.

In Richmond, 1990 heralded the opening of North America's largest enclosed mall, built with the Asian community in mind. It's the **Aberdeen Centre** at 4151 Hazelbridge Way, which includes shops, restaurants and a bowling alley — plus a restaurant *overlooking* the bowling alley. Another large development in Richmond is the **Yaohan Centre**, built with investment money from Japan, but catering largely to Chinese-Canadians. A visit to Yaohan Centre on Richmond's main drag (No 3 Road) feels exactly like being in the heart of CityPlaza, a huge mall on Taikoo Shing Road in Hong Kong that features, among other things, an ice skating rink. The Yaohan experience is virtual immersion: Many shoppers and sales clerks speak very little English.

President's Plaza on No 3 Road was built by Taiwan entrepreneur Jack Lee and houses a Buddhist group, as well as shops and businesses.

RELIGIOUS CENTRES

There are vast numbers of Chinese places of worship, and many forms of worship, for that matter. Enjoy the peaceful surroundings at the **Ching Chung Taoist Church** on the second and third floors, 223 Keefer St (681-6166; fax 681-8686). Donations are welcome, though not required, and there is lots of free literature to take away. Another temple worth seeing, if only for its palatial architecture, is the **Kuan Yin Buddhist Temple** at 9160 Steveston Highway, Richmond (274-2822; fax 271-2338). Inside its entrance, there's an immense white and gold marble statue of Buddha Sakyamuni, and the Main Gracious Hall is itself filled with statuary, paintings and religious artifacts. Call ahead for group tours; otherwise, individuals may visit anytime from 10 to 5.

Basel Hakka Lutheran Church, at 823 Jackson Ave (255-5988 fax & phone) is the only church in Canada providing services in the Hakka language (a Chinese minority). Other noteworthy churches are **Bodhi Rey Tsang Temple**, a Buddhist temple at 514 Keefer St (255-3811; fax 255-8894), which offers free vegetarian food at noon Sundays, followed by group mediation at 1 pm; **Chown Memorial & Chinese United Church** at 3591 Cambie St (876-7114), which holds services in Cantonese, Mandarin and English; **Christ Church of China** at 300 East Pender St (254-4219; fax 254-4218), with services in both Cantonese and in English; **Fung Loy Kok Taoist Temple** at 220-440 West Hastings St (681-6609); **Providence Maitriyeh Buddhist Temple** at 3495 East Hastings St (298-8162; fax 298-8102); **St. Francis Xavier Chinese Parish** at 431 Princess St (254-2727 fax & phone), a Catholic parish with services in Mandarin and Cantonese; and **Taiwanese United Church in Greater Vancouver** at 3821 Lister St, Burnaby (321-7048; fax 437-1571) which holds services in the Fujian language.

For religious artifacts, temple gods, joss money, wind chimes, incense and incense-burners, try **Agata Enterprises/Hing Loong** at 135 East Pender St (688-3300 or 662-3300; fax 662-3832); **Buddha Supplies Centre** at 4158 Main St (873-8169) or **Lotus Pond Religion Centre** at 259 East Hastings St (681-9665 or 683-6802).

CULTURAL LIFE

Chinese Cultural Centres
50 East Pender St (687-0729; fax 687-6260)
860, 4400 Hazelbridge Way, Richmond (278-0873; same fax)

With the Pender Street location as its original headquarters, the Chinese Cultural Centre is integrally involved in the community's festivals, its relationship with the city and the preservation of its traditions. It welcomes anyone interested in learning Mandarin and Cantonese, Tai chi and the martial arts, and such fine arts as calligraphy. Call for details about classes and upcoming performances by theatrical, dance and other artistic troupes.

Dr Sun Yat-Sen Classical Chinese Garden
578 Carrall St (662-3207; fax 682-4008)

The Sun Yat-Sen garden is well worth a visit (the brochure assures you "refreshment for the heart"). It is patterned after private classical gardens developed in the City of Suzhou during the Ming Dynasty (1368-1644), and was built in 1985-86 using materials, tools and techniques dating back to the original period. A guided tour of the gardens is included in the price of admission: $4.50 for adults; seniors free on the third Wednesday of each month. Open daily. Use of the adjacent park is free. In its own way, the gift shop is also spectacular.

FESTIVALS

The extraordinarily colourful (and noisy) **Chinese New Year Festivities** are centred in Chinatown — with a parade that draws tens of thousands of spectators — but it extends across the Lower Mainland, wherever Chinese Canadians maintain a significant presence; check with Chinese-oriented malls or places of worship for details, if the idea of a downtown crush is off-putting. (The Chinese Cultural Centres are always a dependable source of information.) Incidentally, the New Year falls between January 21 and February 19, depending on the phases of the moon.

Since Expo in 1986, the annual **Dragon Boat Festival and Race** has made the third weekend in June another must-see on Vancouver's calendar; it is now the largest such event in North America. Song and dance troupes perform at Plaza of Nations, and the race — based on a tradition going back some 2000 years — can easily be viewed from any number of points nearby. As June approaches, contact the Festival Society 501, 1155 West Pender St (688-2382), which can always use volunteers.

The **Moon Festival**, held between the middle of August and the middle of September, honours the immortal Moon Goddess; in tribute, the CCC usually orchestrates some sort of concert, highlighted by traditionally costumed dancers.

The **Taiwanese Cultural Festival** at the Richmond Gateway Theatre, 6500 Gilbert Road (276-6506) is held annually during the first two weeks of July. Events include dance troupes, video screenings, a music festival and exhibits of aboriginal folklore and art.

MEDIA & LANGUAGE

Among the newspapers available, all are in Chinese, so we have assumed they will not be useful to those who can't read the language. For those studying the spoken languages of Asia, however, there are a number of radio shows: **Overseas Chinese Voice** (203 East Pender St (688-7733; fax 688-0345) airs Monday to Saturday from 9 pm to 6 am on **CHMB** AM 1320; **Canadian Chinese Radio** is on **CJVB** AM 1470 (cable 103.5 FM) Monday to Saturday from 10 pm to 6 am (2615 Aberdeen Ctr, 4151 Hazelbridge Way, Richmond, 270-3639; fax 270-9689); on Sundays **Chinese Voice Alive**, Cantonese religious programming airs on the same station (688-9931 for details); and *Morning Voice* airs weekday mornings on Co-op Radio on 104.7 FM (684-8494).

Chinese Community Television (Cantonese & Mandarin) airs daily on the **Rogers Multicultural Channel**; the producer is Wayne Lee (pager 667-0283; fax 438-8869).

Conversational Chinese lessons can be had for $2.50 an hour at the **Little Mountain Neighbourhood House Learning Centre**, at 3957 Main St. Call Irene Lui at 879-7104 or 324-0887.

RESTAURANTS

High-end

Some of the most extravagant, haute cuisine experiences in the Vancouver area take place in Chinese restaurants, such as at **Kirin** (dramatic table-side presentations on some featured dishes) at 1166 Alberni St (682-8833) or City Square, 201, 555 West 12th Ave (879-8038); **Spicy Court Chinese Restaurant**, offering Szechuan and Cantonese cuisine at 5638 Cambie St (325-1189 or 325-0320); **Sun Sui Wah Seafood Restaurant** for seafood specialties at either 4818 Main St (872-8822) or Alderbridge Plaza, 102, 4940 No 3 Road, Richmond (273-8208); Albert Cheung's sumptuous new **Dynasty**, where Tai Chin Hin used to be — at 888 Burrard St (681-8283); or **Wonton King** (try the Peking duck in crepes or the spareribs in salt and chilies) at 620 S E Marine Drive (321-4433).

One of the best places we know for fine dining with the family is Tony Vong's new location of **Vong's** at 4298 Fraser St (879-4298). You haven't truly lived until you've eaten some of Tony's signature deep-fried curried wontons (the curry is inside the wonton — a welcome surprise). Or try the upscale **Fortune House** at 608, 650 West 41st Ave (266-7728) for the scallop dumplings or excellent dim sum.

In Richmond, many like the buffet at **Foody Goody**, 8120 Lansdowne Road (231-9893; fax 231-8983) and the classic Chinese food at **Top Gun**, 2100, 4151 Hazelbridge Way (273-2883).

Dim Sum

In Cantonese, *dim sum* means to touch or warm someone's heart, as the English use the term "sweet nothings." Generally, dim sum are small steamed or fried Chinese dumplings with various fillings, often pork, crab or shrimp. (Westerners might think of them as "tea sandwiches" or hors d'oeuvres.) The dumplings are displayed to dining patrons on special trolleys. Traditionally, members of our Chinese community — and increasing numbers of non-Chinese — go for dim sum as a Sunday brunch, but other times are quickly becoming routine. Many places serve dim sum daily at lunchtime.

Some years ago, it was impossible to truly explain to Vancouverites who had not been to China what it felt like to be in a restaurant as big as a city block, with carts of dim sum being wheeled around between tables as you could flag down your choice. Now, there are dozens of excellent dim sum places, among them **Gum Yip Chinese** at 710 Twelfth St, New West (540-1618); **Flamingo** at 3469 Fraser St (877-1231) or 7510 Cambie St (325-4511 or 325-4618); and **The Pink Pearl** — huge, long-established (and still going strong) at 1132 East Hastings St (253-4316). Free parking in their adjacent lot; reservations advised.

The most popular dim sum place in town these days seems to be **Park Lock Seafood Restaurant** at 544 Main St (688-1581), where the uninitiated can refer to a simple printed guide.

Take-out and Frozen Dim Sum

Smaller dim sum establishments are primarily for take-out customers, although there may be a few tables. A top dim sum take-out place in Chinatown is **Ho Wah Bakery**, 137 East Pender St (684-8862), where there are fresh steam buns, sticky rice buns, deep-fried red bean dumplings, crispy melon cakes, and a whole, wall-sized freezer filled with shrink-wrapped, take-home, ready-to-heat dim sum. Other candidates are **Joy Chinese Dim Sum**, 3827 Main St (874-2371); **Max King Bakery** — dim sum servings each $1.90 at 277 East Pender St (684-2178); and **Yummy's Dim Sum**, 2708 Main St, 875-0771).

Wonton & Noodle Houses

These are the places to visit when you want a fully tummy but don't have a full wallet. In short, they offer cheap, healthy and filling fare. One of our favourites is Eddie **Tang's Noodle House**, at 2805-2807 West Broadway (so clean it's worth mentioning; no MSG, 737-1278). Other good choices are **Hon's Wun-tun House**, #108, 268 Keefer St. (688-0871); and **Hoy's Wonton (Plus) House**, which offers free delivery and specials priced at $1.99 to $4.50, at 1202 Kingsway (874-4433). **Kent's Kitchen** is simply packed for dine-in or take-out, and rice with two toppings is $3.75, all at 232 Keefer St (669-2237); and **King Heng Noodles** offers *twai teow, you mian, loa shu fen* (different kinds of noodles) and a hot buffet or two toppings on rice for only $3.75 all day, at 617 Gore St (681-3188)

Supplying many of the above restaurants is **Asia Pacific Foods** at 855 East Hastings St (255-7136; fax 255-8282); meanwhile, off-the-street customers are welcome. Offerings include fast-frozen food, particularly the famous Nanxiang steamed "stuff-bun," plus wonton, steamed dumpling, spring roll, dumpling soup, boiled dumpling, etc. The Nanxiang steamed stuff-bun is world-renowned — made by a former Shanghai *Ma-ling* (member of an elite corps of chefs), according to a prized recipe handed down for over 200 years.

Hot Pot Houses

This special form of Chinese dining usually involves built-in burners at each table and powerful ventilation — making the numbers of these establishments understandably small. Patrons cook their own raw food (which is ordered in various combinations from an a la carte menu) in boiling vats of broth. If the concept appeals to you, try **Landmark Hot Pot House**, Vancouver's original hot pot house at 4023 Cambie St (872-2868); **Maple Garden Hot Pot Restaurant** (splendid food and service at 4260 No 3 Road, Richmond, 273-3202, fax 278-3329); and **Ten Ten Hot Pot** at 101, 1788 West Broadway (730-0388), which is generally open till midnight.

Vegetarian

Because Buddhists prefer a vegetarian diet, the city has many excellent Chinese vegetarian restaurants with a truly interesting variety of alternatives to meat. The **Bo-jik**, for one, has elevated vegetarian fare to an haute cuisine level; find it at 820 West Broadway (872-5556). The most recent addition to the scene is the excellent **Bo Kong Vegetarian Restaurant** at 3068 Main St (876-3088). You should also try **Bodai Vegetarian Restaurant** (the original and still one of the top Buddhist restaurants in town) at 337 East Hastings St (682-2666), not to be confused with **Bodhi Vegetarian Cuisine** at 5701 Granville St (261-3388; fax 266-6661).

Szechuan

Ah, we do love hot and spicy food. Our favourites for years have been the two locations of **Won More**, one upstairs at 201, 1184 Denman St (688-8856), and the newer breakaway version at 1944 West 4th Ave (737-2889). Right across the street from the latter is another prime Szechuan place (with an excellent hot and sour soup, we might add) called **The Great Wok** (1961 West 4th Ave, 739-7668). And we do like the food at **Moutai Mandarin Restaurant**, 1710 Davie St (681-2288).

However, we've recently discovered a new "best Szechuan." The place looks fairly unprepossessing, yet the food is original, fabulous, and modestly priced: **Wing Wah Shanghai Szechuan Restaurant** at 260 East Broadway (879-9168); if you crave spicy, try the "orange peel beef."

Other Szechuan places worth noting: **New Grand View Szechuan**, 60 West Broadway (879-8885); and **Szechuan Chongqing** (not quite what it was in the old days on Victoria Drive) at 1668 West Broadway (734-1668; fax 734-8018 & delivery 734-2668) or 4519 Kingsway, Burnaby (434-1668 or 434-2668; fax 434-1660).

Seafood

Chinese gourmets prefer seafood so fresh that in Hong Kong suburbs like Sai Kung or Lei Yei Mun, they actually select their live dinner from huge tanks on the sidewalk, and the "catch" is immediately cooked to order. Among Vancouver's excellent Chinese seafood establishments are **Lock Yuen Seafood Restaurant** at 1625 Kingsway (876-9119); and the inimitable **Park Lock Seafood Restaurant** in Chinatown at 544 Main St (688-1581), where you should be prepared to stand on queue at busy times. Former Dynasty chef, Lam Kam Shing and partner/Maitre d' Simon Lee offer a vast menu of traditional southern Chinese seafood specialties at **Grand King Seafood Restaurant**, 705 West Broadway, 876-7855, where the chicken congee and the dim sum are excellent — and reservations are recommended.

Though we were distressed when they put those glass awnings on a cherished heritage edifice, we have to admit that the dining experience at **Imperial Chinese Seafood Restaurant** is beyond reproach. Find it in the art deco Marine Building at 355 Burrard St (688-8191).

Mongolian

These places cater to the large appetite, in most cases offering you a choice of fixings from a selection of meats, seafood vegetables and noodles.

Great Wall Mongolian BBQ
717 Denman St (688-2121)

Here you'll find an all-you-can-eat lunch for $6.95, or dinner for $9.95, all in Mongolian BBQ style.

Mongolie Grill
467 West Broadway (874-6121)
818 Thurlow St (683-8834)
100, 8400 Alexander Rd, Richmond (276-0303)

Our favourite of the three locations is the one in Richmond, just off No 3 Road (the ventilation is better). The idea is to serve yourself from the various stainless steel tubs of cut veggies, meats, seafood and sauces. Your order is then weighed (you pay by the 100 gm) and custom-cooked before you on the equivalent of a giant upside-down wok. A fun place to take out-of-towners.

Bakery/Restaurants

In Hong Kong, some old-style bakeries have a rear or upstairs area wherein you may enjoy tea and buns inexpensively. When you see "Hong Kong-style coffee" on the menu, brace yourself for a very strong brew. You can also request a "mixture" (half tea, half coffee), common there but an unusual combination for the uninitiated Western palate.

Among the other bakery/restaurants noted for this kind of mid-shopping treat are **The Boss**, 532/534 Main St (683-3860; fax 688-2677); **Loong Foong**, 247 Keefer St (688-0837) and **Maxim's Bakery & Restaurant** 257 Keefer St (688-6281 or 687-0949).

Miscellaneous

For solid family dining, you can't beat **Shanghai Palace Restaurant**, long established in its Marpole location at 8012 Granville St (261-6328). Just to confuse you, another reliably good (albeit smaller) operation is **Shanghai Garden Restaurant** at 3932 Fraser St (873-6123), where the pot stickers are exemplary. **Foo's** in Chinatown at 72 East Pender St (685-1511) and **Fortune City** at 2132 East Hastings St (251-3322) have always been reliable.

Peripathetic restaurateur Ed Lum (formerly of Beijing Restaurant) has set up **Chinese Bistro Moderne** in an upstairs space at

1128 Alberni St (683-8222), fusing the cafe concept with high calibre cuisine (try the spicy chili prawns). And then there's **Mitzie's Restaurant** at 179 East Pender St (689-9763, 683-6662, 683-6670), which is typical of the restaurants you find in Hong Kong itself.

FOOD STORES

Tofu sources

The best sources for tofu are locations of **Sunrise Market's Tofu Factory** at 729 Powell St (254-8888; fax 251-1083) and Chi Tong Chan's **Superior Tofu Ltd** at 438 Main St (682-8867), #1030 Aberdeen Centre, Richmond (279-5567) or at the main "factory" at 1469 Venables St (251-1888; office or fax 251-1806). Sunrise, by the way, offers a "Tofu recipe line" at 253-2326, and includes soy beverages and tofu desserts in its product line.

Meat & Sausages

Carley Quality Meats
293/295 East Georgia St (689-2813)
260 East Georgia St (684-3122)
377 East Broadway (875-9833)

The first Chinatown location combines fast food take-out, with sales of Chinese sausage, BBQ pork, duck and BBQ sausage, quail's eggs, chicken or fish dumplings for the hot pot and chicken feet (a bargain at $1 a bag). Whole roasting chickens can go for just $3 each. The second Chinatown store has more groceries, like canned curry, cooking wine, Robertson's jellies (mango and pineapple), Mount Elephant chili and ketchup in a nice ceramic container for $1.89. The Broadway location is similar to each of these, but combined with Gar Way Market, a large grocery store.

Chong Hing Co
246 Keefer St (681-1336)

Here you'll find fresh BBQ meats, sausage, pig's feet, deep-fried chicken feet and some unusual tinned goods from Mainland

China. We also discovered our favourite Singapore Hut brand curry sauce here at $1.79.

Dollar Meat Store
266 East Pender St (681-1052, 681-8442, 681-0536)

This sister operation to Man Sing Meats (below) is owned by the same family, that of King Wong, a prominent businessman. This is a large store with lots of BBQ meats, pressed duck and Chinese sausage.

Krehmer's Quality Meats
2585 216th St, Langley (533-9899)

Here's where we've found fresh sausages made with spicy lemon grass and Chinese sausages, all at direct-from-the-factory prices. Oriental sausages must be custom-ordered ahead of time, and it takes a week to 10 days until they're available, since the new owners contract it out to an Asian couple who make sausages to order.

Le Kiu Poultry & Grocery
254 East Pender St (683-7451)

This is a poultry outlet with chicken and other birds dressed and ready for cooking, fresh or frozen. Le Kiu Importing is two doors down at 262.

Man Sing Meat Centre
224 East Pender St (681-4491 or 687-5252)

It's hard not to just stand and watch the 20 or so butchers hard at work in neat white caps serving throngs of customers who obviously consider the roast pork the best in town. Man Sing also has barbecue pork, roast or BBQ duck, pressed duck, Chinese sausage and other succulent delicacies.

Sing Chong Food Centre
253 Keefer St (684-0253)

There's usually a whole BBQ piglet in the butcher's window, and you can watch him slice fresh ribs off one by one for his customers. There's also BBQ meat and boneless pork.

Sun Tong
8251 Westminster Hwy, Richmond (273-9822)

Here they sell fresh meats and live seafood from a very large, clean store. Look for the big yellow awning.

Fresh Fish & Seafood

Kam Tong Enterprises
276 East Pender St (683-0033; fax 683-0833)

BBQ meats, fresh seafood, live prawns, iced rock cod and live crab are among the offerings here.

King's Seafood
670 Kingsway (872-2029; fax 873-1727)

A no-nonsense fish market, this place looks like a tiled bathroom filled with tanks of live crustaceans, fish, squid and other delicacies, as well as frozen salmon, ling cod and more. Prices are posted on a daily specials board on the wall.

New Chong Lung Seafoods & Meats
595 Gore St (phone unavailable)

They pack fresh and smoked salmon for travel, and their other seafood always looks exceptionally fresh. They also carry live and frozen geoduck, BBQ meats and an assortment of Chinese sausage.

Pender Seafoods
284 East Pender St (687-5946)

Hard-to-find fresh skate wing, plus choice smelts, live ling cod, halibut and sea bass.

Bakeries

Special occasion cakes in Chinese bakeries are good value and nothing short of elaborate in both design and execution. Secondly, there are usually whole racks of dun tarts (egg custard), coconut tarts, cocktail buns, steamed pork buns, black bean or melon cakes, almond cookies and more. One observation: You can't always tell a Chinese bakery from its name; a prime example is **Casa Mia Bakery** at 2758 Kingsway (436-2255), where a specialty is Taiwan-style Chinese donuts. **Amy's Cake Shop** at 3086 Cambie St (872-4716 or 872-8833) and 1000, 3700 No 3 Road, Richmond (278-3232) sells award-winning cakes; particularly popular are the good-luck plum cakes and the sweet potato cake. Don't miss **Anna's Cake House**, at 666 East Broadway (876-6532), 5510 Cambie St (325-8214), and 155, 8141 Westminster Hwy, Richmond (276-0544). We were very much taken with the jelly rolls and rolls made with lemon, mango or walnut cream at **Keefer Bakery**, 251 East Georgia St (685-2117). **Sally's Cake House** at 291 East Pender St (684-9308) prides itself on its policy of "no preservatives."

Supermarkets

Chinese supermarkets are really super-super-*super*-markets. Vast. Crammed. It's easy to spend hours in the following.

Pak Kai Enterprises
12, 2755 Lougheed Hwy, Port Coquitlam (942-9338 or 944-7368)

This mega-store in Poco Place Mall (near London Drugs) is a staggering experience for the uninitiated. It's well-stocked with inventory of foods, sauces, fresh seafood, herbs, meats, produce and seasonal specialties — and it's always packed with customers.

South China Foods
#212, 2800 East 1st Ave (251-1333; fax 251-6799)

Probably the largest single collection of Asian foods, condiments, sauces, spices and paraphernalia (rice cookers, bamboo steamers, woks, stirring and skimming implements) in the entire Lower Mainland. Perfect for those who need these foods in bulk — and the lowest prices on various kinds of rice we've found anywhere. The seafood, BBQ and poultry sections close daily at 7 pm.

South China Seas Trading Company
1689 Johnston St, Granville Island (681-5402)

Owner Kay Leong scours Pacific Rim countries for the best and most exotic spices and condiments available. Kay will give you endless amounts of free advice on how to use the items she sells — it's not uncommon for Kay and her staff to bail out regular customers with no-fail recipes at the last minute before a major dinner party (They'll even give you on-the-phone coaching if something you attempt falls short of your expectations). The inventory includes spices, fresh herbs, condiments, sauces, noodles and prepared ethnic items from Asia. Fresh herbs are generally flown in directly from the country of origin — like Thai basil; *galangal* (or "kah", a ginger-like, peppery spice) from Thailand; *atemoya* (like custard apple or cherimoya) from Fiji or Hawaii; Kaffir lime leaves; pea eggplant ("gully peas"), which grows wild in the Caribbean; or scotch bonnets (also known as Congo chilies or Mexican habaneros) from Africa via Jamaica and the Yucatan.

Sun Wah Super Market
268 Keefer St (688-9598)

This huge supermarket is tucked into the basement of an office building and parking complex in the heart of Chinatown. We discovered large ceramic egg pots there at the low sale price of $19.99 and various painted tins, including some with handles that could be recycled as lunch pails and quite impress the youngsters.

Super Choice Foods
6457 Fraser St (321-3899)

Here's an assortment of Chinese specialties, some produce, frozen seafood (squid, prawns, sea-cucumber, fish), BBQ pork and duck, fresh pork and chicken, and uncommon items like pork lungs and chicken feet. They also offer take-out deli-style Chinese food.

T & T Supermarket
Metrotown, 470, 4800 Kingsway, Burnaby (436-4881; fax 436-0717)
President's Place, 8181 Cambie Road, Richmond (279-1818; fax 279-0008)

14, 13331 Vulcan Way, Richmond (276-9889; fax 276-1627)

The gigantic grocery store under Zellers at Metrotown carries an immense assortment of ginseng, plus live fish, take-away food (cooked while you wait) and enormous numbers of grocery items. The Richmond branches (one at No 3 Road and Cambie, and the other behind Yaohan Centre) are equally impressive for their size and diversity of stock.

Vikon Foods
Mandarin Centre, 611 Main St, lower level (688-2362)

Everything from superior fresh produce to rice cookers, herbals, spices and rows of freezers full of staple foods. Downstairs.

Two other Asian food stores worth seeking out are **China Can Supermarket**, 102, 4600 No 3 Road, Richmond (270-8183; fax 278-3188); and **Pepper Pot Food & Spice Co**, Lonsdale Quay, 105, 123 Carrie Cates Court, North Van (986-1877).

Grocery & Produce Stores

Unlike the giant supermarkets, these are usually vendors whose stalls spill out onto the sidewalk. Prices are excellent; freshness superb. **Tak Sing Co** at 212 East Georgia St (684-2353; fax 685-2396) borders on supermarket-size, stocking a huge selection of rice, rice flour, fish gravy, chili oil, Singapore curry, seaweed, spices, chili radish in soy, and salted bamboo shoots in chili oil.

Generally conforming to this category, though, are **Bonanza Market**, 265 East Hastings St (688-6824 or 669-8854); and **Red Star Vegetable, Fruit & Meat**, 751 Gore St (681-8538); **Yuen Tong Co**, (if only for its *mongtong* or durian pudding) at 236 East Pender St.

Don't overlook the street market set up to sell farm-fresh produce on Saturdays next to **Gar Lock Seafood & Meat** at East Georgia and Gore.

Miscellaneous Specialty Foods

Fresh Egg Mart
269 East Georgia St (685-1925)

As suggested by the name, they sell every kind and size of egg you might fancy (including quail and duck, for instance), plus gigantic sacks of rice, salt, sugar and bulk vegetable oil. Cash and carry.

Le Kiu Grocery
262 East Pender St (683-7451)

This other half of the Le Kiu poultry operation is the main grocery action: Salted duck eggs, spices and ingredients from all over South East Asia, Thailand, Indonesia and Japan. We found some spicy "Jufran Banana Sauce" we'd never seen before.

Soon Cheong Trading Centre
242 East Pender St (685-4333; fax 669-8933)

This bustling grocery store sells persimmons, lotus seeds coated with sugar, coconut strips, red pumpkin seeds, lotus root, candied watermelon rind and candied kumquats, among other traditional food items.

HEALTH & FITNESS

Health Foods & Herbalists

Our Chinese friends are among the most health-conscious we know, and in this age of enlightened, pro-active food and lifestyle choices, that's saying a lot.

Hing Wah Limited
506 Main (683-3838)

This shop is filled with herbal remedies, dried seahorses, dried snakes, lizards, ginseng and more than 20 varieties of tea. We found black seaweed imported from China (the long strands, like the vermicelli they also sell, represent wishes for the long life of family and guests).

This is also the location of the practise of the famous Dr. Wu, an herbalist so renowned that people come from a number of U.S. states as well as from throughout B.C. to queue up for hours for a consultation. It's first come, first served (take a number on arrival); prescribed herbs are then chopped up and dispensed.

Kiu Shun Trading Co
512 Main St (669-1834; fax 669-6779)
261/269 Keefer (head office, 682-2621; fax 684-8237)

This is a renowned herbal store in Chinatown, due to its large selection of dried seafood, swallow's nest, ginseng, deer horn, kirin horn, Chinese herbs & health foods, and giant dried shark's fins in cases on the wall. Little English spoken, but the staff will try their best to communicate. Ask for Stephen Wong or General Manager Forvic Wong or Albert, all of whom do speak English.

Kang King Traditional Chinese Medicine, Health & Beauty is a new facility at 4750 Main St (875-6138). Other notable shops are **Cheong Wing Herb Co Ltd** for ginseng, dried herbs, noodles, cuttlefish and ginger at 286 Keefer St (687-2513); **Ngai Hoi Trading**, 217 Keefer St (687-3286 or 689-8028); **Pak Chong Enterprises**, 434 Main St (684-6264); and **Tong Fong Hung Medicine Co**, a large store with herbs, health foods, dried seafood at 536 Main St.

The best buys on dried mushrooms in bulk are at **Beijing Trading Co**, 89 East Pender St (684-2736 or 684-3563).

Traditional Chinese Medicine, Doctors & Practitioners

Various Chinese treatments, such as *moxibustion* (detoxifying with burning herbs), *Qi Gong* (Qi is vital energy; when balanced, harmony is achieved), herbal detoxifying, *Zhi Neng* and reflexology are offered by a number of qualified practitioners:

Kwak's Traditional Chinese Medicine Clinic
603 East Broadway (872-1227)

Dr. Fred Kwak offers a full range of traditional treatments, with a focus on back and joint pain.

Nafisa Lakhani
Suite 206, 2025 West 42nd Ave (261-6833)

This doctor of traditional Chinese medicine focusses on herbology, diet therapy and food cures and accepts authorized ICBC claims.

Dr. Zhang Dian Tong
206A, 2525 Pine St (731-2202)

Dr. Zhang is a Qi Gong Master.

Traditional Chinese Medicine Association of B.C.
301, 1847 West Broadway (732-4874)

Their referral service can recommend numerous practitioners, or you call directly to any of the Drs. Wu (Annie, David, Eunice or Joseph) at 107, 1956 West Broadway (732-8968), or to Dr. Jiang Ting Ting at 958 West 8th Ave (738-1012). The referral service has many other practitioners to recommend.

Wild Rose Centre of Natural Healing
1745 West 4th Ave (734-4596; fax 734-4597)

Classes are offered in their college portion, and free information evenings introduce novices to healing practices.

YCY Prosperity
548 Main St (685-3778; fax 683-1918)
YCY Chinese Medicine & Health Care Centre
123 East Pender St (685-1871
YCY Better Health Centre
President Plaza, 1150, 8181 Cambie Road, Richmond (270-8841)

This group of treatment centres offers the services of Solomon Yeung, emphasizing energy channels, treatment points, herbology and health care products.

Acupuncture

Acupuncture, acupressure and other forms of therapy are becoming increasingly accepted in North America. Vancouver has a plethora of such establishments. Here are a number of reputable places.

Ngai Hoi Trading
217 Keefer St (687-3286; 689-8028)

Treatments in orthopedics, acupuncture and massage by appointment at the rear of the store; herbal remedies include many kinds of dried mushrooms.

Solomon Yeung/YCY
548 Main St (685-3778; fax 683-1918)

Acupuncture, acupressure, treatments and supplies are available here, both wholesale and retail. Yeung also works from two other locations (see traditional Chinese practitioners, above, for details).

Fitness & Martial Arts

Black Belt Shop
1, 31550 South Fraser Way, Clearbrook (855-6733)

Videos, weapons, training charts and apparatus, uniforms and books.

D T Lim's Tae Kwon-Do Academy
(formerly Sun E. Choi Tae Kwon-Do Academy)
3058 Kingsway (433-8800)

Grand Master Lim has numerous championships under his belt and decades of experience coaching and training athletes. He develops your skills while building your self confidence, patience and discipline. For more info, call Talking Yellow Pages at 299-9000, #8811.

Golden Arrow Martial Arts Supplies
2234 East Hastings St (254-6910)

Uniforms, sparring gear, training equipment and weapons, books and videos.

Kuan Way Martial Arts Supplies
28 East Pender St (682-3329; fax 682-3351)

This shop — probably intimidating to passers-by — features technique charts, costumes, swords, how-to videos and books.

Praying Mantis Kung Fu Academy
West End Community Centre, 870 Denman St (220-4779)

Kung Fu Master Sifu Jon Funk is a direct descendant of Wong Long, the founder of this form of martial arts. Classes begin periodically, and men and women of all sizes and abilities can call for a free beginner's lesson. Primary focus is on grappling, forms, weapons and sparring, and techniques taught may be successfully employed by both men and women of all sizes and abilities.

White Crane Kung Fu
2440 Main St (872-8720)

Grand Master Vincent Chow is an herbalist and massage therapist whose approach to martial arts is meant to heal as well as train and discipline. He claims to offer mental discipline, inner power, youthful vigour and more.

SHOPPING

Tea Places & Tea Sets

Gim Lee Yuen
47 East Pender St (685-9743)

Kwok Luen Lam imports impressive antique teapots made from natural clay (though they look like ancient metal, and just as heavy) and whole tea and dinner sets of fine porcelain, modestly priced from $23.50 (24 pieces) to $375 (92-piece set). Most of the china is sold by the piece.

Ten Lee Hong Enterprises Tea & Ginseng
500 Main St (689-7598; fax 689-8596)

Just opened in August, 1995, this place is fully stocked with tea, ginseng and dried herbs, plus an attractive assortment of porcelain tea services.

Ten Ren Tea & Ginseng Co
550 Main St (684-1566; fax 684-7348)

We've actually been to this place's sister operation in Hong Kong, and this one is every bit as authentic. If they have time, they will honour you with a Chinese tea ceremony. At the very least, attentive staff rush to you with tiny samples cups of tea. Great selection. Lots of porcelain or clay tea services and accessories for sale, too. A free pamphlet, *The Art of Tea Making*, is available at the counter.

Others worth noting are **Fook Ming Tong Tea Shop**, 680, 4400 Hazelbridge Way, Richmond (270-3191) and **Super Fine Tea Co** for its a nice selection of ceremonial tea sets at 275 East Georgia St (687-4181).

Bookstores

For the immersion experience, nothing beats videos, books and comic books — although be forewarned that though the books are usually Chinese-language, most comics in Chinese bookstores are actually Japanese.

Kiu Yick Bookshop
272 East Pender St (688-5912 or 669-7114; fax: 688-9955)

This upstairs bookstore in the heart of Chinatown sells good-luck money packets, paperbacks, magazines and greeting cards, as well as housing a bustling travel service and the Nam Young Tong Association.

Pioneer Book Store
229 Keefer St (662-7696)

There's the South China Morning Post at the door, and a wealth of Chinese magazines, girlie mags (*Penthouse*, but then there's also *Cosmopolitan*), and a large reference section with items such as the German-Chinese dictionary we found. Comics and paperbacks are mostly Japanese.

Sino United Publishing
78-80 East Pender St (688-3785; fax 688-0798)

Books and magazines, stationery and stamps, musical tapes and

CDs, greeting cards and gifts are all here, well-ordered, in this large store.

Van Chinatown Books & Gift Shop
341 Gore St (684-3982)

Situated in the old Orange Hall Building (built 1907), this place trades, buys and sells new and used English language and Chinese books.

Others are: **KC Book Co** (ask for manager Wing Mah at 105 East Pender St, 684-7959); **Imperial Bookstore Co** at 617 Main St (669-8638); and **World Journal**, CDs, cassettes and books at 157 East Pender St (688-3018; fax 681-9961).

Music

H Q Electronics
546 Main St (681-1432)

Chinese language audio tapes, CDs (three for $23), collectors' cards, laser discs, concert videos, vinyl LPs, electrical equipment, karaoke supplies (mikes, etc).

MAL
115 East Pender St (688-2831; fax 688-2863)

Certainly Vancouver's largest Chinese-language music store, this place features the latest Hong Kong CDs, cassettes, laser discs and a grand assortment of audio equipment.

Ngai Lum Musical Society
529 Carrall St (689-3559)

Choose the right day and you'll hear the haunting strains of their music emanating from this rehearsal space. They are available for public performances.

Videos

Dreams Laser Video & Rico Films Production (Canada)
4209 Fraser St (872-7737 or 872-8893)

6760 No 3 Road, Richmond (270-1862)

This place produces films and rents everything from family fare to X-rated material. The Vancouver location has more tapes and some laser discs; the Richmond one rents mainly laser disc movies, all in Chinese language.

VLC Video, Laser & Compact Disc Centre
Burnaby: 2748 Kingsway (438-8243)

A TVB outlet (one of the main television channels in Hong Kong), this place rents both Chinese and videos, laser discs and CDs.

Other video stores worth finding are **Buddy's Video** at 5890 Cambie St (321-1818); **China Video** carrying Chinese language CDs and videos (both sales and rental) at 3371B Kingsway, Burnaby (431-6829); and **Galaxy Video** 3343 Kingsway (436-9433).

Fine Art, Art Supplies & Framing Services

Please note that arts-and-craft items and Chinese *chops* are in the shopping section following this one.

CC Arts Gallery
20 East Pender (669-2601; fax 436-3284)

Vancouver gallery's new director is Ming Y. Ng, who also provides custom framing and matting services and Chinese silk mounting. To reach Mr. Ng at home for special orders, call 298-6813.

Chan's Gallery
525 Main St (684-6851)

Known as a top place for expert framing and fine art. Though the place looks tiny, all the best local Chinese artists have their work framed here. Mr. Chan is always busy, yet he handles all orders promptly and professionally. He also has a small (but wonderful) collection of unique paintings and art pieces from Mainland China.

Dragon Arts
27 East Pender St (689-7188; fax 689-7181)

Shawn Wong's shop provides custom framing, signs and calligraphy, plus Chinese and Western art supplies. They also sell paintings, easels and pre-carved chops with Chinese zodiac signs — custom carved ones start at $25.

Oriental Arts & Antiques Auctioneer
123B East Pender St (688-6848; fax 688-6887 or 321-5189)

This enterprise belongs to philanthropist Benson Wong; it is also the home to the Vancouver Chinese Art Gallery, so some of the artwork is for sale and other pieces are only on display.

Shu Ren Environmental Arts
9400 Dolphin Ave, Richmond (272-4253 fax & phone)

Arthur S.R. Cheng is an award-winning, locally based sculptor, painter and landscape designer who works in granite, marble, bronze and lately in B.C. cedar. He also does woodblock prints, oil paintings and freeform sketches. He currently specializes in portraits, head sculptures and busts. Arthur designed the entire Chinese Eternal Garden at 14644 72nd Ave, Surrey, including the wayside pavilion and wooden bridge. Commissions accepted. Call ahead to visit his Richmond studio.

Tsi Art Chai Art Gallery
78-80 East Pender St (688-3785; fax 688-0798)

This gallery shares space with Sino United Publishing (basically a books and stationery store). Stock of the art gallery includes Chinese paintings and calligraphy and some fine art and gift items. They also sell Chinese writing brushes, ink and fine art or rice papers.

Also check out the collection of Chinese fine art and pottery at **Tai Ping Trading Co**, 41 East Pender St (682-8598; fax 682-8511).

Gold stores

The Chinese take their fine jewellery very seriously, never settling for the usual North American standard of 10 or 14 karat gold, but insisting on the best: 24 karat. These stores also offer some of the finest craftsmanship and attention to detail in town. Though prices may not be the lowest, quality is tops. Among the best ones are: **Bo Lok Jewellers** (ignore the low-rent neighbourhood, and go for the value) at 871 East Hastings St (254-8023); **Chow Sang Sang** expert advice and evaluation of gemstones, too, at 2516 Granville St (733-2718 or 733-6162); **Golden Art & Gems** at 131 East Pender St (689-3371); **Ultimate 24 Karat Gold Shop**, 523 Main St (688-1860); and **Wing Wah Jewellery**, 40 East Pender St (682-3836).

Chops

Artland
111 East Pender St (688-0383)

We'd heard you could buy chops in town and finally discovered this place — and they cost even less than you'd pay in Hong Kong. Chops are chunks of granite or marble, often topped with a carving of the zodiac animal for the recipient's birth-year. It takes one hour for owner Mrs. Ng to carve words or symbols into the bottom so it can be used as a stamp, or you can buy some common words pre-carved into samples on the spot. With ink, case and carving, prices start under $30. Single custom-carved chops (unadorned by fancy carving on top) cost $20 and the pre-carved plain ones (with characters meaning "long life," "happy" or "good luck") are only $8. Mrs. Ng also does expert picture framing at modest prices.

Another place for chops (they call them "stone stamps") is **Universal Arts**, 49 East Pender St (681-2939).

Shoes & Wigs

Bennie's
445 Main St (669-5774)
1655, 4151 Hazelbridge Way (270-3817)

This otherwise standard shoe store specializes in small sizes and shoes for hard-to-fit feet. Small sizes are increasingly difficult to locate these days in Vancouver.

A great selection of cheap shoes, flip-flops, umbrellas and purses

— just like a Hong Kong street market — is at Anna Chan's Chi Shing Trading Co, 294/296 Keefer St (683-0978). Other branches are at 255 Union St (687-6301) and 100, 629 Main St (683-3287).

Hing Lin Wig Shop
17 East Pender St (684-2917)

The best prices in town for wigs. They also sell hairpieces and hair weaves from a huge stock.

Arts & Crafts

Asia Imports
155 West Hastings St (687-4912)
30 East Pender St (687-8823)

Fine, hand-made quilts, embroidered silk blouses, cutwork pillows, embroidered table linens, duvet covers, exotic kimonos, jade, ivory, cloisonne and other precious items are showcased here. Expensive, but top-notch goods. The best collections of Battenburg-style lace and cutwork in town.

Cathay Importers
104 East Pender St (684-2632)
37 West Pender St (684-9711)

The best Chinatown source for baskets. They also sell rattan furniture, bamboo and wicker products, bird cages, twig reindeer, inexpensive excelsior (shredded cellophane for gift baskets), beach mats, seagrass matting, paper blinds, straw hats, chinawares, novelties and toys. A good place to buy stocking stuffers and party favours.

Another recommended source for cheap toys (wooden snakes, colourful kites, travel games, novelties) is **China West**, 41 East Pender St (681-9665). Lots of wicker and gift stock (dusty but good prices) are at **Sang Cheung Co**, 83 East Pender St (688-5734; fax 298-8448).

China Arts & Crafts Importers
895 East Hastings St (251-2554)

This large operation imports vast quantities of dinnerware, art, carvings (stone, wood and jade), furniture, authentic camphor wood hope chests, marble tables and fireplaces, wall screens and room dividers, vases and more and sells at exceptionally low prices. For example, porcelain flower pot sets were three for $5, a 14-inch vases was $7 and ceramic soup spoons were a mere ten cents apiece. Hope chests ranged from $129 to $289, or about half what we've seen them for elsewhere.

Also try: **Chinese Jade & Crafts**, 38 Pender St (662-8893); **Panda Emporium**, 51 East Pender St (687-5734; fax 298-8448; and for a vast array of rosewood furniture and enormous porcelain vases, visit **Yeu Hua Handicrafts**, 173 East Pender St (662-3832; fax 662-3830).

Chung Kiu Chinese Products Emporium
495 Main St (682-7990)

This place looks exactly like the Chinese Arts & Crafts shops in Hong Kong, with everything from jade carvings and silk imports to silk-covered boxes, fans, rosewood chopsticks and more.

Hing Lung Foods
512 Main St (688-3300)

Though it's a typical grocery store, this is our Chinatown source for bright and inexpensive gift wrap (at the back).

Kitchenware

Ming Wo
23 East Pender St (683-7268)

The prominent Wong family's Ming Wo chain was launched by this single shop in Chinatown in 1919, and for many years it was virtually the only place in town offering a really broad assortment of professional quality cookware and utensils for both home and restaurant use. Today, there are Ming Wo stores in shopping malls all over the Lower Mainland. Our favourites are the South Granville location (with its stock skewed to appeal to preppie residents in the area) and this original Chinatown branch. Need a wok? No place cheaper. An 18-inch wooden spoon? This is the source.

For ceramics, porcelain ware, mah jong sets, thrift-priced sandals and housewares, we like: The inexpensive trinkets and bowls at **Fortune City Bargain Centre**, 248 East Georgia St (683-3611); Catherine Wong's well-priced cookware at **Hing Loong Co**, 135 East Pender St (688-3300 or 662-3300; fax 662-3832); egg pots at $9.90 or three for $17.50 at **N & S Trading Co**, 122 East Pender St (669-0124); large porcelain Vases from Mainland China at **Rong Hua Porcelain Enterprises,** 5632 Victoria Dr (323-8592); kitchen ware at **Save N Shop Home Necessities**, 261 East Pender St (683-8870); rice-cookers, portable gas or electric burners and much kitchenware at **Vigor Trading**, 110, 8211 Westminster Hwy, Richmond (276-2168); and the specialty condiments, housewares, steamers and cleavers at **Yuen Fong**, 242 East Pender St (683-6858).

FAR EASTERN

JAPANESE

We may never get over the vision — some 20 years ago — of watching a friend's mother weeping in her Shaughnessy garden, as she recalled how her revered Japanese gardener came to her on the eve of his removal to a detention camp in the B.C. Interior and asked her if she would store for him several priceless trees and ornamental shrubs until his release. She loved gardening; the man was both a mentor and teacher to her, not just an employee. She insisted on purchasing the plants — as much to assuage her creeping sense of shame as to spare the man further indignity. The trees still stand in that Shaughnessy garden. The gardener did not survive to reclaim them.

Such is the prickling guilt that many longtime B.C. residents share when it comes to recalling the treatment suffered by the Japanese during the Second World War. Both first-generation immigrants (*Issei*) and *Nisei* (next generation) were treated equally badly. Vancouverite Roy Miki, a *Sansei* Japanese (the second generation born in Canada), lobbied tirelessly for redress, which was finally achieved in 1988.

By now, the once-thriving Japanese communities of Powell Street and Steveston Village in Richmond have declined to a handful of businesses or remnants of the past. In each of these areas, however, grand cultural events are held to mark important festivals or memories.

FESTIVALS

Powell Street Festival
Oppenheimer Park, bounded by 400-block Powell, Cordova, Dunlevy and Jackson Ave (details: 682-4335)

Usually held the first Saturday and Sunday of August, this free street fair includes everything from *origami* (the Japanese art of paper-folding) to crafts, food booths, children's entertainment, *taiko* (music), martial arts displays, kite-flying, painting demonstrations and educational films, tours and storytelling. Organized by the Powell Street Festival Society at 450, 1050 Alberni St (682-4335; fax 688-4529). The 19th annual festival, held in 1995 with a peace theme, saw celebrants fold 1000 paper cranes for peace. Inspirational lanterns were also launched at Sunset Beach.

Steveston Salmon Festival
Various venues and streets in Steveston (Maureen: 277-6812)

The 50th annual festival was celebrated in 1995 in downtown Steveston — in an area roughly between Chatham and Moncton streets and between 3rd Ave and Railway Ave. Dates are generally the last week of June through the Canada Day weekend, with venues including the indoor tennis courts, the community centre building, Garry Point Park, a bingo tent operated by the local Lions Club, an outdoor carnival, traditional barbecue salmon bake, a chowder contest, garden festival, children's swap meet, watermelon booth, Japanese cultural show (origami, ikebana, bonsai, martial arts, Japanese dolls), all capped off by a grand display of fireworks at dusk on Canada Day. There's also the annual King of the Fraser competition. Though most events are free, some (like the Miss Richmond/Salmon Queen Reunion and dinner dance) require tickets (call the number above for details).

ATTRACTION

Nitobe Garden
6804 S W Marine Drive, UBC (822-6038)

These elegant-yet-relaxing gardens exemplify the classic, formal Japanese garden. Open daily from 10 to 6; Admission is $2.25 for adults, $1.50 students and seniors. Twice a year, when the UBC Botanical Gardens holds its plant sales (spring and fall), admission is free.

ORGANIZATIONS

Tonarigumi (Japanese Community Volunteers' Association)
378 Powell St (687-2172; fax 687-2168)

This is a direct social service agency provides information, counselling, interpretation, and other services in Japanese. For English-speaking Vancouverites, this is the best local source of information about Japanese Canadians and their programs. Its director, Takeo Yamashiro, has worked tirelessly for the Japanese community for more than 20 years.

Among the various business groups catering to the needs of the Japanese community are the **Japanese Businessmen's Association (Konwakai)** at 404, 999 Canada Place (682-0562; fax 641-1216); **Kiyu-Kai Business Association** (call 264-0273 for details); and **Vancouver Japanese Gardeners Association** at 1, 4289 Slocan St (439-7990 or 430-4117).

The **National Nikkei Heritage Centre (Japanese Canadian Citizens Association)** at 511 East Broadway (874-8187) is the Japanese Canadian Citizen's Association. Housing the Japanese Canadian archives, it is primarily an advocacy group, focussing on human rights, cultural and social issues.

NNHC at #435, 1050 Alberni St (681-9194) is the parent office of the National Nikkei Heritage Centre; it is currently building a multi-complex centre for the Japanese community in Burnaby, which will include both a cultural centre and a seniors' residence.

Among the many Japanese-language publications are **The Bulletin** 348 Powell St, Vancouver V6A 1G4 (681-5222; fax 682-

5220); **The Canada Jiho**, 699, 999 Canada Place (641-1339), a weekly newspaper;

Canada-Japan Business Journal, 370, 220 Cambie St, Vancouver V6B 2M9 (688-2486; fax 688-1487); **Canada West Tourist News** at Box 28, 128, 1050 West Pender St, Vancouver V6E 3S7 (688-7636; fax 688-4775); and **Vancouver Shinpo**, 1336A East Hastings St, Vancouver V5L 1S3 (255-6822; fax 255-9505), a weekly newspaper.

The **Rogers Multicultural Channel** airs *Japanese Community Television*, daily except Monday and Wednesday. Producer Naoto Horita can be reached at 641-1322; fax 641-1310.

SHOPPING

Little Ginza

The most concentrated retail district has been nicknamed "Little Ginza," thanks to its resemblance to Tokyo's famous shopping district. This part of the West End seems devoted solely to Japanese tourists (selling salmon-to-ship, furs, high-end clothing, etc.), but if you want a taste of the real thing, it's your best bet. Among the many shopping and dining choices are **Dreams Discount Gift Shop** at 722 Thurlow St (687-3375; fax 687-6640); **Eager Beaver** at 123, 755 Burrard St (669-2223); **Gyoza Paradise Restaurant** at 824 Thurlow St (669-8586); **Hunting World Leathers** at 1055 Alberni St; **Ichibankan Japanese Restaurant** at 770 Thurlow St (682-6262); **Japanese Steak House** at 1042 Alberni St (684-2451); **New Tokyo Craft, Gift & Fur Shop** at 1055 Alberni St (669-0618 or 669-3615); **New Tokyo Gift Shop** at 1055 Alberni St (669-1655); **OK Gift Shop/Fur Shop** at 1054 Alberni St (689-5513); **Rodeo Collection** at 110, 1080 Alberni (682-8783); **Saitoh Canada** at 107, 755 Burrard St (685-6661 or 683-6389; **Salmon Village** at 779 Thurlow St (685-3378), or 1057 Alberni St (685-7778); fax 685-5524) **Sapporo Canadiana** at 125, 1011 Alberni St (687-3321; fax 687-3326); **Sapporo Gift Shop** at 801 West Georgia St (685-0710); and **Tokyo-Do Gift Shop** at 1210, 777 Hornby St (687-7879; fax 687-1778).

Giftwares & Japanese Imports

Kaya Kaya
2039 West 4th Ave (732-1816)

Antique Japanese furniture and Tansu chests set the mood, rice paper screens gently divide the room, and there's an area devoted entirely to colourful glass wares and Ikeban vases. The gracious and savvy owner, Michiko Sakata, scours haunts back in her native Japan to find the finest porcelain; she also custom-imports for several luxury hotel chains across Canada and the U.S. Among the treasures are ceremonial tea services, exquisite woven clothing by Japanese Weaver Mitsue (including some charming and serviceable vests), unusual terra cotta planters, lacquer trays, and a host of dramatic and offbeat crafts you'll find nowhere else in town.

Japanese china, lacquerware, giftware and art pieces can also be found at **Japanese Accents Kiku**, 1532 Marine Drive, West Van (925-2584) and **Murata Art** at 392/394 Powell St (688-1117).

Paper-making

Kakali Handmade Paper Studio
Granville Island, 1249 Cartwright St (682-5274)

Sharyn Yuen has attained legendary status in the dozen or so years her Kakali classes have been teaching Vancouverites how to make and use paper in the time-worn fashion of the Japanese artisan. Sharyn's sister operation is **Paper-Ya**, a retail shop at 9, 1666 Johnston St (684-2531), that sells many of these papers and other gifts, too.

Sharyn has announced she will soon be closing Kakali's workshop facilities, yet she pledges to continue to offer supplies by phone or mail order from the former Kakali premises. In addition, the Hollander beater (used for making paper pulp) remains in its old location and is available for rent by prior booking. Postal code for mail ordering is V6H 3R7.

FISHING SUPPLIES

The Japanese have long been expert commercial fishermen. One of the oldest marine supply stores catering to this industry is **Nikka Industries**, with branches at 611 Powell St (251-2466; fax 251-7226) and in Steveston at 3551 Moncton St (271-6332; fax 271-1217).

FOOD STORES

Fujiya
203, 403 North Road, Coquitlam (931-3713)
Fujiya Store
100, 8211 Westminster Hwy, Richmond (270-3715)
Fujiya Fish & Japanese Foods
912 Clark Drive (251-3711)

These are the cheapest sources for Japanese foods and pearl rice in town. They also have weekly specials, and carry a wide variety of inexpensive kitchenware, steamers, woks, kitchen tools and the like. We found the best buys in sushi supplies here, including those hard-to-find bamboo mats for rolling up *nori sushi* (sea-weed rolls). The Clark Drive location has very inexpensive lunch specials on take-out sushi, too; the *obento* (lunch boxes) are priced at under $5, and are 50% off after 6 pm.

Shimuzu-Shoten Store
349 East Hastings St (689-3471, fax: 689-5328)

This is a great place for Japanese imported foods and housewares, and one of the cheapest places in town for bulk rice.

Yaohan
3700 No 3 Road, Richmond (278-8808)

This huge Japanese mega-store stocks every spice, condiment and soy product you could ever want, plus specials at rock-bottom prices. There's fresh produce, super-fresh seafood and BBQ meats, too. We've found tofu for 49 cents per pound and a great tempura pan for $12.99 on sale. Housewares and novelties are cheap here as well. Find the store in Yaohan Centre, just north of Aberdeen Centre, off Cambie Road. To receive the Yaohan flyer (which lists specials) by mail every two weeks, write to Yaohan Dept., 370, 220 Cambie St., Vancouver V6B 2M9. A "World Gift Catalogue" is available at the store, so you can send presents directly to your friends in Japan.

Sunrise Market
300 Powell St (685-8019)

Because of its extensive array of Japanese foodstuffs, this is where most of Vancouver's Japanese chefs shop. It's a good source of whole ginger and low-priced Japanese Mandarin oranges, in season.

Other dependable food outlets are **Ikkyu Hitoyasumi Grocery** at 1459 West Broadway (731-5519); **Kobayashi Shoten** at 1518 Robson St (683-1019); and **Sakanaya Seafood** at 8435 Granville St (261-7717).

RESTAURANTS

The days when the only place you could eat Japanese food in town — at the **Aki** on Powell Street — are long gone. Today, there are more than 150 Japanese restaurants in the downtown corridor alone, and more seem to open every month. Many of these are tiny noodle shops or sushi joints, but there are also a great many fine restaurants. What makes one of these establishments more inviting than another to local Japanese Vancouverites is often the owner of the restaurant, who more often than not also wears the chef's hat and wields the knife. In sushi places, this factor often determines whether a business thrives, or not.

The reason is simple: In Japanese culture, sushi chefs are more than mere cooks; he (the sushi chef is always male) performs as a social interlocutor — almost like a local newscaster for the community. He shares gossip, listens as a neighbourhood bartender might, and offers counselling on family and personal problems — and sage advice, while periodically whacking at a piece of prime fish or seaweed roll.

Among the Japanese restaurants that have enjoyed continued success over the past decade — and whose owners are also the chefs — are **Koko** (starring Koji Shimamura at 2053 East Hastings St, 251-1328); **Sakae** (Keisuke Mori, 745 Thurlow St, 669-0067 and in Richmond at 120, 8360 Granville Ave, 278-8070); **Shijo** (Keiichiro Yamasaki, 202, 1926 West 4th Ave, 732-4676); and last, but certainly not least, **Tojo's** (Hidekazu Tojo, at 777 West Broadway, 872-8050 or 872-8051). The last, by the way is considered Vancouver's best — certainly one of the most expensive, but worth it. Besides the excellent food, Tojo himself remains one of the prime attractions.

Fine Dining

As with Chinese food, some dishes may contain MSG (monosodium glutamate), which is known in Japanese as *aji-no-moto*. If you don't like MSG, remember to ask if it's used, when you order: It can always be omitted.

Bon Japanese Restaurant
53 West Broadway (872-0088 or 872-4435)

The dishes are the usual first-class sushi—except that the chef here adds something special: choreography, if you will. He dances as he works, and every movement is rhythmic. Great entertainment, which we think adds to the digestive process. He also offers the best combination *maki* (rolled sushi) deal in town.

Dai Masu
525 West Broadway (875-0077; fax 875-0063)

Dine-in or take-out at this fine Japanese restaurant featuring *robata* (entrees, dinner-only), teriyaki, gyoza, sushi, sashimi and a wonderful *yaki udon* (noodle soup). Their "eye-openers" start not too early — 11:30 am — and are available for dine-in only.

Kobe Japanese Steak & Seafood House
1042 Alberni St (684-2451)

Samurai-garbed chefs liven up the atmosphere of this long-time tourist favourite. Chefs perform with flashing blades — you watch as your meal is cooked in front of you. Kobe steak is among the finest in the world (expensive, too). The New York cut, for example, will run you about $25 per person (entree only). Add chicken or seafood in a combo and the price goes up. Reservations recommended.

Misaki at the Pan Pacific
999 Canada Place (662-8111)

Just opened at the end of August, 1995, this posh environment caters to the wealthiest of tourists — but those who also know their food.

Other top-end restaurants with strong followings include **Chiyoda** at 200, 1050 Alberni St (688-5050); **Kakiemon**, where you often see Japanese businessmen entertaining important clients, at 200 Burrard St (688-6866); **Koji** at 630 Hornby St (685-7355); **Sagano**, which offers a mountain view from its patio at 601 West Broadway (876-9267) and **Suehiro Japanese Restaurant** at 10251 St Edwards Drive, Richmond (276-1163) offers *tappan yaki* style cuisine, where the chef performs at your table and grills the food.

Sushi Restaurants & Noodle Cafes

The aforementioned Koji Shimamura, who now runs **Koko** at 2053 East Hastings St, popularized sushi in Vancouver during the years when he was running Koji's. He is a veteran of more than 33 years as a sushi chef, and most of the other sushi chefs in town once worked under him and studied his technique. Although his place is not fancy at all, his sushi is always fresh and very reasonably priced compared to other top-end Japanese restaurants.

E-Hak Japanese Restaurant
1095 Kingsway (873-1734)

The dinner special here is $7.95 for sushi, tempura, teriyaki, udon and gyoza.

Japanese Deli House
381 Powell St (681-6484)

3017 St John's St, Port Moody (469-6484)
Japanese Deli House Take-out
381 Powell St (662-7422; fax 682-7621)

All-you-can-eat sushi for a fixed price. You have to finish your rice serving with each course, however, which makes pigging out a bit difficult.

Kappa Japanese Restaurant
4067 Cambie St (872-4744; fax 876-0329)

Considered by many one of the best sushi places in town. Closed Mondays.

Momiji
3550 Fraser St (872-2027)

A very popular Japanese noodle house, thanks to gigantic portions (giant bowls of udon or yakisoba) and low prices. They used to close at the oddest times; now that they've regulated their hours, it's a more reliable place to visit.

Musashi Japanese Restaurant
780 Denman St (687-0634)

This is the place all the local sushi chefs go when they're not rolling and chopping at their own restaurants. It used to be a dinky little place but was expanded last year. Top-rated items: the *toro* (tuna) and *oma bi* (raw shrimp) sushi. Prices are rock-bottom: *nigiri* (sliced tuna, shrimp, geoduck, etc) is usually $1 per piece; *maki* (rolled sushi), cut into four bite-sized nibbles ranges from $2 to $4.50.

Octopus's Garden
1995 Cornwall Ave (734-8971)

Good sushi, affordable prices. Big with the Gen-X crowd. Bright and clean, and every seat affords a good view of the passing parade on Cornwall.

Pacific Royal Buffet
195 West Broadway (879-7337)

Sashimi and sushi available every night. Fixed menu prices (all you can eat) are $7.99 for lunch and $12.99 for dinner (M-W) or $14.99 (Th-Sun). Lots of free parking. As well, special "theme" nights honour Thai, Indonesian, Vietnamese, Korean and Singapore cuisines.

Shiro Japanese Restaurant
3096 Cambie St (874-0027)

"Shiro's" may be small, and you may expect to wait a bit for your table, but it's well worth it; better sushi is hard to find.

Tokyo Joe's Take-out
5105 Kingsway (pick-up order by phone 434-6020; by fax 434-8185)

From *udon* (noodle soup) to *tempura* (deep fried) or *yakisoba* (fried noodles), and of course, sushi (rolled, cone-style, vegetarian, spicy, *sashimi* (raw fish) — everything is available on a take-out or dine-in basis. Call or fax ahead, and they'll have your order waiting. They also do all manner of lunch boxes (served all day), combination sushi plates, and offer party trays at reasonable prices. Closed Sundays.

Tsunami
238, 1025 Robson St (687-8744)

Touted as "Vancouver's only floating sushi bar," it's a great place to bring visitors; you sit up at the sushi bar and watch the boats float around.

Other sushi places of note are **Fujiya** (as mentioned above — great deals on obento); **I love sushi** for robata, tempura, teriyaki, sashimi and 99-cent take-out sushi at 8251 Westminster Hwy, Richmond (273-3500); good spicy rolls at **Minato Sushi**, 992 West Broadway (732-6554 or 732-6532); **Misaki Japanese Deli**, 115, 3800 Bayview St, Steveston (275-5465); **Sushi Boy** for large portions and low price at 101, 409 West Broadway (879-5236; fax 879-5237); **The Sushi Shop** at 116, 1610 Robson St (682-7280); **Tokyo Ichiban** at 170, 8380 Lansdowne Road, Richmond (279-8802) or 222, 4501 North Road, Burnaby (421-6622; fax 421-6629);

Vancouver Sushiman at 25 Victoria Drive (255-5188; fax 255-5138); and **Yoshimi Restaurant** at 410 Sixth St, New West (540-9540).

Miscellaneous

Finally, varied food styles can be enjoyed at **Crazy Spaghetti House Raku**, 838 Thurlow St (685-8817), which features Japanese "pub-food," including oden, yakitori, onigiri, etc.; **Papa's and Mama's Japanese Kitchen**, 1434 Lonsdale Ave, North Van (986-1118) and **Hachibei**, 778 West 16th Ave (879-8821), both of which serve home-style fare; **Harbour Moon** at 1230 Robson St (688-8777), a noodle house popular with young people; and **Tokachi Japanese Restaurant**, 10767A King George Hwy, Surrey (951-3800).

BOOKSTORES

Anime Jyanai
2547 Renfrew St (253-7831)

This store carries Japanese animation videos, books, posters, games, model kits and video games.

Iwase Books
2535, 3700 No 3 Road, Richmond (231-0717; fax 231-0727)

One of the top Japanese book stores in the world, tucked into the second floor of Yaohan Centre.

Japanese Educational Centre Tenrikyo
3690 Nanaimo St (433-4773)

A good source for books and texts.

Japanese Language & Books
3647 Main St (874-3366)

A tiny store simply crammed with books, teaching and other curriculum materials and stationery supplies.

Sophia Book Store
725 Nelson St (684-4032)

This downtown store specializes in volumes about Japan and the Far East, plus language books and many books penned in Japanese.

LANGUAGE CLASSES

Considered the best place for language classes for business people and those planning to visit, live or work in Japan is **David Lam Centre** at SFU's downtown campus, Harbour Centre, 555 West Hastings St (291-4585; fax 291-5659). Or investigate the **Japanese Language Centre**, 93 Peveril Ave (874-5830); **Steveston Japanese Language School**, 4255 Moncton St (274-4374); or **Vancouver Japanese School** at 119, 530 East 41st Ave (327-0333; fax 327-0318).

MARTIAL ARTS & FITNESS

A number of associations help regulate this growing fitness and discipline field. Among them are **Aikido Federation of B.C.** at 432-6770; **Japan Karate Assn of BC** at 11767, 225th St, Maple Ridge (463-8939); **Japan Karate Assocation**, Vancouver at 955 Burrard St (681-0221); **Pacific Aikido Kensankai Assn** in Trout Lake Community Centre, at 3350 Victoria Drive (876-9285 or 684-4497); and **World Shorinji Kenpo Organization**, Vancouver Branch at 4076 Kincaid St, Burnaby (451-9491 or 662-8884).

There are also many schools and clubs from which to choose. Here is a sampling: **Aikido with Ki**, 140, 2268 No 5 Road, Richmond (261-3136); **J.K.F. Shito-Ryu Karate-Do Itosu-Kai**, 6184 Ash St (321-1815; fax 685-5130; res 876-0552); **Kingsway Shito-Ryu Itosukai Karate-Do** — they teach aikido, man seikan, fitness and self-defence at 2501 Kingsway (430-4237); **Kyokushin Karate Vancouver College** at 5400 Cartier St (266-6801); **Mansei-Kan Aikido** and **Canada Kingsway Dojo** (housed with other karate schools at 2501 Kingsway, 430-4237); **Seikidokan Judo Club** at 6260 Killarney St (434-9167); **Steveston Judo Club** housed at 4111 Moncton Road, Steveston (277-6812) along with

Steveston Kendo Club; and **Vancouver Kendo Club** at 2929 East 22nd Ave (684-2056).

THERAPEUTIC MASSAGE & SHIATSU

The following are some of Vancouver's many trained, licensed practitioners. Some do home-visit massage. **Hideo Takahasi Acupuncture Clinic** at 300, 1701 West Broadway (736-2430); **Japan Health Centre** at 101, 2524 Cypress St (739-2121); **Japanese Therapeutic Centre**, 2992 East 3rd Ave (253-4671); the very well-regarded **Mizutani Junji** at 896 West King Edward Ave (874-8537); **Sumimoto Oriental Therapeutics**, 408, 1541 West Broadway (734-7537); and **Tokyo Health Sauna Club** at 2737 West 4th Ave (739-5882).

ENTERTAINMENT & KARAOKE

The Japanese popularized *karaoke* (singing along in public to pre-recorded hit parade songs), and the tradition continues here in such clubs as **Daruma Restaurant** 2528 Kingsway (436-5597); **Harajuku** at 1256 Robson St (685-5818); **Hollywood North**, which always looks deserted from the outside, but inside it's hopping at 856 Seymour St (682-7722); **Queen Bee Karaoke** at 756 Kingsway (closed Mondays); and **Tokyo Lounge** at 350, 1050 Alberni St (689-0002). It is often possible to book a private room, do you don't have to warble in front of strangers.

VIDEO RENTALS

Among the dependable places to rent Japanese-language videos are **Anime Jyanai** at 2547 Renfrew St (253-7831); **Kiku Japanese Video** at 2980 East 22nd Ave (433-0011); **Sakura Video**, 1782 Alberni St (324-1455); and **Videomatica** at 1855 West 4th Ave (734-0411).

KOREAN

Vancouver's Korean residents have grown from several hundred refugee immigrants in the early '60s to a community of almost 10,000 today.

ORGANIZATIONS

The Korean Society of BC
1320 East Hastings St, 255-3443; fax 255-3739)

This group hosts an annual festival (usually in late June) at the Bonsor Sports Complex, 6550 Bonsor Ave, Burnaby. Attractions include Tae-Kwon-Do martial arts demonstrations, sporting events, and the traditional Korean barbecue, *bulkokee*. Other locations offer dance and musical performances in the evening. Most of the events and activities are free. Call the society for details, or watch for posters in the Bonsor vicinity. The Korean Society also provides services for seniors (for details, call 255-6313) and publishes a community telephone directory.

Korea Trade Centre
1710, 505 Burrard St (683-1820; fax 687-6249)

Primarily an arm of an international trade group helping Koreans develop trade links to this country, this group also facilitates import-export inquiries, trade missions to Korea, and offers assistance and counselling for those planning to do business there. Naturally, they can help with inquiries about Korean customs and traditions—either here in Vancouver or across the Pacific.

CULTURAL & RELIGIOUS

Probably the first Korean religious organization established in the Vancouver area was the **Korean Canadian** congregation, later merged to become **Renfrew and Korean United Church** at 2855 East 1st Ave (255-7002). Services are still held in Korean on

Sundays at noon. (Korean congregations meet in 17 churches representing virtually every branch of Christianity.) As well, there is the **Korean Ban-Seok Alliance Church** at 8611 Armstrong Ave, Burnaby (524-6415 or 437-3056) and the **Korean Deung Dae Church** at 7772 Graham Ave, Burnaby (439-6719).

There are a few weekly Korean-language newspapers: **Korean Canadian News** at 7982 Edmonds St, Burnaby V3N 1C2 (522-7699; fax 522-5849); **The Koreanna Sunday News** at 5628 Killarney St, Vancouver V5R 3W2 (436-9274; 436-9284); **The Korean Times** at 308, 877 East Hastings St (251-5929; fax 731-2965); and **The Vancouver Korean Press** at 207, 2043 Quebec St, Vancouver V5T 2Z6 (877-1178; fax 877-1128).

Korean TV can be viewed on **Rogers Multicultural Channel** every day except Monday. Producer of *TV Korea* is Charles Chi (220-6611; fax 583-1232).

RESTAURANTS

Bulkokee (or bulgogi) is a Korean specialty involving marinated beef and a slow-barbecue method.

Arirang House
2211 Cambie St (879-0990)

You've seen this place dozens of times at the 2nd Avenue end of the Cambie Bridge. Like most Korean BBQ places, you cook the food yourself, at your own table, *bulkokee*-style. Try the Jumuluck garlic lovers dish (marinated beef, lettuce and garlic galore), sided with the traditional *kimchi* (spicy-hot pickle). Expensive in the evening; lunch buffet is a welcome bargain. Fully licensed.

Bulkokee BBQ House
410 Sixth St, New West (540-9540)

This place is combined with a Japanese restaurant, offering BBQ-at-your-table bulkokee and sushi.

Bulkokee Restaurant
1480 West 11th Ave (736-0634)

This place, naturally, specializes in *bulkokee* that melts in your mouth. Again, food is cooked right at your table.

Korea Jung Restaurant
5152 Kingsway, Burnaby (451-4598)

Situated in a former funeral home with heritage stained glass, owners Nam and Yoon Cho offer the usual BBQ at your table, *jongol* (hot pot), *pajun* (seafood and veggie pancake), and *ojing bockum* (pan-fried squid). Dinner is on the pricey side. Daily lunch specials are a better deal at $5.95.

Seoul House Garden Korean Restaurant
36 East Broadway (874-4131)

Not to be confused with the next entry, this one offers BBQ bulkokee, which you prepare in your private room. They also serve sushi.

Seoul House Korean Restaurant
1215 West Broadway (738-8285 or 739-9001)

Private Tatami rooms and Vancouver's "best karaoke sing-along system" are the draw here, along with authentic Korean BBQ dinners, sushi and other traditional Korean dishes.

Shil-la Korean Restaurant
208, 333 East Broadway (875-6649; fax 875-9886)

The nominal sign outside says "Shin-la," but this is the right place. The upstairs restaurant is surprisingly large, with many private rooms wherein you do your own barbecuing. It offers a full *shil-la* (Korean-style buffet) including prawns, scallops, kalbi, bul go gi (bulkokee), futo make, California roll and tempura — many items you may be familiar with from Japanese restaurants. They also have Korean style BBQ kalbi and sushi. Private booths are available for up to eight people.

Sorabol Korean Restaurant
301, 403 North Road, Coquitlam (936-3778)

They call their BBQ *bulgogi*, but it's all the same to us. Also try their kalbi, noodle hot pot, *kimchi* and *bibim bab*. Sorabol has locations in places as diverse as Atlanta, Georgia and Beijing, not to mention Seoul — and, of course, Coquitlam.

Other worthy Korean restaurants include **Chun's Korean Garden Restaurant** 3918 Fraser St (876-6212); **Da Rae Korean Restaurant** 3510 Kingsway (435-6664); **Il Uk Jo Korean-Japanese Restaurant** 15188 Fraser Hwy, Surrey (583-9622 or 583-9632); **Korean Barbecue House**, 8291 Ackroyd Road, Richmond (270-6776); **Korean Gardens**, 843 East Hastings St (255-5022); and **See's Korean Garden** 1150 Kingsway (874-2377).

SHOPPING

Deerland Canada Import & Export
2, 843 East Hastings St (255-7808; fax 255-0116; cel 290-1282)

This is a large importer of Korean ginseng, health and beauty products. Another such business is **Korean Ginseng Centre**, 7188 Curragh Ave, Burnaby (438-1054).

Hyun Dae Japanese Korean Food Market
3373 Fraser St (874-1651)

Typical grocery store, with emphasis on Korean and Japanese foods. Free parking at rear. Another is **Seoul Food Market** at 677 East Broadway (873-1438 or 873-1448).

Two gift stores: **Koreana & Japanese Food & Gifts**, 102, 1050 Kingsway (875-8444) and **Seoul Gifts**, at 32 East Broadway (874-9911; fax 874-9322).

ENTERTAINMENT & FITNESS

Lucky Star Karaoke Box
208, 1050 Kingsway (872-6888)

Tae Kwon Do Schools
1760 Kingsway (873-5355)

A beginner's package costs $24.95 — including a free uniform.

LATIN AMERICAN

CULTURAL

Our Spanish-speaking community is served by *Accento Latino*, on the **Rogers Multicultural Channel**, with programming on Monday, Tuesday and Thursday. Call for details: 272-7337. On radio, there's *Latino Soy* on Saturdays, **CJVB AM 1470** (cable 103.3 FM) at 8 pm. There's also a Latin music radio show (*salsa, merengue, cumbia, reggae*) on **CITR 101.9 FM** on Tuesdays from 9 to 10 pm.

The **Latino Theatre Group** offers various theatrical presentations, sometimes at La Quena at 1111 Commercial Drive (info: 251-2006).

Newspapers and Magazines from Argentina (La Nacion, Gente); Chile (El Mercurio, Tercera); Peru (El Comercio, La Republica); Colombia (Especatador, Colombiano); El Salvador (Diario de Hoy, La Prensa); Mexico (Excelsior, El Sol de Mexico), Guatemala (Prensa Libra, Hoy) and others are available at **Baires Imports**, 1855 Commercial Drive (254-9695; fax 253-9694).

Locally, **Conexion Latina** is published bi-monthly with a circulation of 5,000. Half of the newspaper is in English; flip it over mid-way through and the rest is in Spanish. A subscription costs $16 for six issues to: Latin America Connexions, 2344 Spruce St, Vancouver V6H 2P2 (733-3367; fax 733-1852). Fluent readers, writers, proofreaders in English or Spanish (and translators) are invited to volunteer for a variety of tasks.

MEXICAN

Although Spanish explorers were the first to visit the Northwest coast — and had some very interesting dealings with Native peoples of this region (early cross-cultural exchanges, of a sort) — our Hispanic population today is relatively modest, with a total of about 6,000 people, of whom about 1,100 are Mexican.

Mexican Society of Vancouver
6362 Royal Oak Ave, Burnaby (433-0625)

This society organizes cultural occasions, such as the celebrations for Independence Day in Mexico (usually mid-September) with such events as the dinner-dance held this year at the Gizeh Temple Hall in Burnaby. Tickets were sold right out before the 1995 event, so if you're interested, call to inquire in plenty of time. President (phone number above) is Martha Foufoulas; vice-president is Aida Lainas (942-9597); and treasurer is Arcelia Vagge (438-7933).

RESTAURANTS

Fine Dining

Cafe Norte
Edgemont Village, 3108 Edgemont Blvd, North Van (255-1188)

Undoubtedly Vancouver's very best and most exactingly authentic Mexican restaurant, this one is tucked away in Edgemont Village — call ahead for directions. Owner Philip Mitchell scours

Central America and the American Southwest for new recipes every year. The only place serving Mexican food that we could honestly dub "cuisine." Surprisingly, the atmosphere can be discreet enough for a romantic rendezvous, or when you prefer it, boisterous and fun.

Las Margaritas Restaurante Y Cantina
1999 West 4th Ave (734-7117)

Owner Dan Rodriguez has been in the restaurant business most of his life in locations from Los Angeles to Europe. There are combo plates, all the conventional dishes one expects, and many new twists or entirely unanticipated menu items. For instance, there's a wide choice of vegetarian meals, many innovative seafood dishes, and the best salsa in town — no contest. A great patio in fair weather, and the perfect place for a celebratory meal with the gang from the office.

Tio Pepe
1134 Commercial Drive (254-8999)

This tiny place offers several Mexican dishes straight from the Yucatan — and unique in Vancouver: Try the *pascaya con huevo* (date palm shoots fried in egg batter and sided with fresh tomato salsa) or the lamb marinated in a mixture of wine, spices and oranges, then charbroiled to perfection. Tio Pepe's habanero sauce is searingly hot, but if you prefer a milder cuisine, you can have it that way, too.

Family-style, moderately priced

Andale's
1175 Davie St (682-8820)
3211 West Broadway (738-9782)

This place features good, reliable family fare, with emphasis on the Spanish influence in Mexican cuisine. Specialties include a fine *paella* (Spanish-style fish stew), *mole poblano* (a stew combining the flavours of chocolate and ancho chilies), and an outstanding *zarzuela de mariscos* (shellfish stew).

Burro's On Burrard
2015 Burrard St (739-3147)

This recent arrival offers "real Mexican, not California-style" food and live entertainment every evening (usually starting around 8 pm). Open late.

Cafe Quetzal
3289 Main St (873-6261)

Standard taco-and-enchilada Mexican fare, but easy on the wallet. Excellent coffee. Their generous Mexican breakfasts are served daily from 10 to 1, including such fare are *casamiento*, two corn tortillas, beans-and-rice, two eggs over easy, topped with fresh salsa and crema. Cost: a modest $5.25.

El Cantina Mexicano Restaurant
2052 Kingsway (874-3232)

Modestly priced and modestly spiced is how we would portray this family dining spot. Customary dishes.

Hombre's Mexican Restaurant
49 West Cordova St (669-3229)

"Absolutely authentic" are the words that come to mind to describe this place. Try the cream of garlic soup — unbelievable!

Fast Food & Take-out Style

Compadres Mexicatessen
3788 West 10th Ave (222-2997)

Take-out or dine-in at this bona fide Mexican deli. Call ahead to have your take-out food ready-and-waiting. Features include four different burritos, tacos, quesadillas and enchilladas. Take-out provisions include salsa and taco chips, guacamole or rice and black beans.

Conquistador Mexican Deli
616 Davie St (689-3228)

Dine-in or take-out excellent Mexican food. Some groceries and produce, too.

Mexi Deli Canada
4655 Arbutus St (266-4049)

Take-out or dine-in (it's a tiny place, with only eight seats), and enjoy authentic Mexican food. In the little strip mall just south of Arbutus Village.

Mucho Gusto Mexican Delicatessen
2909 West 1st Ave (739-4639)
Lonsdale Quay, 151, 123 Carrie Cates Court, North Van (986-6344)
1474 Marine Drive, West Van (925-6151)

Chorizos, salsas, corn chips, chilies and all kinds of Mexican food are available here.

Nazare Market Mexican Style BBQ Chicken
1408 Commercial Drive (251-1844)
#2, 3871 Moncton St (275-3871)

Debbie and Jerry's take-out chicken has been much-lauded by various newspaper polls. If you like it spicy, ask for it "with medicine." This chicken is a truly fabulous treat: tender, flavourful, delicious.

Poncho's & Nazare Mexican Style BBQ Chicken and Cuisine
825 Denman St (685-4442)

We've decide to award this the longest-name-for-a-cafe distinction. They offer take-out or dine-in. *Mixta* (tossed salad), chicken and various combos are all good value. Or for a special taste treat, try the *camarones al ajillo* (prawns with garlic sauce). They also sell a whole range of salsas, from mild to hot, in various sizes for take-out.

FOOD STORES

Los Guerreros Mexican Food Products
102, 3317 Kingsway (451-7850)

The sign says *su tienda latina*, so you know they understand Spanish-style cookery and have wonderful *fruitas y verduras frescas* (fresh produce). There's *masa mixta* (flour), *horcheta* (a drink made with melon seeds, lemon, lime and sugar), *tamalitos de elote* (small, sweet corn tamales), *panela* (raw, brown sugar), and *yerba mate* (something like a cross between coffee and tea). Food products featured here are from Mexico, Central and South America.

Que Pasa Mexican Foods
3315 Cambie (874-0064)

Que Pasa is our premier source for spices and ingredients needed for Central American cookery. We found *epazote*, crushed *habaneros*, Manzanilla tea, *pasilla*, *tepin* and a practical *molcajete* — a kind of mortar and pestle for grinding rice into flour.

There are unusual books, a tiny palm-sized English-Spanish dictionary, a notice board and reference library for in-store customer use, plus pinatas, Mexican plates, candles, marguarita glasses many Mexican deli items (and fresh homemade cornbread muffins), bags of corn husks for tamales, chunky olive salsa, wooden chocolate beaters and Que Pasa's own, superlative tortilla chips.

For those with a sweet tooth, there's *camote* (sweet potato and sugar), *jamoncillo* (evaporated milk, sugar, corn syrup and vanilla) and *piloncillo* (unrefined brown sugar).

Salza Mexican Products
4140 Hastings St, Burnaby (299-4690)

Here you'll find Mexican food, canned goods, a few arts & crafts items, and beverages imported from Mexico and parts of Central and South America.

SHOPPING

Mexican Sol
1485 Welch St, North Van (990-9055; fax 990-9077)

This is a wholesale and retail importing operation, which carries terra cotta tiles, glassware, clay pots, and furniture made from pine or wrought iron.

Mexico Arte
Gastown, 28 Water St (687-1346)
1767 West 3rd Ave (739-1767)
2248 West 4th Ave (731-5374)
849 Park Royal North, West Van (922-4007)

A fine collection of art and artifacts imported from Mexico, including pottery, rugs, charming blue-glass ware, serapes, carvings and jewellery. The Park Royal branch has the largest inventory of stock and an interesting variety of crucifixes.

CENTRAL & SOUTH AMERICAN

There are some 4,500 Vancouver residents originally from Salvador, Chile, Peru, Guatemala, Nicaragua, Brazil and Columbia, making our Hispanic or Spanish-speaking neighbours a force to be reckoned with.

Mundo & Familia is a bi-weekly newspaper published by Canar Co, at 7, 8415 Granville St, Vancouver V6P 4Z9 (322-0285; fax 322-3362). A subscription costs $15 for 12 issues.

There's also **La Prensa** from 8191 Gilbert Road, Richmond V7C 3W8 (271-7242), **El Contacto Directo** (published for Vancouver and Bellingham regions) from 2827 East 14th Ave, Vancouver, V6A 4B6 ($25 a year, 438-4864) and the **Guida Telfonica Hispanica** from 9017 Altair Place, Burnaby, V4J 1A8 (421-4803; fax 273-4817).

An annual **Latin American Carnival** is held in early August in a rented hall. Last year, it was at the Maritime Labour Centre at 1880 Triumph (Info: 640-1372 or 420-8847).

ORGANIZATIONS & CULTURAL SUPPORT

Language Classes

Spanish classes are available for children to adults at the **Centro**

Cultural Hispano in New West (931-1425). **Patricia Martinez** teaches in Kerrisdale (info 264-7587).

Organizations

The many groups serving Vancouver's Hispanic community are often defined by their names: **Aquelarre: Latin American Women's Cultural Society**, which also publishes a magazine at 301, 1720 Grant St (251-6678); **Canadian Association for Latin American and Caribbean Studies** operates at SFU's Latin American & Caribbean Studies; **Canadian Latin American Cultural Society** at 1111 Commercial Drive (251-6626); **Central American Support Committee** at P.O. Box 1446, Stn E, Victoria V8W 2X2 (474-5403); **Centre for Co-operation with El Salvador** at 1244 East 43rd Ave (325-1094); **Club Uruguay Cultural Society of B.C.** at 1370 Delta Ave, Burnaby (298-6078), or contact society president Alberto Langone at 941-7671; **Hispanic Community Centre of B.C.** at 1380 West 73rd Ave (261-4869); and **Latin American Community Council** — contact T. Median or H. Mendoza c/o P.O. Box 65916, Station F, Vancouver V5N 5K5.

RESTAURANTS

El Cocal Restaurante y Pupuseria
1037 Commercial Drive (255-4580)

Salvadorean and Mexican *(platillos Salvadorenos y Mexicanos)* food *con sabor Latino* (with a Latin flavour) is served such as: *pupusas* (hand-made Salvadorean tortillas with fillings), *tamales, yuca* (cassava, kind of like sweet tuber), *enchiladas, tacos, sopa de mariscos* (like a seafood bisque), *sopa de patas* (thick soup), *burritos, quesadillas Salvadorendos.*

La Quena Coffee House
1111 Commercial Drive (251-6626)

Inexpensive and delicious is how we'd sum this place up. It's run co-op style, in a '60s-beatnik-coffee-house atmosphere, so service may be hit-and-miss, but the big bowls of steaming veggie soup and house specials are worth hassling to find a parking spot in front, on The Drive. Evenings they sometimes schedule in South American music or a Latin American performance of some kind. Also great for breakfast.

Mirasol Peruvian Restaurant
181 East 16th Ave (874-3463)

Vancouver's only Peruvian restaurant also happens to offer excellent cuisine. Among the wonders on their menu are a stuffed chicken, peppers, cheese and cream sauce stew, and superlative stuffed mussels.

SHOPPING

El Mundo
2600 West 4th Ave (731-4800)

This brand new shop is filled with "world imports" — chiefly clothing and art from Central and South America.

Expo Latin American Food
2, 9303 Nowell St, Chilliwack (793-2221)

Here's a place to buy real *masa harina* (the limed flour for making tortillas), Mexican chilies, frijoles and imported foodstuffs from Guatemala and other Central American countries.

Latin Supermarket
1680 East 13th Ave (874-8618)

Friendly staff will help you find everything you need in the way of groceries and fresh produce from Central and South American countries. Find it at the corner of 13th and Commercial.

San Marcos Bakery
1303 Commercial Drive (255-9145)

Here you'll find a great assortment of Salvadorean baked goods.

VIDEOS & MUSIC

Los Olivares
2048 Commercial Drive (255-3224)

Here's a source for hard-to-find Spanish recordings, CDs and cassettes *en Espanol*.

Pacific Cinematheque
1131 Howe St (688-8202; fax 688-8204; taped info 688-3456)

They keep a modest number of Spanish-language films and videos on hand for loan. Periodically, there's a film festival (last year a Venezuelan one ran for several weekends in June and July).

Pancho's Videos
1265 Kingsway (877-7740; fax 877-7760)

Spanish-language videos for rent. The sign declares: "Spanish movies our specialty."

Pepe's Video
4183 Fraser St (874-7088)

Both music CDs and cassettes are available here (*musica en Espanol*), plus *peliculas en Enspanol y Ingles* (Spanish and English movies).

Polo Market
6475 Fraser St (321-7117)

Fresh produce spills out onto the sidewalk from the front of this store, which offers an odd mix of Latin American and Indian specialty foods, bulk foods, and to top the whole thing off, rentals of videos in Spanish.

Son Canela Orquesta
Info: 431-8907

This Latin American dance band is available for fiestas, social events and parties. They perform *merengue, salsa, cumbia, bomba, soca* and *palo de mayo*.

Two other music groups available for hire are **Groupo Cultural "Los Andes"** at 6, 404 East 33rd Ave c/o Rubin Conteras (business 324-9717 or 321-5203; residence 327 9828); and **Kin-la-Lat Guatemalan Cultural Society** at 3891 Main St c/o Tito (879-7104) or Sandra (872-0297).

CARIBBEAN

The city's energetic Caribbean community is exceptionally well-organized, and supports a wide range of activities, restaurants and shops.

Its special-interest monthly newspaper, **The Afro News**, is a useful source of events for the upcoming month. For distribution nearest you, write c/o P.O. Box 1101, Aldergrove, V4W 2V1 (or call 856-4838; fax 856-1074).

Co-op Radio (102.7FM) features *Roots Reggae* on Fridays starting at midnight; *The Reggae Show* airs Saturday from 6 to 7:30 pm, and *Caribbean Sounds* airs Saturday from 9:30 to 11 pm.

The Barbados Cultural Association of B.C. holds meetings every second Monday at 7:30 pm at Mount Pleasant Neighbourhood House at 800 East Broadway (879-8208), and organizes dances, picnics and boat cruises. Mailing address: 19984 76th Ave, Langley, V2Y 1S1 (533-4622).

The Canadian-Cuban Friendship Association promotes relations between Canada and Cuba on a variety of fronts: tourism, business, education and sports. Mailing address: Box 57063, 2458

East Hastings St, V5K 3G6 (253-4628). Their annual Garden Party (the 35th was held in 1995) includes dinner and is usually held late in July. Call for details as the time approaches.

The Jamaican Caribbean Association meets on an irregular basis; call 521-8793. Mailing address: 7067 Ramsay Ave, Burnaby, V5E 3L3.

The Trinidad and Tobago Cultural Society of B.C. meets at 1 pm on the third Sunday of the month at the South Arm Community Association (8880 Williams in Richmond). Mailing address: 230, 11180 Voyageur Way, Richmond, V6X 3N8 (273-0874; fax 273-9855). President is Finderson Alves.

FESTIVALS

The annual **Caribbean Days** is organized by the Trinidad and Tobago Cultural Society. (In 1995, it was a two-day event, held on the last weekend in July, packed with people, many of them in fabulous costumes.) The first day's events, held at The Plaza of Nations (dubbed "Plazarama"), included a song-and-dance spectacular, with a Carnival costume parade competition, steel bands and an Afro-Caribbean dance troupe. On the second day, the action moved to Waterfront Park in North Vancouver, highlighted by Caribbean food, steel band music, limbo contests, and arts and crafts.

Also in mid-July each year is the **Caribbean Boat Cruise**, organized by the same people, in association with the Trinidad Chinese Club. Tickets can usually be purchased in many of the restaurants listed below.

FOOD STORES

Calypso Foods
216, 12837 76th Ave, Surrey (599-5996)

Despite being located in an industrial complex, this is a cosy spot with a few tables for the dine-in trade; they are also food wholesalers and do catering, importing their ingredients from the Caribbean and preparing all the dishes themselves. Specialties are the Jamaican patties — half circles of a lightly curried flaky pastry with fillings of beef, chicken, ackee and saltfish, *callaloo* (similar to spinach) and plantain — served hot or frozen for takeout. The patties can also be slipped inside a coco bread bun for a typical Jamaican snack. Jerk chicken (which refers to the seasoning mix, not the temperament of the chicken) is available as a meal with "rice 'n' peas" or can be bought by the pound. Also: stew peas with pig's tails and *spinners* (dumplings); a wonderfully appetizing selection of baked goods, such as *hardo* bread, a dense loaf that toasts very well; *bulla* cake (made with molasses and ginger; *gizzadas* (coconut and ginger tarts); Jamaican rum fruit cake; fruit sticks (twists of pastry with guava or apricot jam on them); and plantain tarts.

Nice 'n' Spicy
12864 96th Ave, Surrey (930-0368)

Located in the Cedar Hills Plaza, Nice 'n' Spicy makes for one-stop Caribbean shopping: wholesale, retail, catering, grocery items and foodstuffs, cook books, reggae tapes, CDs and T-shirts. Packaged herbs and spices are available. Irish Moss, for instance, is boiled to make a drink that has a milkshake-like consistency; it is said that it will "build up the back" or make men more potent. Search Me Heart is used to make a kind of bush tea, and there are prepackaged ingredients for making "chocolate tea" (such as cocoa nuts, cinnamon and nutmeg). There are mixes to make *festival* (a type of deep-fried dumpling) and freezers full of goat fish, salted fish, mackerel, and yellow tail snapper, as well as callaloo and okra. Sunday brunch is from noon to 5 pm; on the menu are several incredibly labour-intensive dishes that most aficionados don't have time to prepare at home. The rest of the week, there's jerk chicken or pork, curried chicken or goat, chicken roti, meat loaf (baked bread dough with a spicy beef filling rolled throughout it) and beef, chicken or vegetable patties. Tropical fruit-flavoured ice cream is available in the cone or to go from the freezer section: mango, guava, soursop, jackfruit, coconut and the Jamaican favourites, *avulsion* or grapenut flavours. Every once in a while, the owner, Andrew Yap-Chung, gets the urge to entertain in a big way and throws a Caribbean food festival in the mall parking lot. (The events are so popular they may have outgrown their space, so Yap-Chung is considering one of the local parks instead.) There's live entertainment, booths with Caribbean items for sale and, of course, Nice 'n' Spicy food and refreshments. By the way, when you're in the store, pick up the brochure that lists Jamaican patois — like "full-a-mout," which means all mouth, boastful or of no substance.

Pappy's Caribbean Market
1003 Royal Ave, New West (522-9480)

Strange as it may seem, this place combines Caribbean and Newfoundland influences in a spice-and-grocery store that is surely without parallel in the Lower Mainland. Yarmouth, Nova Scotia-born John Robbins and his wife Savi, who is from Trinidad and Tobago, sell bulk spices, a large variety of packaged dried beans and whole dried corn, frozen Jamaican patties, breadfruit, soursop pulp, conch and even flying fish fillets. The fresh produce includes okra, scotch bonnet peppers and curry leaves. There's an assortment of hot sauces, tamarind pepper sauce or pickle, cans of guava jam or melon jam with ginger, tins of Jamaican-style curry, cosmetics for dark skin, and cassette tapes and records.

Quality Foods
5481 No 3 Road, Richmond (273-1712; fax 273-1728)

Though this store is predominantly East Indian and Fijian in content, West Indians in Richmond frequent this store for most of their supplies. In addition to the expected chick peas, chili peppers, okra, plantain, taro leaves and fresh and frozen cassava, they sell frozen Jamaican patties, salted cod fish, salted pig tails and salt beef. There's a little deli at the back (for dine-in or take-out).

RESTAURANTS

Callaloo Caribbean Food & Cappuccino Bar
3365 Cambie St (876-8277)

The roti at this tiny restaurant are huge — a good 30 cm across, layered with yellow split peas, curry and spicy seasonings. This is the place to sample such Creole dishes as *pelau* (pilau) and *callaloo*.

The former is a dish of rice and pigeon peas; the latter is similar to gumbo — combining callaloo bush, okra, fresh crab, coconut milk, herbs and spices. Other specialties of owners Patrick Rochard and Tosca Baggoo include *aloo* pies (a type of spicy perogy) with tamarind chutney, *cassava pone* (Trinidadian pudding with cassava, coconut and raisins). Drinks: soursop, *mauby* (from the bark of the carob tree) and peanut punch drinks.

Caribbean Cafe
1003 Royal Ave, New West (525-6558)

Located above Pappy's Newfoundland & Caribbean Market, the cafe reflects the Latin American and African influences in the islands, but also includes the classic dishes: Caribbean salad made from banana, chickpeas and fruit, callaloo soup (callaloo, okra and shrimp), aloo pie, calypso chicken and jerk chicken, shrimp or goat curry. Also on the menu is Jamaica's national dish: ackee and codfish. (Ackee is a red pod that when ripe opens to reveal the yellow edible part, which tastes a bit like eggs. It can be deadly if eaten before mature.) For dessert: cassava pone, coconut or mango ice cream. Red Stripe and Carib beer are available.

Nuff Nice Ness Restaurant
1861 Commercial Drive (255-4211)
2365 Burrard St (730-1012)
412 Columbia St, New West (525-2622)

The daily specials at these tiny popular diners and take-out joints include curry chicken or goat, red snapper, oxtail, jerk chicken, ackee and saltfish, and chicken roti (chicken wrapped in a flour and chick pea dough wrapper). There are beef, chicken or vegetable Jamaican patties, and you can wash it all down with Ting (a grapefruit soda), Jamaican ginger beer (ginger ale with an attitude) and Kola Champagne (an orange drink).

P Gees Jamaican Restaurant
724 Nelson St (669-7810)

The classic dishes here include *escoveitched* fish (halibut or red snapper, marinated and fried in a seasoned sauce), ackee (by itself or with saltfish), oxtail served in gravy, jerk chicken and *ital* stew (kidney beans with vegetables stewed in coconut cream). For dessert: Jamaican sweet potato pudding, plantain tart and Jamaican fruit cake.

Patty Shop
4019 Macdonald St (738-2142)

Jamaican patties feature a spicy filling — usually ground meat — tucked into a folded-over circle of curry pastry. At the Patty Shop (which sells only patties), there are enough varieties for the staff to offer a different special for each day of the week. The patties come in a regular size or a mini version that is great as an appetizer, and they're available fresh from the oven or frozen by the dozen.

Roti Bistro
1966 West 4th Ave (731-0222)

Roti is a traditional accompaniment to Southern Caribbean curries. There are two varieties: *dalpourie* roti, which is similar to a crepe and is wrapped around curried chicken, shrimp, goat or, when available, conch; and *paratha* roti, which is a flaky bread that is dipped into the curry of your choice. Drinks include peanut punch (made from milk and peanuts), sorrel (a bright red drink made from the rosella plant, a member of the hibiscus family) and mauby.

Roti Man
#4, 10302 135 St, Surrey (581-2444)

This location (formerly on 108th and recently moved to near the SkyTrain station), serves such West Indian specialties as *samosas* (deep fried pastry triangles filled with either beef or vegetable), curried shrimp or goat and, of course, roti filled with chicken, beef, shrimp, goat or vegetables. Jerk chicken is served with either rice or bake (fried bread). They also sell music tapes.

Taste of Jamaica
941 Davie St (683-3464)

This tiny restaurant (just seven tables) serves all the traditional dishes, especially ackee codfish (with fried plantain dumplings) and curried goat (served with peas 'n' rice). They will make combination dishes on request, so you can try different items.

MUSICIANS FOR HIRE

If you're planning a party with an islands theme, consider hiring a musical troupe that will serenade your guests — and likely get them all up dancing.

Afro-Caribbean Drum & Dance Ensemble
Combining the rhythms of Afro-Caribbean, Latin and funk, this five-woman group displays dances including the Samba, Lambada, Limbo and La Bamba. For bookings, call 255-1469.

Fernandes & Company
The band specializes in soca, calypso, reggae, meringue, salsa and zouk, and will perform steel pan music for small parties. Contact Bernard at 588-2010.

Orquesta B.C. Salsa
This 12-piece orchestra focusses on the latest salsas, meringues and cumbia dance beats. Call Julio Portillo at 327-5324 or Francisco Ayala at 322-1796 for bookings.

Soul Survivors
A five-member steel drums band, with the recent addition of electric bass and drums. Their repertoire includes everything from calypso, jazz, reggae and classical to soca and funk. Contact Tony Blackman at 522-8630.

Tropical Breeze Band
This very popular, seven-member band (together since 1986), specializes in calypso, soca and reggae. Contact Sam Hope at 936-8374.

Tropitonics Caribbean Steel Band
This eight-member band promised to "mash down da place," when they played Caribbean Days — and did. They offer a wide

range of rhythms — from upbeat tempos like soca, reggae and calypso to slow boleros. Call Ron at 525-4022 or Mike at 522-4399.

SHOPPING

Roots 'N Culture
Metrotown, F109, 4820 Kingsway (436-3992)

Promoted as your "one stop culture shop," here's where you'll find the latest reggae, soca, African and Latin CDs, books, posters and cards, plus hip hop fashions, custom-design caps, over 200 designs of reggae-inspired T-shirts, and an assortment of incense and oils.

FIRST NATIONS

We considered *not* including First Nations in this book for one good reason: unlike the rest of the groups, who to one degree or another share an immigrant history, the province's aboriginal people were, after all, *here first*. We decided, though, that the Lower Mainland's First Nations represent such a vibrant and vital component of our cultural mosaic — and one that few Vancouverites, let alone tourists, are familiar with — that the book would be seriously incomplete without this chapter.

NEWSPAPERS, FRIENDSHIP CENTRES & COMMUNITY INFORMATION

Aboriginal Expressions
101, 96 East Broadway (876-1212)

This free community paper features editorial, articles, poetry and a notice board section identifying dates of meetings for various native groups.

Kahtou News
Mailing address: P.O. Box 192 5526 Sinku Dr, Sechelt VON 3AO
203, 540 Burrard St (684-7375; fax 684-5375)

Calling itself the "Voice of B.C.'s First Nations," this monthly paper has a circulation of over 12,000 and includes articles, poetry and special features on education, business and cultural issues. In a section called "Talking stick" — the aboriginal equivalent of the soap box — are unedited commentaries by readers.

The Native Voice
319 Seymour Blvd, North Van (987-9115)
415B West Esplanade Ave, North Van (983-3137)
200, 1755 East Hastings St, Vancouver V5L 1T1 (255-3137; fax 251-7107)

Published bi-monthly in English by the Native Brotherhood of B.C. Subscription is $20 per year, attention editor Maurice Nehanee.

Nanatsiaq News
P.O. Box 8, Iqaluit, NWT, X0A 0H0 (819-979-5357; fax 819-979-4763)

This weekly paper in English and *Inuktitut* (the Inuit language) is circulated in every community in Nunavut (soon to be the Inuit territory — the eastern portion of what we have known as NWT, including all the Arctic Islands, and all around Hudson's Bay), plus Yellowknife and throughout B.C. and other parts of Canada. Readership is chiefly Inuit, but essential for those who want to learn about Canada's north. *Iqaluit* (where it's published), by the way, means "place where there are many fish."

Other publications worth noting are: **First Nations Drum** at 222, 810 West Broadway (669-5582); **Native Issues Monthly** at 822 East 10th Ave (873-1408); and **Tansai Journal** at 13565 King George Hwy, Surrey (581-2522).

Vancouver Aboriginal Friendship Centre Society
1607 East Hastings St (251-4844)

Executive Director Robert Harry runs this centre and its many events and programs; the president is Minnie Kullman. There's usually host a pre-Christmas food and craft fair at the centre in early December. Call for details.

Another open-to-the-public event is the VAFCS's Annual General meeting (usually held mid-September), which is followed by a customary banquet of First Nation foods. There is no cost to attend or share in the feast/festivities.

Two other crossroads of community interaction are **Louis Riel Metis Centre** at 207, 13638 Grosvenor Road, Surrey (581-2522; fax 582-4820) and **Valley Native Friendship Centre**, c/o 1607 East Hastings St (251-4844).

RADIO

Co-op Radio (102.7 FM) at 337 Carrall St (684-8494) offers two shows with a First Nations focus: *When Spirits Whisper*, highlighting local native arts, music and culture, airs Wednesday evenings 11 to midnight; and *Kiahowyah*, which deals with current events and public affairs, is broadcast Thursday evenings from 5 to 6 pm.

EVENTS & OUTINGS

Coast Salish Boat Tours
Call Toivo Hutikka, Scowlitz band office (826-5813)

If you've ever wanted to visit ancient Indian pit houses and 2500-year-old *middens* (burial mounds), or view the origins of native pictographs and legends, here's your chance. Pioneered under the direction of Dr. Michael Blake from UBC's anthropology department, the boat tours set off in the Fraser Valley near Kilby, last three hours and cost $120. Guide is *Sto:lo* (Coast Salish) Indian Toivo Hutikka, who is very knowledgeable about local legends and heritage.

Elders' Gathering
Organized by LNN Local 111 (876-1212)

This annual celebration features "bone games," storytelling and various competitions and demonstrations. It was held in late June last year, at the Capilano Reserve Park in North Van.

Urban Native Education Centre's Annual First Peoples Cultural Festival

285 East 5th Ave (873-3772 or 873-3761; fax 873-9152)
3035 Ghum-Lye Drive, North Van (929-9513; fax 929-8681)
Tickets: Native Education Centre, 285 East 5th Ave (873-3772 or 873-3761; fax 873-9152)

Held at the Squamish First Nations Capilano Long House in North Vancouver, usually the last Saturday in May. There are displays of arts and crafts and a BBQ salmon dinner, followed by First Nations singers and dancers.

UBC Museum of Anthropology
UBC, 6393 N W Marine Dr (822-5087)

Key to its attractions is a large display of First Nations art, some of it ancient. The museum organizes a number of special events throughout the year (call for details), and its gift shop has a remarkable selection of Inuit and Native Indian art and folk art for sale. There are usually a number of Indian masks available for collectors, although in mid-summer they're sometimes temporarily sold out of mask stock. Call ahead.

NATIVE MUSIC, DRUMMING AND DANCE

Many groups and individuals are willing to provide performances of music, drumming, chanting and traditional dance. One contact person is **Donald Morin** (876-1627), an interdisciplinary Cree performing artist who has been involved with **Red Slam Jam** (a big Native festival), Headlines Theatre and assorted native programs (talent, arts, culture, entertainment). Donald, in turn, has access to various native talent and technical people, most of whom are — in his words — "very grounded in tradition."

Actress-writer **Gunargie O'Sullivan** (684-8494) is also involved with Red Slam Jam and knows pretty well everyone of significance in the dance and Native production arena. Gunargie hosts co-op radio's *When Spirits Whisper* and welcomes news of upcoming events or skills (especially Native language ones).

Florence Thomas (462-0883), from the Quantlen reservation, organizes pow-wows in Langley and represents the Fraser Valley Drummers.

STORES & ART GALLERIES

Appleton Auctions Galleries
1451 Hornby St (685-1715; 685-1721)

After more than 30 years at their old Seymour Street location, Ron and Harry Appleton have recently relocated here, just up from the Kettle of Fish. They have long been known as the premier dealer in Canadian Inuit carvings, offering artisan-direct prices from one of the largest collections in Canada. They also sell Inuit wall hangings and North West Coast Indian masks.

Canoe Pass Gallery
115, 3866 Bayview St, Richmond (272-0095)

Here we found carvings, a good collection of books about Westcoast peoples and art, clothing, vests and scares using the same types of applique techniques found on button blankets, and lovely hand-knit hats and slippers.

Chief's Mask
Gastown, 75 Water St (687-4100)

Somewhat touristy by location, this place still carries some lovely art, a good selection of books on aboriginal issues, and many well-constructed, traditional dream-catchers.

First Peoples Art Ltd
Gastown, 102, 12 Water St (662-7854)

Stone and wood carvings; art prints; music on Cds and cassette tapes; and T-shirts with native prints. There's a good selection of jewellery, too. A catalogue is available.

Fitzcrombie's Fine Art
1165 Robson St (688-9200)

The focus here is on small decorative items, masks, decorated paddles, art cards, prints and books.

Freda Nahanee
424 West 3rd St, North Van (988-4735)

Freda herself knits, and she also represents a collective of women who craft those famous Cowichan Indian sweaters, ranging in price from $180 to $225. Call for directions to her North Van studio, which is in the basement of her home.

Heritage Canada
Gastown, 356 Water St (669-6375)

Decorated drums and small bentwood boxes, art prints and jewellery.

Hill's Indian Crafts
Gastown, 165 Water St (685-4249)

Established in 1946, they boast of having "Vancouver's largest collection of genuine Northwest Coast Indian Arts and Crafts." We've found totem poles in myriad sizes, and hand-knit and spun Cowichan sweaters; the entire top floor is given over to a gallery of Northwest Coast Indian art, wood and soapstone carvings, and Nootka-style woven baskets.

Images for a Canadian Heritage
Gastown, 164 Water St (685-7046)

This is a large presentation of Inuit sculpture, wood and argillite carvings, contemporary pottery, limited-edition prints and original art.

The Inuit Gallery of Vancouver
Gastown, 345 Water St (688-7323)

Set up much more like a gallery than other Gastown stores, this place bills itself as "Canada's foremost collection of masterwork Northwest Coast Indian and Eskimo art." One entire wall is devoted to finely carved masks; each item is tagged with the name of the artist and tribal affiliation.

Kanata Hand Knit
130, 11811 Voyageur Way, Richmond (273-3929; fax 272-4658)

Bargain-priced hand-knit Indian sweaters, from $70.

Khot-Ha-Cha Coast Salish Handicrafts
270 Whonoak St, West Van (987-3339)

Hand-knit Cowichan sweaters start here at $160. The shop is tricky to find: It's located one block south of Marine Drive. Find the four-way stop at Capilano, turn right at Maguire (next block), and the location is right behind the high-rise known as Plaza Towers.

Native Indian Collectible Art
139U, 4820 Kingsway, Burnaby (433-1861)

A few very small pieces of Inuit stonecarving, lots of woodblock prints, and a number of Indian masks and ceremonial drums. Not a bad collection, but the prices are tourist-level.

3 Vets
2200 Yukon St (872-5475; fax: 872-7605)

3 Vets is a Vancouver tradition for inexpensive outdoor clothing, footwear and equipment. But one of the surprises here is the collection of museum-quality native Indian artifacts, many of which are available for purchase.

RESTAURANTS & FOOD

The Gathering Place Cafe
3013 Sleil-Watuth Rd, North Van (929-9421)

Right on the reserve of the Tsleil-Waututh Nation is a pre-fab-style diner you'd never find if you hadn't read about it here. Given the truck-stop atmosphere, the food is substantial, tasty and inexpensive: "Mom's Kitchen" chili, salmon and bannock bread, and an extraordinary venison stew if they have it. Also recommended: the *Xosun* (pronounced "Hoshun") juice — a soapberry derivative that's slightly tart and not too sweet. For dessert: lemon meringue pie or chocolate-honey cheesecake.

Liliget Feast House (formerly Quilicum)
1724 Davie St (681-7044)

Vancouver's premier "Westcoast native restaurant" has been through many incarnations. It's a reliable — and comfortable — environment in which to enjoy such specialties as herring roe on kelp (a greasy dish cooked in oolichan oil), smoked oolichans (an oily fish, highly regarded for its healing properties), rabbit, cariboo, goat, fabulous BBQ salmon, poached halibut, wild rice and edible fern fronds. The delicious fried bannock bread is prepared according to an ancient recipe. Dolly Watts, who used to run "Grandma's Bannock" (a catering outfit), is involved in this venture.

Salishan Seafood
3903 Ke-kait Pl, Musqueam/Southlands (264-0021; 264-9194)

Best prices in town for smoked Pacific salmon, frozen sockeye, Indian candy (double-smoked salmon), sliced smoked salmon (lox), and many items packaged in beautiful cedar gift boxes. This native Indian family fishes all its own product, then takes it to Maple Ridge for custom smoking. Call ahead for directions; they can even fax you a little map to guide you through the Musqueam reservation, which can be confusing to the first-time visitor.

Minnie Kullman
2, 3798 Laurel St, Burnaby (433-3194; fax 433-9697)

Minnie offers catering services with her partner Joan Walters. The pair are able to provide salmon BBQ and bannock, as well as other Native Indian specialty foods for groups large or small. Perfect for the company picnic or to impress out-of-town visitors. Among the traditional Native foods are herring roe, smoked salmon, dried salmon jerky, smoked oolichans, seaweed in chunks or seaweed soup (with salmon eggs), dried herring roe with oolichan grease and for dessert, soapberries (Indian ice cream).

Other reliable caterers are Wilfred Baker (**Squamish Nation**) at 980-6780; Noni Hall (**First Nations Catering**, who did a great job for the Dragon Boat Festival last year); and Alice Adolf (**Musqueam Band**) who is a good contact for food services in the Native Indian community, at 872-2797.

CALENDAR OF ETHNIC, RELIGIOUS AND COMMUNITY EVENTS

We are indebted to David Spence for his advice and assistance with this chapter. His detailed **Multifaith Calendar** is published annually in August and costs $12.95 by mail to: Multifaith Calendar Committee, 33 Arrowwood Place, Port Moody, V3H 4J1 (469-1164).

Another excellent reference book on the subject of celebrations is **The Folklore of World Holidays**, edited by Margaret Read MacDonald (Gale Research, 1992).

Or look for **Let's Celebrate!** by Caroline Parry (Kids Can Press, 1987).

Though most holy days are set according to the solar calendar, some groups — the Chinese, Jewish and those of the Baha'i faith, for instance — follow a lunar calendar instead, so we can only give an approximate range of dates. Canadian aboriginal peoples also employ unorthodox customs for determining special dates; we have included only those we could pin down.

For specific details on any of the festivities outlined below, please consult the chapter about the ethnic group in question.

JANUARY

January 1: A feast day to celebrate the New Year for Koreans and Japanese. Koreans call it **Solnal**.

January 6: **Epiphany** (on the Georgian calendar) is celebrated. (Austrians burn incense on the Virgil of Epiphany, while the French celebrate with a special cake, *galette*, hymns and songs and call the day *Les Rois*.)

January 6: **Three Kings Day** (Spanish, Belgium, Mexican). It's also **Godchildren's Day** in the Greek community (godparents send gifts to their godchildren, sometimes including a *photiki*, or string of fruits and candies with a candle on its end), and among Italians, this is the day to give gifts to police.

The English celebrate the evening of January 5 to January 6 as **Twelfth Night**, as do the Danes (where girls are said to dream of their future husbands), and Icelanders celebrate the **Dream of the Magi**.

January 7: **The Burning of the Green** is a post-Christmas gathering (and a time-honoured Vancouver tradition) that takes place at Deas Island park. Participants bring their drying-out Christmas trees to add to a giant bonfire. The inspiration might have come from the English **St. Distaff's Day** when women routinely returned to their spinning work and the menfolk amused themselves by plotting to set fire to their wives' flax.

January 7: **Julian Christmas** is celebrated locally by Ukrainians and other Eastern Orthodox Christians.

January 7: Ethiopians celebrate **Ganna** (Genna), with a competitive game similar to hockey followed by religious services.

Our East Indian community celebrates *Pongal* or the **Indian harvest festival** on January 14 or 15.

Maghi, in mid-January, commemorates the martyrdom-in-battle of 40 Sihks who laid down their lives for Guru Gobind Singh Ji.

January 15: Japanese observe *Seijin-No-Hi* or **Adult's Day**. All who have reached age 20 during the previous year show off their finery — traditional kimonos are worn.

January 19: Julian calendar **Epiphany** (or Theophany in orthodox churches).

Followers of Islam begin the holy month of **Ramadan** in late January (date determined by lunar calendar) — during that month devotees forego food and water during daylight hours.

January 24: **Vasanta Panchami** venerates the Hindu deity Saraswati, the Goddess of Learning.

January 25: Many Scots stab the *haggis* and kick up their heels on **Robbie Burns Night**.

January 26: **Australia Day** commemorates the first British arrivals (by ship in 1788).

Jews worldwide celebrate **Tu B'Shevat** (according to a lunar calendar) between January 20 and February 7. It's known as the tree festival (cedars for boys, cypresses for girls). Local celebrations are held at most synagogues.

FEBRUARY

February 2: Whether you observe it as **Groundhog's Day** or **Candlemas** (Candelaria), it's both a pagan festival (observed by followers of Wicca) and a time for purification (according to Christian beliefs, Mary underwent ritual purification 40 days after childbirth on this day). Greeks believe that whatever the weather on Candlemas, it will remain for 40 days. The Spanish elaborately decorate the candles used and display them in their homes all year. And the French stage a mock bear-hunt for **Le Chandeleur**.

February 3: The Shinto "bean-throwing" festival, or **Setsubun-sai**, which marks the end of winter. Beans are thrown into each room of the house with the shout "Devils out, fortune in!"

Christians observe **Lent** seven weeks before Easter.

Shrove Tuesday, A Christian holiday just before Lent, is also called **Pancake Day.** In England, the Shrove Tuesday Pancake Race at Olney is believed to have a history of over 500 years. The Swedish, instead, eat a meat stew on this day.

Ash Wednesday is the first day of Lent on the Christian calendar.

February 15: **Nirvana Day** among the Mahayana Buddhist.

Also mid-February is **Shiva Ratri** (also known as **Mahashivaratri**, or the Hindu night of the great Lord Shiva).

Laylat al-Qadr (The Night of Power) in mid-February, commemorates the first revelations of the Koran (Islamic scriptures) to Prophet Muhammad.

The first day of the first month of the Chinese lunar calendar is a religious and cultural celebration for the Chinese, Vietnamese and many of Vancouver's Koreans. **Chinese New Year** falls between January 21 and February 19, depending on the phases of the moon. Locally, it's celebrated with feasts, fireworks and dragon dances. Gifts and "lucky money" packets are exchanged.

The Icelandic festival to celebrate the end of winter is called **Thorrablot** and is held in a local hall annually on a date falling anytime between the end of February and the end of March.

The Jewish **Purim** (Festival of Esther) — celebrated with food and stories — is held mid-February to mid-March.

MARCH

In preparation for **Naw Ruz** (see below), people of the Baha'i faith fast from early March for 19 days, during daylight hours. The first day of the fast is called **Ala** (Loftiness).

March 1: The Welsh observe **St. David's Day** (the patron saint of Wales).

March 3: The Japanese spring festival called **Hina Matsuri** (Girl's Day or Dolls' Day).

Palm Sunday falls a week before Easter, or the sixth Sunday in Lent.

March 17: **St. Patrick's Day** (the patron saint of Ireland) is celebrated with the wearing of the green.

No Ruz (Navrouz), the Persian New Year's celebration (or Farmer's Day), is observed by people from Iran, Iraq and Afghanistan between March 20 and April 2. Kashmiris call the holiday **Nav Roz**, while the Baha'i say **Naw Ruz**.

The harvest festival in India takes place in February or March. It's called **Holi** and honours the Goddess/Demoness Holika.

Easter is celebrated by Christians on a Sunday between March 22 and April 30.

March 25: **Greek Independence Day**.

APRIL

The Jewish **Passover** (**Pesach**) falls on a date determined by a lunar calendar, usually late March or mid-April. It commemorates the departure of the Israelites from slavery in ancient Egypt.

In early April, Czech children burn straw effigies decorated with rags and eggshells to symbolize the **Death of Winter**.

Mahavir Jayanti is the observance of Lord Mahavir's birthday in April. It is celebrated by Jains.

April 2: The end of **Sizdeh Bedar**, a Middle-Eastern New Year celebration.

April 13: **Vaisakhi** or the Hindu harvest festival.

Thai New Year — around April 13 — is called **Songkran**.

April 13 or 14 is **Baisakhi** or the **Solar New Year** for Hindus, Buddhists, Jains and Sikhs.

April 14: **Sri Lankan New Year**.

April 15: The Chinese observe the **Ch'ing Ming Festival**, during which it is traditional to visit and tidy the graves of ancestors.

A 12-day Baha'i festival called **Rizvan** runs late April through early May.

The birth of Sikhism is celebrated in a New Year festival known as **Baisakhi**, usually held around mid-April. There is a parade with costumes, symbolic dress and ornate floats, involving thousands of East Indians.

April 23: **St. George's Day** (patron saint of England).

MAY

May 1: **Vappu**, or Finnish Carnival Day.

May 3: Filipinos mark their spring festival, **Santa Cruzen Day**.

Also scheduled early in May is **Wasak**, the most important day of the year for Buddhists. It coincides with the full moon and marks Buddha's birth. Enlightenment and Final Demise. It's also known as **Buddha's Birthday Festival**.

May 13: The Portuguese celebrate **Our Lady of Fatima Day**.

Ascension Day is celebrated mid-May by Christians, marking the saviour's ascension into heaven. It falls 40 days after Easter, according to the Georgian calendar.

Norwegian Constitution Day, the Norwegian equivalent of Canada Day is celebrated on the closest Sunday to May 17 every year at the Amundsen Centre.

On the Monday before May 24, British Commonwealth countries enjoy the **Victoria Day** holiday.

Pentecost (Whitsunday) is the Christian commemoration of the coming of the Holy Spirit upon the disciples of Jesus following His ascension. It falls 50 days after Easter. The date is late May if you follow the Georgian calendar; early June if you go by the Julian version.

A **First Peoples Cultural Festival** is held at the Squamish First Nations Capilano Long House in North Vancouver, usually the last Saturday in May.

JUNE

June 5: **Danish Constitution Day** is generally celebrated on the first Sunday in June. **Swedish National Day**, by coincidence, falls the next day.

June 10: **Dia de Portugal**, or Portuguese National Day.

The **Philippine Day Festival** is usually the second weekend in June or as close possible to June 12th, which is **Independence Day** in the Philippines (Freedom from Spanish rule was gained on June 12, 1898). The two-day event is held at the Plaza of Nations.

June 17: **Icelandic Independence Day** (freedom from Danish rule).

June 21: **Midsummer's Day**, an ancient Druid festival still celebrated by followers of the Wicca faith.

An annual **Korean festival** (usually in late June) is held at the Bonsor Sports Complex in Burnaby.

An annual **Native Indian Elders' Gathering** features "bone games," storytelling and various competitions and demonstrations in late June, at the Capilano Reserve Park in North Van.

JULY

Italian Week is held at the Italian Cultural Centre in early July.

A multicultural festival is held in July in celebration of **Africa Day**, including food, drumming and arts and crafts.

A **Taiwanese Cultural Festival** is usually held during the first two weeks of July at Richmond Gateway Theatre. Events include dance troupes, video showings, a music festival and exhibit of aboriginal folklore and art.

On July 13 to 15, Japanese observe the **Obon Festival** to honour the spirits of the departed.

Similar memorial days on the 15th of every month are solemnized by Chinese and Vietnamese Buddhists. The Vietnamese mid-July festival is called **Trung Nguyen** or Wandering Souls'

Day (also Hungry Ghosts' Festival or Feast of Souls), during which much food (especially vermicelli soup) is set out to satisfy the appetite of the hungry spirits in their travels.

Greek Summer Fest is an annual mid-July celebration that runs for 10 days.

Also in mid-July each year is the **Caribbean Boat Cruise**, in association with the Trinidad Chinese Club.

The annual **Caribbean Days** event is organized by the Trinidad and Tobago Cultural Society for the last weekend in July, one day at The Plaza of Nations, and the second at Waterfront Park in North Vancouver, highlighted by Caribbean food, steel band music, limbo contests, and arts and crafts.

July 27: **Mawlid al-Nabiy** or the anniversary of the birth of the Prophet Muhammad.

July 30: **Oh-harai-taisai** is a Shinto purification ceremony held so that devotees can relinquish sins committed during the first half of the lunar year — sort of a spiritual housekeeping procedure.

AUGUST

August 1: **Swiss National Day**.

The Powell Street Festival in Oppenheimer Park is regularly held on the first Saturday and Sunday of August. It's a free street fair with a Japanese focus. The 19th annual festival, held in 1995 with the theme "peace," saw celebrants fold 1000 paper cranes for peace. Inspirational lanterns were also launched at Sunset Beach.

An annual **Latin American Carnival** is held in early August in a rented hall. Last year, it was at the Maritime Labour Centre.

The **Moon Festival**, held between the middle of August and the middle of September, honours the immortal Moon Goddess; in tribute, the Chinese Cultural Centre usually orchestrates some sort of concert, highlighted by traditionally costumed dancers.

SEPTEMBER

MASSAC — The Malaysia Singapore Sikh Association of Canada — holds a **pasar malam** or night market, incorporating a food fair — held in late August or early September, in Surrey. Hosts are Malaysian, Singaporean, Indonesian or Thai origin, but their seasonal events are open to everyone.

September 4: **Sri Krishna Jayanti** (also known as **Janmashtami**) is the Hindu observance of the birthday of the God Krishna.

Early September is **Paryushana-parva**, the holiest period of the year for Jains. Seven days later follows **Samvatsari**, a day of penance.

September 11: **Egyptian New Year**.

Celebrations for **Independence Day in Mexico** are usually scheduled for mid-September.

September 16: **Ganesh Chaturthi** is the Hindu celebration of the birth of Ganesha, the God of Success.

September 18: **Chilean New Year**.

Every September, the **Polish Thanksgiving** is celebrated.

Usually, mid-September is the time for **Rosh Hashanah** or Jewish New Year.

Ten days later, the most holy of Jewish days — **Yom Kippur** (the Day of Atonement, characterized by fasting), takes place.

OCTOBER

The Jewish harvest festival of **Sukkot** takes place during a week-long period from late September to early October and is honoured by the building of free-standing, temporary structures and decorating them with harvest produce.

Right after Sukkot is **Simcha Torah**, when Jews roll back the Torah (old testament scroll) and begin synagogue readings anew for the year.

Oktoberfest takes place, naturally enough, in October, and is enjoyed by Germanic people. There's usually a local celebration a week long in duration.

Dia de la Raza is heralded by Latin American and Hispanic people as significant. It's the second Monday in October, coinciding with Columbus Day.

October 31: The Celtic holiday, **Hallowe'en**, is valued by some as a witches' fest and by the rest of the population as Candy Collection Eve. In Vancouver (and we seem to be unique in this tradition, worldwide), fireworks are set off.

NOVEMBER

November 1: **All Saints Day** was proclaimed in the seventh century by Pope Boniface IV to overshadow a pagan festival of the dead on the same day.

November 1: Mexicans honour a similar tradition with **El Dia de los Santos**. Belgians are very dutiful about **Aller Hailigen Dag** (everyone goes to Mass), Bolivians follow **Kawsasqanchis** (Our Living With the Dead), and Filipinos visit ancestors' graves at the cemetery.

November 2: Christians also participate in **All Souls' Day**, by cleaning graves of deceased relatives. The Italian equivalent is **Giono dei Morti** and for Mexicans it's **El Dia de los Muertos**.

November 5: Bonfires are set alight on the coast of Newfoundland on **Bonfire Night**, clearly influenced by **Guy Fawkes Day**, which is boisterously observed throughout the British Commonwealth, particularly by the English and New Zealanders.

Diwali (or **Deepavali**, Festival of Light) is an important event observed in late October or early November by most Indo-Canadians, but most important to the Hindu members of that population. Traditions of the autumn festival — the first day of the New Year in India, include lighting lamps to welcome the Hindu goddess Lakshmi (or Laxmi, Goddess of Wealth). In Bengal province, it is instead dedicated to the Goddess Kali. In Jainism, the holiday is known as **Dipavali** or the Festival of Lamps, and glorifies the "light of knowledge" attained by Lord Mahavira.

Frequently slated for mid-November, Vancouver's Thai community organizes a local **Loi Krathong** observance during which the public is invited to launch little paper boats designed to carry a lit candle, incense and flowers. The location is usually English Bay or from a launch point on Granville Island, or both. A food event is typically part of the festivities.

November 30: Scots respect **St. Andrew's Day** (patron saint of Scotland).

DECEMBER

The first day of **Advent** begins the approximately four-week preparation for the Christian celebration of Christmas.

Normally falling in late November or early December, the Jewish **Channukah** (Festival of Lights) recalls a miracle during the seige of a holy temple. Candles are lit for eight nights, and each evening children receive small gifts and Channukah *gelt* (chocolate money).

Ml'raj al-Nabiy commemorates the ascension of the Prophet Muhammad to heaven, following his night journey from Mecca to Jerusalem, as told in the Koran. It is observed in early December.

December 13: The annual **Lucia Festival** (also known as **St. Lucia's Day**), a traditional Swedish Christmastime celebration, is often at a Vancouver hotel. This date was considered the longest day of the year under the old calendar, so early Norsemen drank to call back the sun god, and they wore hideous masks to scare away the creatures of the underworld.

December 22: In the Shinto faith, the **Grand Ceremony of the Winter Solstice** is observed, to celebrate the joy of the ending of the yin period of the sun.

MASSAC — The Malaysia Singapore Sikh Association of Canada —usually hosts a big public event near Christmas or New Year.

December 25: **Christmas** is one of the biggest Christian festivals, celebrating as it does the birth of Jesus. This is the date according to the Georgian calendar.

December 26: **Kwanza** is an Afro-Canadian festival. Candles are lit for seven days representing each of the principles of Kwanza: unity, self-determination, co-operation, sharing, purpose, creativity and faith.

December 26: The anniversary of the death of the Prophet Zarathustra (Zoroaster) — the inspiration for the Zoroastrianism faith.

December 26: On **St. Stephen's Day**, Irish lads practice "hunting the wren" (begging a penny to bury a dead bird), while Poles toss rice at each other as a blessing.

December 30: The Irish celebrate the birth of **St. Lynne McNamara**.

December 31: **New Year's Eve** is the subject of revelry almost universally, in observances ranging from protecting the farm from fire (Denmark) to smashing pots at midnight (Italy — and a very common practice in Vancouver). In Iceland, canny celebrants sit in the crossroads so that elves will be forced to offer them gifts of gold and treasures in order that they might pass by. In Ireland, a great supper is eaten on the theory that the new year would continue as it began. Russians chase away the demons. And the Scots simply get crazy during what they refer to as "The Daft Days."

INDEX

101 Yek O Yek Deli & Bulk Food 86

1st Avenue Deli   42

24-Hour Video   71

3 Vets   219

78th Fraser Highlanders, The   9

A

A & S Meats   111

A Bosa & Co   68

A Golden Star Jewellery   107

Abercorn Inn   36

Aberdeen Centre, The   146, 155, 181

Aboriginal Expressions   213

Acropol   77

Adega Restaurant   58

Afghan Association of B.C., The 93

Afghan Fast Foods   93

Afghan Horseman Restaurant   93

Afghani   93–94

Africa-Canada Development & Information Services Assn   79

African Canadian Assn of BC   79

African Market   82

African National Congress   79

African   79–83

Afro Canadian Restaurant   80

Afro News, The   205

Afro-Caribbean Drum & Dance Ensemble   211

Agata Enterprises/Hing Loong 147

Aikido Federation of B.C.   187

Aikido with Ki   187

Ajay Food Store   111

Akbar's Own Dining Room   113

Aki   181

Al Halal Meats   87

Al-Aqsa Specialty Foods   87

Alabaster   63

Aldo's Pasta Bar & Italian Restaurant   66

Alex's Restaurant   141

Alice Adolf   221

Aling Pining Foods and Video Rentals   139

All India Foods   111

All India Sweets   109

Alliance Française   24

Amapola Magasin   138

Amy's Cake Shop   158

Anatoli Souvlaki   77

Andale's   60, 195

Anime Jyanai   186, 188

Anna's Cake House   158

Annapurna   116

Anton's Pasta Bar   66

Appleton Auctions Galleries   217

Aquelarre: Latin American Women's Cultural Society 200

Arab Community Centre Association   85

Arabic peoples   85–86

Ararat Oriental Rug Co   94

Arirang House   190

Artland   170

Ashiana Tandoori   115

Ashiana Tandoori Restaurant & Sweet Shop   115

Ashoka 106
Ashoka Boutique 106
Asia Imports 171
Asia Pacific Foods 151
Asian Publications 117
Asian Video 108
Auring 141
Austria-Vancouver Club 30
Aviv Kosher Meats 97
Awaaz 117
Ayalamp 108

B
B'nai Yehudah 94
B.C. Highland Games 7
B.C. Market 86
B.C. Muslim Association 85
Babushka's Kitchen 52
Bach Dang Ice Cream Cafe 126
Baires Imports 193
Bali Bali 137
Bali Bali Galleria 137
Bali House 136
Banana Leaf Malaysian Cuisine 135
Bandi's 46
Bao Chao Spring Roll Specialty House 126
Barbados Cultural Association of B.C., The 205
Basel Hakka Lutheran Church 146
Bavaria House Restaurant 34
Bavaria Restaurant, The 33
Bavarian Bakery & Delicatessen 33
Bee Kim Heng Beef & Pork Jerky Ltd 132
Beef Bowl Restaurant 125
Beijing Trading Co 162
Belgian Canadian Association 24
Belgian 24–25, 63
Bengali 117

Bennie's 170
Benny's Bagels 97
Best Bi Foods 28
Beth Israel 94, 102
Beth Tikvah 102
Bhaia Sweet Shop & Restaurant 109
Bharti Art Jewellers 107
Bhatti's Bombay Jewellers 107
Bianca Maria 68
Bianco Nero 63
Bijan Specialty Foods 89
Black Belt Shop 164
Black Forest Delicatessen 33
Black Forest Restaurant 34
Blarney Stone, The 6
Bo Kong Vegetarian Restaurant 152
Bo Lok Jewellers 170
Bo-jik 152
Bodai Vegetarian Restaurant 152
Bodhi Rey Tsang Temple 147
Bodhi Vegetarian Cuisine 152
"Bollywood" 108
Bombay Sweets Cash & Carry 109
Bon Bon Bakery 70
Bon Japanese Restaurant 182
Bon Ton 21
Bonanza Market 160
Bonjour Books 23
Boracay Cafe 141
Boua Thai 130
Boulangerie la Parisienne 22
Bouquet 20
Brazilian 55–56
Bride & Groom Shop, The 106
Brig-a-Doon Bakery 8
British Ex-Serviceman's Association, The 1
British Home Store 2
British Isles 1, 23
Broadway Bakery & Pastries 74

Buddha Supplies Centre   147
Buddy's Video   168
Bulkokee BBQ House   190
Bulkokee Restaurant   190
Bulldog Vancouver, The   27
Bun Bo Hue   124
Burro's On Burrard   196

C
Cafe Anh Kong   126
Cafe Calabria   68
Cafe D'Lite   133
Café de Paris   19
Cafe Diem Hua   127
Café il Nido   63
Cafe Norte   194
Cafe Quetzal   196
Cafe Thanh Loan   125
Caffe Roma   68
Cakes To Go   101
Calabria Bakery   57
Callaloo Caribbean Food &
    Cappuccino Bar   208
Calvin's   37
Calypso Foods   206
Cambodian   121–129
Canada Jiho, The   178
Canada Kingsway Dojo   187
Canada West Tourist News   178
Canada-Japan Business Journal
    178
Canadian Association for Latin
    American and Caribbean
    Studies (SFU's Latin American
    & Caribbean Studies)   200
Canadian Chinese Radio   149
Canadian Croatian Business
    Association   41
Canadian Latin American
    Cultural Society   200
Canadian Parents for French, BC
    24
Canadian Slovak League   44

Canadian Zionist Federation, The
    96
Canadian-Cuban Friendship
    Association, The   205
Canoe Pass Gallery   217
Capilano Reserve Park   216, 229
Caren's Cooking School   23
Caribbean   205–211, 230, 241
Caribbean Boat Cruise   206, 230
Caribbean Cafe   209
Caribbean Days   206, 211, 230
Carley Quality Meats   155
Carmelo's Bakery   56
Casa Mia Bakery   158
Casablanca   122
Caspian Restaurant   90
Cathay Importers   171
Cazba Restaurant   91
CC Arts Gallery   168
Cedars of Lebanon Restaurant
    87
Celtic Connection, The   2
Central American Support
    Committee   200
Central American   198,
    200–201
Centre Culturel Francophone de
    Vancouver   18
Centre for Co-operation with El
    Salvador   200
Centro Cultural Hispano
    199–200
Chan's Gallery   168
Château Bakery   22
Cheesecake Etc   101
Cheo Leo Banh Mi & Cafe   126
Cheong Wing Herb Co Ltd   162
Chez Lin   123
Chevalier Creations   71
Chez Lin   123
Chi Shing Trading Co   171
Chief's Mask   217
Chili Club   131

China Arts & Crafts Importers 171
China Can Supermarket 160
China Video 168
China West 171
Chinatown 69, 94, 137, 145–146, 148, 151, 153–155, 159, 162, 166–167, 171–172
Chinese 145–173, 223, 226–227, 229–230
Chinese Bistro Moderne 154
Chinese Cultural Centres 147–148
Chinese Jade & Crafts 172
Chinese New Year Festivities 148
Chinese Voice Alive 149
Ching Chung Taoist Church 146
Chiyoda 183
Chong Hing Co 155
Chow Sang Sang 170
Chown Memorial & Chinese United Church 147
Christ Church of China 147
Chun's Korean Garden Restaurant 192
Chung Kiu Chinese Products Emporium 172
Cielo's 60
Cincin Ristorante 64
Cinco Estrelas Restaurant 58
Cioffi's Meat Market & Deli 68
Cipriano's Ristorante & Pizzeria 66
CJVB Radio 30, 73, 103
Classic Cakes 101
Club Uruguay Cultural Society of B.C. 200
Coast Salish Boat Tours 215
Cockney Kings Fish and Chips 4
Compadres Mexicatessen 196
Conexion Latina 194
Conquistador Mexican Deli 196

Continental Coffee 68
Conversational Chinese lessons 149
Cottage Tea Room, The 5
Country Deli 33
Crabtree & Evelyn 3
Crazy Spaghetti House Raku 186
Croatian Cultural Centre 41
Croatian Folk Festival 42
Croatian 41–44
Cuu Long 123
Czech and Slovak 44–45
Czech 44–46, 227
Czechoslovak Association of Canada, The 44

D

D C Duby Patisserie Bruxelles 25
D T Lim's Tae Kwon-Do Academy 164
Da Pasta Bar on Yew 67
Da Pasta Bar 67
Da Rae Korean Restaurant 192
Dai Masu 182
Damini Jewellers 107
Danes 11, 224
Danex Polish Delicatessen 48
Daniel Le Chocolat Belge 25
Danish Bakery 14
Danish Community Centre of Vancouver, The 12
Danish Pastry Shop, The 14
Daruma Restaurant 188
David Lam Centre 187
Dawat 113
De Dutch Pannekoek House 27
De Hollandse Coffee Shop 27
Deerland Canada Import & Export 192
Der Olde Klok 29

Deserts Middle East Vegetarian Restaurant   86
Deutsche Press   30
Deutsches Haus   31
Doaba Sweets   109
Dollar Meat Store   156
Dollenkamps European Bakery   28
Dolly Watts   220
Dolphin Cinemas   108
Donald Morin   216
Dover Arms, The   6
Dr Sun Yat-Sen Classical Chinese Garden   147
Dr. Zhang Dian Tong   163
Dragon Arts   168
Dragon Boat Festival and Race   148
Dreams Discount Gift Shop   178
Dreams Laser Video & Rico Films Production (Canada)   167–168
DuBrulle French Culinary School   23
Duna Delicatessen and Gift Shop   46
Duso's Italian   69
Dussa Delicatessen   33
Dutch   26–29
Dutch Wooden Shoe Cafe   28
Dynasty   120, 148–149, 153

E
E-Hak Japanese Restaurant   183
Eager Beaver   178
East African flair   79, 82
East Indian   103–117
Ecco Il Pane   70
Edinburgh Tartan Gift Shop   8
El Cantina Mexicano Restaurant   196
El Caravan   88
El Cocal Restaurante y Pupuseria   200

El Contacto Directo   60, 199
El Contacto Directo   60, 199
El Mundo   201
Elders' Gathering   215, 229
Elmasu Food Importers   86
English   1–6, 224, 232–233
English butcher   23
Ethiopian Community of BC   79
Ethnic Food at South Vancouver Neighbourhood House   114
Expo Latin American Food   201

F
Falafel King, The   88
Falcone Bros Meat Market   69
Far-Met Importers   22
Fassil Ethiopian Restaurant   80
Féderation des Francophones de CB   18
Federation of Irish Associations and Societies   6
Fernandes & Company   211
Fiji Canada Association, The   118
Fiji Fresh   118
Fiji Islands Guru Lucky Sweets   119
Fiji Sun, The   118
Fijian   118–119, 208
Filipinas Video   143
Filipino Association in B.C., The   137
Filipino Canadian Business Directory, The   137
Filipino Canadian Cultural Society, The   137
Filipino Diamonds Society of B.C.   142
Filipino   132, 137–143
Finnish Bethel Church   12
Finnish Lutheran Church   12
Finnish Mission Assembly   12
Finns   11

First African Diaspora Dance
Workshop 83
First Nations 213–217, 219, 221,
228
First Nations Catering 221
First Nations Drum 214
First Peoples Art Ltd 217
First Peoples Cultural Festival
216, 228
Fish & Chips 4
Fitzcrombie's Fine Art 218
Flamingo 150
Flavors 83
Florence Thomas 217
Flying Fashion 107
Foo's 154
Foody Goody 150
Fook Ming Tong Tea Shop 166
Fortuna Bakery 57
Fortune City Bargain Centre 173
Fortune City 154, 173
Fortune House 150
Fraser Bakery and Konditorei 31
Fraser BBQ & Fresh Meat 141
Fraser Halal Meats 87
Fraserview Sausage &
Delicatessen 32
Freda Nahanee 218
French 17–23, 224–225
Fresh Egg Mart 160
Freybe Sausage 32
Frontier Cloth House 105
Fujiya 180, 185
Fung Loy Kok Taoist Temple
147
Furugh Books 92

G
Galaxy Video 168
Galing-galing Restaurant 142
Gar Lock Seafood & Meat 160
Gathering Place Cafe, The 219
Gazeta informacyjna 48

Genevieve Lemarchand 0
German 30–35, 37, 44, 46–47
Ghanaian Cultural Association of
BC 79
Gim Lee Yuen 165
Gizella's 37
Goethe Institute, The 31
Golda's Delicatessen 98
Golden Arrow Martial Arts
Supplies 164
Golden Art & Gems 170
Goldilocks Bake Shop 139
Good News Foreign Nations
Baptist Church 56
Goulash House Restaurant 47
Govinda's 116
Grace International Baptist
Church 138
Grand King Seafood Restaurant
153
Grandma's Bannock 220
Great Wall Mongolian BBQ 153
Great Wok, The 152
Greek 72–77, 224, 227, 230
Greek Canadian Voice, The 73
Greek Community of East
Vancouver, The 72–73
Greektown 72–73
Green Market 108
Groupo Cultural "Los Andes"
203
Guida Telfonica Hispanica 199
Gujrati 117
Gum Yip Chinese 150
Gunargie O'Sullivan 216
Guru Lucky Sweets 110, 119
Guyanese Canadian Assn of BC
79
Gyoza Paradise Restaurant 178

H
H Q Electronics 167
Ha Do Video 128

Hachibei   186
Hadassah Bazaar   102
Hai Au Music Centre   128
Hai Kee Cambodian &
    Vietnamese Restaurant   122
Halal Meats & Deli   86–87
Han Kook Video & Book Centre
    128
Happy Vietnam Family
    Restaurant   123
Harajuku   188
Harbour Moon   186
Hardawar Sweet Shop &
    Restaurant   110
Hari Om's Jewellers   107
Heaven & Earth India Curry
    House   115
Heidelberg House   34
Hellenic Canadian Congress of
    B.C., The   72
Hellenic Centre, The   72
Heritage Canada   218
Hermitage, The   20
Hideo Takahasi Acupuncture
    Clinic, The   188
Hill's Indian Crafts   218
Hillel Foundation B'nai Brith, The
    102
Hindi   103, 108, 117–118
Hing Lin Wig Shop   171
Hing Loong Co   173
Hing Lung Foods   172
Hing Wah Limited   161
Hispanic Community Centre of
    B.C.   200
Hispanic   59–60, 194, 199–200,
    232
Ho Wah Bakery   151
Holland Calling   26
Holland Shopping Centre Langley
    28
Holland Shopping Centre   28
Hollywood North   188

Holy Family Church   59
Holy Trinity Ukrainian Orthodox
    Cathedral   51
Hombre's Mexican Restaurant
    196
Hon's Wun-tun House   151
House of Brussels Chocolates
    25–26
House of McLaren   8
Hoy's Wonton (Plus) House   151
Hrvatski Glas/Voice of Canadian-
    American Croatians   42
Hungarian Cultural Society of
    Greater Vancouver, The   45
Hungarian-Calvin Presbyterian
    Church   46
Hungarian   45–47
Hunky Bill's House of Perogies
    52
Hunting World Leathers   178
Hyun Dae Japanese Korean Food
    Market   192

I
I Love Bagels   98
I love sushi   185
Icelandic Canadian Club of British
    Columbia, The   12
Icelandic   11–14, 226, 229
Ichibankan Japanese Restaurant
    178
Iglesio Ni Cristo   138
Ikea   14
Ikkyu Hitoyasumi Grocery   181
Il Caffe di Milano   68
Il Giardino   64
Il Uk Jo Korean-Japanese
    Restaurant   192
Images for a Canadian Heritage
    218
Immaculate Heart of Mary
    Croatian Catholic Church
    41–42

Imperial Bookstore Co 167
Imperial Chinese Seafood
Restaurant 153
India Fine Cuisine Punjab 113
India Gate 115
India Video & Gift Shop 108
India Village 114
Indo Canadian Business Pages,
The 104
Indo Canadian Voice 117
Indo Fiji Supermarket 119
Indonesian Evangelical Church
136
International Sausage Co 33
Inuit Gallery of Vancouver, The
218
Inuit 214, 216–219
Iran Super 89
Iranian 88–92
Irish 1, 6–7, 234
Irish Fancy Store 7
Irish Sporting & Social Club, The
7
Isaac Waldman Jewish Public
Library, The 101
Isle of Man, the 10
Ital Cream 70
Italian 62–72, 229, 232, 238
Italia Pasticeria Bakery & Deli
70
Italian Cultural Centre 62, 229
Italian Market Day 62
Italian-Canadian Winemakers
Club, The 62
Iwase Books 186

J
J & B Foods 111
J Beethoven's Pizza Gourmet 98
J, Z & N Deli 48
J.K.F. Shito-Ryu Karate-Do Itosu-
Kai 187
Jagga Sweets & Cuisine 110

Jagoda European Deli 49
Jak en Poy 141
Jamaican Caribbean Association,
The 206
Japan Health Centre 188
Japan Karate Assn of BC 187
Japan Karate Assocation 187
Japanese 175–188, 224–226,
229–230
Japanese Accents Kiku 179
Japanese Businessmen's
Association 177
Japanese Canadian Citizens
Association 177
Japanese Community Volunteers'
Association 177
Japanese Deli House 183–184
Japanese Educational Centre
Tenrikyo 186
Japanese Language & Books
186–187
Japanese Language Centre 187
Japanese Steak House 178
Japanese Therapeutic Centre
188
Jeet Video & Food Market 108
Jerusalem Bakery 86
Jewish 94–102, 223, 226–227,
231, 233
Jewish Arts Festival, The 95
Jewish Beaux Arts, The 95
Jewish Community Centre, The
94–96
Jewish Family Service Agency
95
Jewish Film Festival 95
Jewish Folk Choir, The 95
Jewish Genealogical Institute of
B.C., The 96
Jewish Western Bulletin, The 96
Joe's 68, 70, 185
John's Meats & Groceries 56
Jolly Coachman Pub, The 6

Jolly Foods   14
Jolly Taxpayer, The   6
Josie's Specialty Foods   141
Joudy's   76
Joy Chinese Dim Sum   151
Joyal Import-Export   108
Judith Chan   36

K
Kababsara Restaurant   90
Kabayan   141
Kafe Europa   45
Kahtou News   214
Kakali Handmade Paper Studio   179
Kakiemon   183
Kalamata Greek Taverna   77
Kalamata   76–77
Kam Tong Enterprises   157
Kamal's Video Palace   108
Kanada Kurier   30
Kanata Hand Knit   219
Kang King Traditional Chinese Medicine, Health & Beauty   162
Kapit Bahay   139
Kaplan's Deli   98
Kappa Japanese Restaurant   184
Kavkas   53
Kaya Kaya   179
KC Book Co   167
Keefer Bakery   158
Kent's Kitchen   151
Keren Or   96
Kerrisdale Meat Market   3
Khalsa Diwan Society, The   104
Khot-Ha-Cha Coast Salish Handicrafts   219
Kien Giang Video Rental   128
Kiku Japanese Video   188
Kilimanjaro   81
Kim Chau Delicatessen   126
Kim Chee Oriental Deli   126

Kim Dinh Oriental Noodle House   124
Kim Hai/Tiem Vang   128
Kim's Jewellers   128
Kin-la-Lat Guatemalan Cultural Society   203
King's Fare   4
King's Seafood   157
King Heng Noodles   151
Kingsway Shito-Ryu Itosukai Karate-Do   187
Kirin   149
Kiu Shun Trading Co   162
Kiu Yick Bookshop   166
Kiyu-Kai Business Association   177
Kobayashi Shoten   181
Kobe Japanese Steak & Seafood House   182
Kohinoor Grocery   87
Koji   182–183
Koko   182–183
Kolbeh Deli & Restaurant   91
Konwakai   177
Korea Jung Restaurant   191
Korea Trade Centre   189
Korean   189–192, 229
Korean Ban-Seok Alliance Church   190
Korean Barbecue House   192
Korean Canadian News   190
Korean Deung Dae Church   190
Korean Gardens   192
Korean Ginseng Centre   192
Korean Society of BC, The   189
Korean Times, The   190
Koreana & Japanese Food & Gifts   192
Koreanna Sunday News, The   190
Krehmer's Quality Meats   156
Kuan Way Martial Arts Supplies   164

Kuan Yin Buddhist Temple, The
146
Kulacs International Restaurant
47
Kurt's Clock Repairs 38
Kwak's Traditional Chinese
Medicine Clinic 162
Kyokushin Karate Vancouver
College 187

L
L'Eco D'Italia 62
La Baguette et L'Echalotte 22
La Barka 43
La Belle Auberge 20
La Casa Gelato 71
La Charcuterie 14
La Cuisine de Saint-Germain 21
La Grotta del Formaggio 62, 69
La Lorraine 21
La Page d'Or 100–101
La Prensa 193, 199
La Quena Coffee House 200
La Toque Blanche 21
Laboratoires St. Ives S.A. 38
Laidlaw's Scottish Bakery 9
Lala's Perogy Express 52
Laleh Bakery, The 90
Landmark Hot Pot House 152
Lang Van Video & Book Store
128
Las Margaritas Restaurante Y
Cantina 195
Las Tapas 60
Latin American 193, 199–202,
230, 232
Latin America Connexions 194
Latin American Community
Council 200
Latin Supermarket 57, 201
Latino Theatre Group, The 193
Lau's Musical Association 128
Lazy Gourmet, The 101

Le Crocodile 19
Le Gavroche 19
Le Grec 76
Le Kiu Grocery 161
Le Kiu Poultry & Grocery 156,
161
Le Soleil de Colombie 18
Lebanese 85, 87–88
Lebanese Canadian Society of
B.C., The 87
Lei Yei Mun 153
Lemon Grass Vietnamese Cafe
126
Leone 71
Lesley Stowe Fine Foods 23
Liliget Feast House 220
Lisbon Bakery 57
Lista Telefonico
Portuguese/Brazileira 55
"Little Ginza" 178
"Little India" 104, 107
Little Mountain Neighbourhood
House Learning Centre 149
Lock Yuen Seafood Restaurant
153
Lombardo's Ristorante & Pizzeria
67
Loong Foong 154
Los Guerreros Mexican Food
Products 197
Los Olivares 202
Lotus Eaters 129
Lotus Pond Religion Centre 147
Louis Riel Metis Centre 215
Lucky Foods 120
Lucky Star Karaoke Box 192
Luquan Vietnamese Restaurant
127
Luxmiis 120

M
Lynne McNamara 234
MacKinnon Bakery 9

Mad Butcher, The   87
Madina Halal Meats &
    Delicatessen   87
Main Jewellers   107
Maison de la Francophonie
    17–18, 23
MAL   167
Malaysia Cuisine   135
Malaysian   129, 133–135,
    231
Malaysian Singapore Brunei
    Cultural Association, The
    134
Malinee's Thai Food   131
Man Sing Meat Centre   156
Mandarin Centre   160
Manhattan Books & Magazines
    23
Manila Food Market   141
Manila Food Mart   140
Manila Mini Mart   143
Mann Bros. Meat Shop & Video
    Store   108
Mansei-Kan Aikido   187
Maple Garden Hot Pot Restaurant
    152
Maria's Taverna   77
Mario's Gelati   71
Marks and Spencer   3
Martini's   67, 76
MASSAC: The Malaysia
    Singapore Sikh Association of
    Canada   134
Max's Bakery & Delicatessen   98
Max King Bakery   151
Maxim's Bakery & Restaurant
    154
Mayfair News   24
Mazurek Deli   49
Mediterranean Bakery & Cafe
    61
Mediterranean Market   61
Mediterranean Maza Bar   61

Mehfil   117
Meli's Taverna   76
Melonari Custom Made Shoes
    71
Memsaab Boutique   105
Mexi Deli Canada   197
Mexican   194–201, 224
Mexican Society of Vancouver
    194
Mexican Sol   198
Mexico Arte   199
Middle-Eastern   227
Minaret Oriental Carpets   92
Minato Sushi   185
Minerva's Mediterranean Deli
    74
Minerva Imports   74
Ming Wo   172
Minh Dan Jewellery   128
Minh Nhut Jewellery & Gifts
    128
Mini Mart Plus   141
Minnie Kullman   215, 220
Mirasol Peruvian Restaurant
    201
Misaki at the Pan Pacific
    183
Misaki Japanese Deli   185
Misha Video   112
Mitzie's Restaurant   155
Mizutani Junji   188
Mohan Cloth House   105
Momiji   184
Mongolie Grill   154
Moon Festival, The   148, 230
Moore's Bakery & Delicatessen
    9
Mountain Shadow Inn   6
Moustache Cafe   65
Moutai Mandarin Restaurant
    152
Mucho Gusto Mexican
    Delicatessen   197

Mundo & Familia 60, 199
Mundo and Familia 60
Murata Art 179
Musashi Japanese Restaurant
185 184

N
N & S Trading Co 173
Na di Lanka Impexco 120
Nafisa Lakhani 162
Nakornthai 131
Nanatsiaq News 214
Nanda Jewellers 107
Nando's Chickenland 58
Nang Moi 128
National Nikkei Heritage Centre
177
Native Education Centre 216
Native Indian 213–217, 221,
228, 229
Native Indian Collectible Art
219
Native Issues Monthly 214
Native Voice, The 214
Natraj 114
Nazare Market Mexican Style
BBQ Chicken 197
New Chong Lung Seafoods &
Meats 157
New Grand View Szechuan 153
New Tokyo Craft, Gift & Fur
Shop 178
New Tokyo Gift Shop 178
Newstar Tribune 138
Ngai Hoi Trading 162, 163–164
Ngai Lum Musical Society 167
Nhon Hoa BBQ House 126
Nice 'n' Spicy 207–208
Nigeria Cultural Assn of BC 79
Nikka Industries 180
Nirvana 114, 226
Nitobe Garden 177
NNHC 177

Noni Hall 221
Noor Mahal 115
Noorali's International News &
Magazines 117
Norwegians 11
Nossa Sehora de Fatima Roman
Catholic Church 56
Nuff Nice Ness Restaurant 209
Nya Svenska Pressen 12
Nyala Restaurant 80

O
O'Hare's Pub 6
Octopus's Garden 184
OK Gift Shop/Fur Shop 178
Old Country Inn 34
Olivieri Foods 69
Olympia Oyster & Fish Co 4
Opinion 73
Or Shalom 94, 96
Oriental Arts & Antiques
Auctioneer 169
Oromo Community Assn 79
Orquesta B.C. Salsa 211
Othmar Kaegi 36
Our Lady of Fatima Roman
Catholic Church 56
Our Lady of Hungary (Magyarok
Nagyaszonya) Roman Catholic
Church 46
Out of Africa Global Culture 83
Overseas Chinese Voice 149

P
P & G Sausage 32
P Gees Jamaican Restaurant 209
Pabla Trade Centre 105
Pacific Aikido Kensankai Assn
187
Pacific Breeze 142
Pacific Cinematheque 202
Pacific Homeopathic Clinic, The
117

Pacific Review   30
Pacific Royal Buffet   184
Pacyfik   448
Pajo's   4
Pak Chong Enterprises   162
Pak Kai Enterprises   158
Pakistani   108
Paloma   129
Pancho's Videos   202
Panda Emporium   172
Papa's and Mama's Japanese
   Kitchen   186
Paper-Ya   179
Papi's Ristorante Italiano   65
Pappy's Caribbean Market   208
Paradise Imports   43
Park Lock Seafood Restaurant
   150, 153
Pars Deli Mart   89
Parthenon Wholesale and Retail
   Food   74
Pasparos Taverna   77
Patel's Discount Bulk Foods   111
Patisserie Bourdeaux   22
Patricia Martinez   200
Patrides   73
Patty Shop   210
Pazifische Rundschau   30
Pender Seafoods   157
Penny Farthing, The   4
Pepe's Video   202
Pepitas   61
Pepper Pot Food & Spice Co
   160
Perestroika Products Limited   53
Periodico News   56
Perogy's Perogies   52
Persian Moslem Foundation, The
   89
Peter Black & Sons   9
Petticoat Lane   4
Philipinyana Magasin   138
Philippine Chronicle, The   138

Philippine Community Centre
   Society, The   137
Philippine News Canada   138
Philippine Tropic Express & Food
   Store   141
Pho Dong Phuong   125
Pho Hoa   124
Pho Hoang   125
Pho Kim Saigon Chinese &
   Vietnamese Restaurant   125
Pho My Xuan   125
Pho Nam   124
Pho Ngu Binh   125
Pho Quyen   125
Pho Thai Hoa   122, 125
Pho Thai Hoa   122, 125
Pho Thanhg Long   125
Pho Van   125
Pilipinas Specialty Foods   140
Pink Pearl, The   150
Pinoy Video   140
Pioneer Book Store   166
Pita Plus Deli   99
Plaza of Nations, The   36, 138,
   148, 206, 229–230
"Plazarama"   206
Polish   47–51, 231
Polish Bakery & Pastry   50
Polish Bookstore, The   50
Polish Combatants Hall, The   47
Polish Community Centre, The
   47–48
Polish Deli   49
Pollyanna's English Tea Shoppe &
   Restaurant   5
Polo Market   202
Polonia   50
Poncho's & Nazare Mexican Style
   BBQ Chicken and Cuisine
   197
Popovers Plus   99
Portugal Meats & Groceries   57
Portuguese   55–59, 228–229

Portuguese Canadian Seniors
    Foundation, The   55
Portuguese Club of Vancouver,
    The   55
Powell Street Festival   176, 230
Prata-Man Restaurant   133
Praying Mantis Kung Fu Academy
    165
President's Plaza   146
Presyong Palengke   140
Protection of the Blessed Virgin
    Mary Catholic Church   51
Providence Maitriyeh Buddhist
    Temple   147
Punjab Food Centre   112
Punjabi   103, 105, 108, 110, 113,
    117
Punjabi Market   105
Pyasa   81
Pythagoras Greek School   73

Q
Qualitie-Made Bakeries   9
Quality Foods   112, 208
Quality Shoes & Gifts   107
Que Huong   123
Que Pasa Mexican Foods   198
Queen's Cross Neighbourhood
    Pub   6
Queen Bee Karaoke   188
Queen Sheba Ethiopian
    Restaurant   81
Quilicum   220

R
R B Gourmet Butchers   2
R P Market & Video   143
Rasasayang Singapore Restaurant
    133
RDI   18
Red Slam Jam   216
Red Star Vegetable, Fruit & Meat
    160

Regal Theatre, The   108
Renato Pastry Shop   70
Rene's on Broadway   142
Renfrew and Korean United
    Church   189
Restaurant des Gitans   37
Rich Cafe   136
Richmond Gateway Theatre
    148, 229
Richmond Halal Meats   87
Rino's Italian Shoe Centre
    71
Riwaaz Exclusif   106
Roald Amundsen Centre   12
Robin Hood Pub   6
Robson Gourmet Foods   23
Robson Public market   23
Rodeo Collection   178
Rodos Taverna & Souvlaki House
    77
Rogers Multicultural Channel
    12, 30, 48, 56, 62, 89, 93, 103,
    118, 138, 149, 178, 190, 193
Rogue Folk Club, The   1
Rokko Saree & Fabrics   106
Romios Greek Taverna   77
Rong Hua Porcelain Enterprises
    173
Roots 'N Culture   212
Rose Bakery, The   90
Rosie's on Robson at the Rosedale
    Hotel   99, 101
Roti Bistro   210
Roti Man   210
Rubina Tandoori Lazeez Cuisine
    of India   115
Rumah Bali   136
Runeberg Choir, The   12
Rungh Cultural Society   117
Rungh   117
Russian & Ukrainian Restaurant,
    The   53
Russian-Vancouver Magazine   52

Russian   33, 45, 51, 53–54
Rusty Gull Neighbourhood Pub,
    The   6

S
S. Eskandani   92
Sabra Kosher Bakery & Deli
    99
Sagano   183
Sai Kung   153
Saigon Book Store & Video Rental
    128
Saigon Pharmacy   129
Saigon Restaurant   122
Saigon Supermarket   126
Saint Joseph's Roman Catholic
    Church   138
Saitoh Canada   178
Sakae   182
Sakanaya Seafood   181
Sakura Video   188
Salathai   131
Salishan Seafood   220
Sally's Cake House   158
Salmon Village   178
Salvatore Ferragamo   71
Salza Mexican Products   198
Sam Kee Building, The   145
San Marcos Bakery   201
Sandhu's Video   108
Sang Cheung Co   171
Sangam Education & Cultural
    Society, The   118
Santorini Taverna   77
Santos Tapas   59
Sapporo Canadiana   178
Sapporo Gift Shop   178
Sari Sari Store   140
Satnam Foods   112
Save N Shop Home Necessities
    173
Sawasdee   131
Scandinavian Arts   13

Scandinavian Canadian Chamber
    of Commerce, The   11
Scandinavian   11–15
Schara Tzedeck   94
Scheffelaar's   30
Schnees Delicatessen   33
Scotch Shop, The   8
Scottish   1, 7–10
Scottish Cultural Society, The   7,
    10
See's Korean Garden   192
Seikidokan Judo Club   187
Seoul Food Market   192
Seoul Gifts   192
Seoul House Garden Korean
    Restaurant   191
Seoul House Korean Restaurant
    191
Serano Greek Pastry   75
Shaan Video & Gifts   108
Shahnoor Designer Wear   106
Shahrvand-E-Vancouver   88
Shalom Vancouver   95
Shan-E-Punjab Restaurant &
    Sweet Shop   110
Shanghai Garden Restaurant   154
Shanghai Palace Restaurant   154
Shaz Video & Snack House   108
Shensai Carpet Ltd   92
Shijo   182
Shil-la Korean Restaurant   191
Shimuzu-Shoten Store   180
Shingaar Emporium   107
Shiro Japanese Restaurant   185
Shiv Mandir   118
Shu Ren Environmental Arts
    169
Shubh Laxmi Jewellers   107
Siegel's Bagels   100
Simchaphonics, The   95
Sing Chong Food Centre   156
Sing Sing Restaurant   125
Singapore Arts & Crafts   132

Singapore Restaurant 133
Singaporean 129, 132–134, 231
Singh Foods 112
Sino United Publishing 166, 169
Skazska Gallery 53–54
Slavia 45
Slovak 44–45
Société Biculturalle de
    Maillardville 18
Société d'Histoire des Franco
    Columbiens 17–18
Société Fête Columbienne des
    Enfants 18
Society of Saint George, The 2
Socrates Greek School 73
Socrates Greek Taverna 77
Solly's Bagelry 100
Solomon Yeung/YCY 164
Son Canela Orquesta 202
Sons of Norway Sleipner Lodge,
    The 12
Sons of Scotland Benevolent Assn,
    The 7
Soody's Cuisine 91
Soon Cheong Trading Centre
    161
Sophia Book Store 187
Sorabol Korean Restaurant 191
Soul Survivors 211
South American 59, 199, 201,
    203
South China Foods 158
South China Seas Trading
    Company 158
Spanish 59–61, 202, 224–225,
    229
Spanish Catholic Mission 59
Spanish Cultural Centre 59
Spargo's Restaurant 67
Speelman's Bookhouse 29
Spiceland Cash & Carry 112
Spicy Court Chinese Restaurant
    149

Sporting Restaurant Cafe 59
Spumante's Cafe Ristorante 65
Squamish First Nations Capilano
    Long House 216, 228
Squamish Nation 221
SRC-CBUF 18
SRC 18
Sri Lankan 119–120, 227
Sri Lankan Gem Museum 119
St. Casimir's Polish Church 48
St. Elias Orthodox Church 87
St. Francis Xavier Chinese Parish
    147
St. George's Greek Orthodox
    Cathedral 72
St. George's Melkite Greek
    Catholic Mission 87
St. Mark's Lutheran Church 30
St. Nicholas-Demetrios Greek
    Orthodox Church 73
Stage Eireann Dramatic Society,
    The 6
Star Catering Inc 100
Stepho's Souvlaki Greek Taverna
    77
Steven Sadurah's Fancy Jewellers
    107
Steveston Danish Bakery 14
Steveston Japanese Language
    School 187
Steveston Judo Club 187
Steveston Kendo Club 188
Steveston Salmon Festival 176
Steveston Village 176
Strawberry Bakery 57
Sts. Cyril and Methodius Roman
    Catholic Slovak Parish 44
Suehiro Japanese Restaurant
    183
Sumimoto Oriental Therapeutics
    188
Sun E. Choi Tae Kwon-Do
    Academy 164

Sun Sui Wah Seafood Restaurant
   149
Sun Tong   157
Sun Wah Super Market   159
Sun Yin Gems   128
Sunrise Market   136, 155, 181
Sunrise Market's Tofu Factory
   155
Sunrise Videos & Coin Laundry
   128
Super 8 Restaurant   134
Super Choice Foods   159
Super Fine Tea Co   166
Superior Tofu Ltd   155
Supreme Meat   141
Surat Sweet   110
Sushi Boy   185
Sushi Shop, The   185
Svenska Kulturforeningen   11
Sweden House Society, The   11
Swedes   11
Swedish Canadian Rest Home and
   Manor, The   11
Swedish Cultural Society, The
   11
Swedish Press magazine   13
Swedish Press   12–13
Swiss   35–39, 230
Swiss Bakery   37
Swiss Canadian Athletic Club
   35
Swiss Canadian Mountain Range
   Association   35
Swiss Chamber of Commerce,
   The   36
Swiss Choir, The   36
Swiss Crossbow Association   35
Swiss Folk Dancing   36
Swiss Gourmet Restaurant, The
   37
Swiss Herald, The   35
Swiss Herbal Remedies   39
Swiss Outdoors Club   35

Swiss Society of Vancouver, The
   35
Swiss Trade Co   38
Szasz Delicatessen and Restaurant
   47
Szechuan Chongqing   153

T
T & T Supermarket   159
Tae Kwon Do Schools   192
Tagalog   138–139, 143
Tai Ping Trading Co   169
Taiwanese Cultural Festival, The
   148, 229
Taiwanese United Church in
   Greater Vancouver   147
Tak Sangha Indonesian Restaurant
   136
Tak Sing Co   160
Tan Cang   126
Tandoori King   116
Tandoori Taj   116
Tang's Noodle House   151
Tansai Journal   214
Tarogato   45
Tasleem's Video & Gifts   108
Taste of Jamaica   210
Tele-Kosher   100
Temple Sholom   102
Ten Lee Hong Enterprises Tea &
   Ginseng   165
Ten Ren Tea & Ginseng Co   165
Ten Ten Hot Pot   152
Terra International Foods Inc.   50
Thai Cultural Association of
   Vancouver, The   130
Thai House   131
Thai   129–132, 227, 231, 233
Thaler Enterprises   39
Thamil Cultural Society of BC
   79
Thanh Thanh   125
The Boss   154

The Bulletin 177
The CookShop 23
The Diner 5
The Gong 79
The Link 117
Théatre la Seizième 18
Thien Dia Nhan 128
Thoi Su 128
Thuan Phat Enterprises 132
Tiem Vang Jewellers 128
Time & Gold 38
Tio Pepe 195
Tivoli Restaurant & Catering, The 15
Tojo's 182
Tokachi Japanese Restaurant 186
Tokyo Health Sauna Club 188
Tokyo Ichiban 185
Tokyo Joe's Take-out 185
Tokyo Lounge 188
Tokyo-Do Gift Shop 178
Tonarigumi 177
Tong Fong Hung Medicine Co 162
Top Gun 150
Torrefazione Coliera 68
Tosi Italian Food Import Co 69
Touch of Africa 83
Touch of Sweden 13
Towkay Singapore Seafood 134
Traditional Chinese Medicine Association of B.C. 163
Trinidad and Tobago Cultural Society of B.C., The 206
Tropical Breeze Band 211
Tropika Malaysian Cuisine 135
Tropitonics Caribbean Steel Band 211
Trufoods 112
Tsi Art Chai Art Gallery 169
Tsunami 185
Tu Do 128

Tuk Tuk Thai Restaurant 132
Tuong Lai Vietnamese 126
Tzimmes Musical Ensemble 95

U
U Zavoralu 44
UBC Museum of Anthropology 216
Uganda Cultural Assn of BC 79
Ugo & Joe's Market 70
Ukrainian Canadian Congress, The 51
Ukrainian Community Society of Ivan Franko 51
Ukrainian 51–54
Ukrainian Gift Shop 54
Ukrainian Museum of Canada, The 51
Ultimate 24 Karat Gold Shop 170
Union Food Market 57
United Scottish Cultural Society, The 7
Universal Arts 170
University of B.C., The 102
Urban Native Education Centre 216
Urdu 103, 108, 117

V
Valentino's Ice Cream Corner 71
Valley Bakery 28
Valley Native Friendship Centre 215
Van Chinatown Books & Gift Shop 167
Van Den Bosch Patisserie Belge 25
van Kessel's 30
Van Lang Vietnamese Restaurant 123
Vancouver Aboriginal Friendship Centre Society 214

Vancouver Alpen Club
  Restaurant, The   34
Vancouver Alpen Club   31, 34
Vancouver Dorfmusik   36
Vancouver Finlandia Club, The
  12
Vancouver Folk Festival, The
  114–115
Vancouver Japanese Gardeners
  Association   177
Vancouver Japanese School   187
Vancouver Kendo Club   188
Vancouver Kidsbooks   24
Vancouver Korean Press, The
  190
Vancouver Manx Society, The
  10
Vancouver Peretz School, The
  102
Vancouver Public Libraries, The
  18
Vancouver Rug Import   92
Vancouver Shinpo   178
Vancouver Singapore Club   132
Vancouver Sushiman   186
Vancouver Westside German
  School   31
Vanderheide Publishing   29
Vasillis Greek Taverna   77
Vassilis Souvlaki Greek Taverna
  77
Venezia Ice Cream   71
Vicky's Children's Wear   77
Victoria Bakery & Delicatessen
  33
Video Shop, The   108
videos
  Arabic   86
  British Isles   2
  Central American   202
  Chinese   148, 164, 166–168
  Croatian   43
  Dutch   29

East Indian   105, 108, 112
  Filipino   139, 140, 143
  Germanic   31
  Greek   74
  Iranian   89, 90
  Italian   62, 69, 71
  Japanese   186, 188
  Polish   48, 49, 50, 51
  Portuguese   56
  South American   202
  Sri Lankan   120
  Vietnamese   128
Videomatica   72, 188
Viet Hoa Market   127
Viet Nam Thoi Bao   128
Vietnam City   123
Vietnamese   121–129, 132, 185,
  226, 229
Vigor Trading   173
Vij's   116
Vikon Foods   160
Villa del Lupo   64
Vine Yard Restaurant, The   77
Violet Moore (Irish folk dancing)
  7
Vita Meats & Seafood   119
VLC Video, Laser & Compact
  Disc Centre   168
Voice of Palestine, The   86
Vong's   150
Vroni Bernardis   36

W
Walk with Israel, The   96
Wedding & Party Store, The   107
Welsh   1, 5, 10, 226
Welsh Society of Vancouver, The
  10
West Lake Jewellery   128
White Crane Kung Fu   165
White Rock/South Surrey
  Jewish Community Centre,
  The   94

Wild Rose Centre of Natural
Healing 163
Wilfred Baker 221
William Tell, The 35–36
Windjammer Inn 4
Windmill Herald, The 26, 29
Wing Wah Jewellery 170
Wing Wah Shanghai Szechuan
Restaurant 153
WISE Club, The 1
Won More 152
Wonton King 149
World Journal 167
World Shorinji Kenpo
Organization 187

Y
Yaohan 180–181
Yaohan Centre 146, 160, 181,
186

YCY Better Health Centre 163
YCY Chinese Medicine & Health
Care Centre 163
YCY Prosperity 163
Yerushalem Imports 102
Yeu Hua Handicrafts 172
Yoshimi Restaurant 186
Your Place or Mine 77
Yuen Fong 173
Yuen Tong Co 160
Yummy's Dim Sum 151

Z
Zagreb Imports 43
Zagros 91
Zeenaz Restaurant 82
Zeppo's Trattoria 66
Zodiak Fast Foods 87
Zofia Polish Store 451
Zorba's Bakery & Foods Ltd 75

Photocopy this page and mail or fax to:

SERIOUS PUBLISHING
7249 Waverley Ave.,
Burnaby BC   V5J 4A7
fax: (604) 875-007 or 433-5594

Dear Serious Publishing:

Please consider the following suggestion for the next edition of
EXPLORING ETHNIC VANCOUVER

ETHNIC AFFILIATION (i.e. Italian): _____

Name:
Address:
Postal Code:
Phone/Fax

Check most appropriate category:

[   ] Cultural Group
[   ] Festival
[   ] Food Store
[   ] Clothing Store
[   ] Other _____

Please explain why your choice deserves inclusion in our next edition.
Include a name and number (phone/fax) in case we need to contact you for
more details.

_____

_____

_____

_____

Your Name: _____

Your Address: _____

Your Phone/fax: _____

ORDER FORM

SERIOUS PUBLISHING
7249 Waverley Avenue • Burnaby, B.C. • V5J 4A7
(604) 879-0321 • Fax: 875-0007

Qty	Item	Amt
	Exploring Ethnic Vancouver *by Anne Garber & John T.D. Keyes* Recommended and off-the-beaten-track "tastes" of the many ethnic communities that make up Vancouver's cultural mosaic — food, fairs, films, shopping & events. ISBN 0-9695187-8-1	$14.95
	Vancouver's Best Bargains *by Anne Garber & Lorraine Gannon* Everything (and place) you need to know to save money in Vancouver and environs: clothing, food, renovation, kids' stuff, factory outlets & more. ISBN 0-9695187-5-7	$18.95
	Obits: The Way We Say Goodbye *by MaryEllen Gillan* A tender look at Canadian life through the messages created by survivors to honour loved ones who have died. A great resource for bereaved families and grief counsellors. ISBN 0-9695187-6-5	$10.95
	Victoria's Best Bargains *by Anne Garber & John Keyes* Victoria can be frightfully expensive—but not with this indispensable guide to discounters, deals, restaurants and classic British pubs—in hand. ISBN 0-9695187-4-9	$10.95
	101 Uses for a Severed Penis *by Dan Murphy* Cartoonist Murphy turns his considerable wit and talent toward (shall we say) *sensitive* matters in this cutting-edge satire, proving the penis mightier than the sword! ISBN 0-9695187-3-0	$6.95
	Subtotal	

Qty	Item	Amt
	Cheap Eats *by Anne Garber & Marv Newland* Over 130 diners, greasy spoons, cafes,ma-and-pa eateries, cafeterias and other discount dining in and around Vancouver comprehensively reviewed and indexed for easy access. Illustrated. ISBN 0-965187-1-4	$9.95

Subtotal	
Add 20% shipping & handling	
Add 7% GST (Canadian orders only)	
Total (cheque or money order enclosed)	
(American orders, prices in U.S. dollars)	

PLEASE PRINT

NAME_____

STREET_____

CITY & PROV/STATE _____

POSTAL/ZIP CODE _____

FAX (for info on new titles) _____

Note: Payment by Visa to our fax #: (604) 875-0007. Please include your Visa number, expiry date, signature and print the name of the person to whom the card is issued.

"Serious" Phone inquiries: (604) 879-0321

Serious Publishing GST # R 127510964